Praise for Héctor Tobar's
TRANSLATION NATION

"Tobar's book is a **triumph of observation**. In one account after another, from that of the couples who work in a Tyson chicken plant in Alabama, where the author goes 'undercover' as a factory worker, 'hoping to see America through the innocent eyes of the wandering migrant,' to the story of the marine from Guatemala who dies in the Persian Gulf, Tobar vividly and movingly captures the conflict between the immigrant ideal to which America has always aspired and presiding white culture's deep ambivalence about the immigrant presence."
—*The New York Times Book Review*

"Tobar's heartfelt paean is **a worthy contribution** to the growing literature on a rapidly growing population: the newest Americans who will, like generations of immigrants before them, reshape everything from the language we speak to the way we experience culture, politics, and the very space of the streets we live on."
—Rubén Martínez, *Bookforum*

"Attentiveness to the complexity of Hispanic life in the United States is the great virtue of Héctor Tobar's new book *Translation Nation.* . . . Tobar showcases diversity through vivid vignettes of Hispanics currently living and working in different areas of the United States. This book is the perfect corrective to the fuzzy profile of the nation's number one minority group that many Americans carry around in their heads. . . . [*Translation Nation*] **makes the tremendous diversity, dynamism, and geographical breadth of our blossoming Hispanic population come alive.** That's a valuable contribution to understanding where our country is going in this new century, and I am grateful to Tobar for providing it."
—*The Washington Post Book World*

"There is a secret *América* that has a message for America, and Héctor Tobar is its angel. *Translation Nation* will come as a revelation to many Americans. **De Tocqueville, roll over; here comes Tobar.**"
—Thomas Keneally, author of *Schindler's List*

"*Translation Nation* is a **thoughtful, ambitious, and sweeping guide** to our America's future, which Héctor Tobar makes clear is already present." —Richard Rodriguez, author of
Brown: The Last Discovery of America

"Tobar captures . . . the current state of Latino in the United States . . . with **equal measure of insight and élan**, giving the book an infectious optimism, an undeniable sense that the nature and scope of *latinidad* are not only expanding but becoming more inclusive as well. The most compelling passages come when he strays from the familiar to the newest, most tenuous pocked of *latinidad,* encountering individuals who may otherwise have gone unnoticed precisely because they complicate the common notions of Latino identity. . . . *Translation Nation* is a wealth of profiles generally rendered with careful, respectful detail. . . . When looked at collectively, the assemblage highlights the great complexity of the American Latino experience. " —*Los Angeles Times*

"Frankly, I'm jealous as hell of Héctor Tobar. He combines a journalist's eye for the devastasting fact with a poet's eye for the astounding image. *Translation Nation* goes places many of us have not traveled, and once we get there, our jaws often drop. This book may not comfort you, but it will delight you. **It's beautiful.**"
—Luis Alberto Urrea, author of
Across the Wire and *The Devil's Highway*

"The scope of Tobar's book is matched by its superb writing. . . . **A graceful read and a tremendous reporting project**, *Translation Nation* succeeds not just as a Latino-American history, but as a thought-provoking meditation on the contemporary immigrant experience."
—*Time Out New York*

"*Translation Nation* will be looked upon as both **a cornerstone** and a corrective—the kind of book that didn't just document American life, but **showed us the way of the future**, too."
—*The Dallas Morning News*

"One of the book's true gems is Tobar's **gifted, breezy writing** style. His eye for detail intertwined with the storytelling skills of a novelist elevate his story beyond the usual immigrant tale. . . . Those interested in how the United States' largest minority group is influencing America's food, culture, and politics will be well-served by Tobar's literate efforts." —*The Cleveland Plain Dealer*

"Héctor Tobar is a worthy descendant of Che Guevara: Without a motorcycle but with equal brio, he travels the American landscape from west to east in pursuit of an unexplored America, reinvigorated everywhere by Latino immigrants. His chronicles are as agile as they are **unpretentious and thought-provoking**, a welcome respite to the diet of manufactured national identity we're accustomed to." —Ilan Stavans, author of *Spanglish: The Making of a New American Language* and *The Hispanic Condition*

"Tobar's book is not so much a treatise about how things should or should not be as an examination of how things are. Latino-Americans are here to stay, and they are changing the look and feel of America, just as it is changing them in return. . . . The United States faces problems and conflicts already with this mass influx of humanity, and there will be more trouble. But there is also a new vibrancy. Change is a constant, and, for now, the change in America has a decidedly Latin flavor, as Tobar's **good book** makes clear." —*The Charlotte Observer*

"**Armed with the eloquence and journalist's eye** that earned him a Pulitzer Prize . . . Héctor Tobar embarks on a trip across the other America. . . . The subject of Hispanic identity could not be in defter hands than those of Tobar, who brings to this topic the certainty and depth of a writer who has lived the experience he writes about." —*Loft Magazine* (Miami)

"Blending his memories of growing up Guatemalan American . . . with more than a decade spent visiting Latino communities in the United States, this Pulitzer Prize–winning *Los Angeles Times* journalist delivers **an insightful meditation** on the realities of modern-day Latino life." —*Latina* **magazine**

"**Impressive** . . . For those of us who view the dream of racial equality in America as largely unmet, Tobar's guarded optimism provides a glimmer of hope." —*Austin American-Statesman*

"Tobar explores the vast and diverse 'Latin Republic of the United States' in **crisp, energetic prose**. . . . Consciously harking back to Tocqueville and other observers of the American experience, Tobar claims a place for Latinos in the evolving story of what is, after all, a very young nation of immigrants." —*The Arizona Republic*

"*Translation Nation* examines the complexities and contradictions of the immigration process. . . . [Tobar's] accomplishment is making clear how the growing demographics of Latinos is not just about numbers, but also about how a new identity is affecting society. . . . This is a **must-read book**." —*El Paso Times*

"In plain, stirring prose, **this landmark documentary** brings close the universals of exodus and displacement, as Tobar reveals the unsettling particulars of Americans who are restless and always longing for home, whatever that is." —*Booklist* (starred & boxed review)

"**Magnificent** . . . A plea for transnational identity in the spirit of Tobar's hero, Che Guevara." —*Kirkus Reviews*

"**Engrossing** . . . Tobar's nuanced reportage vividly conveys the complexity and pathos of the Latino experience." —*Publishers Weekly*

TRANSLATION

Defining a New American Identity in the Spanish-Speaking United States

NATION

HÉCTOR TOBAR

Riverhead Books · New York

THE BERKLEY PUBLISHING GROUP
Published by the Penguin Group
Penguin Group (USA) Inc.
375 Hudson Street, New York, New York 10014, USA
Penguin Group (Canada), 90 Eglinton Avenue East, Suite 700, Toronto, Ontario M4P 2Y3, Canada
(a division of Pearson Penguin Canada Inc.)
Penguin Books Ltd., 80 Strand, London WC2R 0RL, England
Penguin Group Ireland, 25 St. Stephen's Green, Dublin 2, Ireland (a division of Penguin Books Ltd.)
Penguin Group (Australia), 250 Camberwell Road, Camberwell, Victoria 3124, Australia
(a division of Pearson Australia Group Pty. Ltd.)
Penguin Books India Pvt. Ltd., 11 Community Centre, Panchsheel Park, New Delhi—110 017, India
Penguin Group (NZ), cnr Airborne and Rosedale Roads, Albany, Auckland 1310, New Zealand
(a division of Pearson New Zealand Ltd.)
Penguin Books (South Africa) (Pty.) Ltd., 24 Sturdee Avenue, Rosebank, Johannesburg 2196,
South Africa

Penguin Books Ltd., Registered Offices: 80 Strand, London WC2R 0RL, England

First Riverhead hardcover edition: April 2005
First Riverhead trade paperback edition: April 2006
Riverhead trade paperback ISBN: 1-59448-176-8

The Library of Congress has catalogued the Riverhead hardcover edition as follows:

Tobar, Héctor, date.
Translation nation: defining a new American identity in the Spanish-speaking United States /
Héctor Tobar.
p.   cm.
ISBN 1-57322-305-0
1. Hispanic Americans—Social conditions.   2. Hispanic Americans—Ethnic identity.
3. United States—Ethnic relations.   I. Title.
E184.S75.T63   2005   2004051478
305.868'073—dc22

PRINTED IN THE UNITED STATES OF AMERICA

10 9 8 7 6 5 4 3 2

For Virginia Espino

CONTENTS

Part One

CROSSINGS

Chapter One

AMERICANISMO
City of Peasants

Los Angeles, California

Long before I understood what the word "revolution" meant, when I was a five-year-old boy growing up in the seamier half of Hollywood, California, I knew the face of Che Guevara. In the same way that other boys believed in Santa Claus and the Tooth Fairy, I knew that Che, with his Christ-like martyr's gaze and mane of wavy black hair, had come to help the poor and to make things right in the world. In real life, he was a knot of contradictions too complex to explain to a kindergartner: he was a poet who carried a gun, a dreamer known for his ruthlessness, generous to his friends and intransigent with both allies and enemies. He was a Robespierre in olive drab, who wanted to bring socialism to the Americas. But to me, behind that beard, underneath that black beret and its red star, there was a benevolent savior. Plenty of other people around me believed the same thing: it was the late 1960s, and my father, like most men in their twenties, was an idealist. My mother, his slightly younger wife, was too. Like Che, they were ambitious romantics, although neither one could appreciate this quality in the other.

"Che died for us," my father would say. "He went into the hills and fought as a guerrilla." I was small enough then that I didn't understand the difference between a guerrilla and a gorilla. I imagined a man jumping about the jungle, in imitation of an ape, ambushing the purveyors of evil.

My parents had brought Che with them when they left Guatemala in 1962. He came in their luggage, a spirit of adventure tucked in between their layers of clothes, next to the English dictionary my father brought along, the devotional cards of saints my mother depended on to protect her and her unborn baby. Like my parents, Che was a risk taker, a man with an impulsive streak. As a teenager, he would not hesitate to accept an outrageous dare, like walking on an irrigation pipe suspended over an impossibly deep gorge. A similar impetuousness had placed the young couple who would become my parents in the back of a delivery truck one spring afternoon in 1962, slipping off their clothes just long enough to conceive me while a driving rainstorm beat on the roof of the truck. A few weeks later they were pregnant and married and planning to run away to California. They arrived the week of the Cuban missile crisis, on a Pan American Airways flight that dropped them off at Los Angeles International Airport. Stepping for the first time into the California sunshine, they were greeted by the striking image of the airport's new Theme Building, a structure suspended between two giant arches suggesting the orbits of atoms, the coming "Space Age." My parents, a pair of young adults with a baby on the way, would soon embrace that uniquely California élan that wove together modernity and an incipient rebelliousness. In this new land of cat-eye sunglasses, my mother quickly learned to beehive her hair and to channel the allure of wool dresses that rose suggestively toward her kneecap. She outfitted my father in argyle sweaters no Guatemalan had ever worn before. Che was the most chic thing they had of their own to add to this American stew of coolness. Long before his face started popping up all over California—carried aloft on placards at Los Angeles City College rallies and on dorm room walls in Berkeley—he had been a hero to my father.

"El Che was from Argentina, but he fought in Cuba, and he lived in Guatemala too," my father would say, which would lead me later to ponder a map of the world, wondering how a man could travel such great distances swinging from tree branches, across mountains and jungles.

One of the first secrets I ever kept from my father was that I admired Maury Wills, the shortstop of the Dodgers, and Jerry West of the Lakers as much as, if not more than, El Che. For me the United States was a land ruled by sports heroes and astronauts, where arenas were filled with cheering crowds, and rockets zoomed into space with fiery ascents that caused hundreds of necks to crane upward and mouths to open in awe. I had never seen Che on my television, like my other heroes, who sank baskets from the half-court line and sent baseballs over the fence at the brand new Dodger Stadium, or who walked on the moon as fuzzy silhouettes. I was becoming an American, another species, different from all my ancestors. My mother and father would become Americans too, taking the oath as U.S. citizens within a decade of their arrival, even while believing and telling any Spanish-speaking person they met that they were still *guatemaltecos*. My father, I see now, embraced Che as an antidote to the lure of American culture, to its overwhelming power to amaze and intimidate, especially back then in the 1960s, when America gleamed and dazzled like the chrome bumpers and tail fins of the Fords and Chevrolets he longed to own. To prove he had not become a total *gringo*, my father became a more devout Guevarista, an armchair rebel with a single, loyal follower—me.

An especially self-confident brand of American identity had

reached its apex in the United States, the Anglo-Saxon Protestant worldview celebrated by writers like Samuel Huntington, a civic religion whose holy trinity was the Protestant work ethic, individualism, and an obsession with orderliness in all matters, public and private. Back then, an immigrant like my father needed to be stubborn to keep the person he had been before from being washed out in the laundry. It took work to hold on to the idea that you could be an outsider. "Never forget where you came from," my parents told me, but this was not an easy command to follow, since I was an only child, cut off from all my grandparents, my uncles and aunts, and my cousins by thousands of miles, and by a cultural and language gap that seemed to grow wider every year. Well into the 1970s, I could still count the number of Guatemalans I knew in Los Angeles on one hand. Che stood for the beliefs my family had left behind, a symbol of our Latin American identity during the long years we lived as cultural pioneers, a lonely crew of *chapines* (as Guatemalans call themselves) planting a flag with Che's face on the thirty-fourth parallel of North America.

Everything is different in California today. In the decades since my family arrived in Los Angeles, several accidents of geopolitics and macroeconomics brought millions of people like us to the United States, all to experience a similar kind of attraction and repulsion to American culture, all to remake the idea of themselves and their community with icons like Che, or the mustachioed Mexican revolutionary Emiliano Zapata, or, more recently, the hooded Subcomandante Marcos, who led the Mayan Indian uprising in Chiapas. We have come in so many numbers to California, America's most populous state, filling its cities and towns with our flags and pictures of our heroes, our language, our parades, and our prejudices, and so many other things that are uniquely ours, that even the notion of what it means to be an "American" has begun to change completely. You can see this transformation most dramatically in my hometown, where the Stars and Stripes still flies over the government buildings of the Civic Center downtown, an island of English-speaking culture encircled north, south, east, and west by a sprawl of *latinidad,* Latinness. Billboards for Mexican deejays in excessive Stetsons loom over the thoroughfares, and the Virgin of Guadalupe, the patron saint of Mexico, is posted outside countless liquor stores as a sentinel against graffiti and armed robbery. If you go to the flat plain of South Los Angeles on a Saturday night and stand under the milky light of the streetlamps, or visit the arroyos of Echo Park on a Saturday afternoon, you can close your eyes and feel the rural provinces of Mexico and Central America come to life in the acoustic universe that surrounds you, in the voices and the music of the people who live there.

In the most recent census, the number of Spanish speakers in the city of Los Angeles (1,422,316) was roughly equal to those who spoke only English (1,438,573). The city's top-rated newscast is the Spanish Univision *noticiero,* and the city parks are beginning to resemble the exhausted public spaces of Mexico City. In 1995 Los Angeles County parents registered the name José most often on birth certificates for baby boys. At Griffith Park, where I played as a child, the city Department of Parks and Recreation has placed enormous boulders in the center of the lawns to discourage the most popular municipal pastime, the playing of soccer, a sport unknown in the California of my childhood. Che is stencil-painted across the city more than ever, almost always staring back with the dreamy eyes of his most famous portrait, from a 1960 photograph taken at a funeral in Havana. Four decades removed from that time and place, it is an image ever more stylized, a sort of George Washington in negative image, a Latin icon from the founding of an altogether different republic, staring back at his progeny not from the dollar bill but from countless printed T-shirts, posters, and postcards. Che is the "founding father" symbol of the anti-WASP republic, a nation that embraces informality, excess in emotion, the dissembling force of rebellion, and the idea of strength in collectivity.

Today Los Angeles and California are quietly exporting their people and their way of life eastward across the continent. The city is the starting point of a new identity that is at once Latin American and—though it may not be immediately apparent—intertwined with North American traditions, with Jeffersonian ideals and the civic culture molded in the United States over the past two centuries. Los Angeles is to the twenty-first-century United States what New York City was to the twentieth. It is the crucible where a new national culture is being molded, where its permutations and contradictions can be seen most clearly. Once upon a time it could be said that every American city had a little bit of Ellis Island in it, or even a bit of Little Italy or the Bronx or Harlem. Something similar is happening in the twenty-first century, in which each new day sees another Spanish-speaking Angeleno set off on Interstates 5, 10, 15 from the overcrowded metropolises of our state to the greener pastures of places like Pasco, Washington, or Fayetteville, Arkansas, or even New York City itself, and in so doing helps bring a bit of Los Angeles to those places too.

In the United States and the Los Angeles I knew as a child, there was only one way to become American, the method perfected in New York and other Eastern cities. Most immigrant families stuck to the formula, the one people had followed on a path to Americanness for a century. They stopped speaking Spanish—or Italian, or Armenian, or Greek—and instead embarrassed themselves in front of their children by trying to wrap their Mediterranean or Latin

American mouths around English. Their children would retain only a handful of phrases from the mother tongue, and would know the culture of the Old Country primarily as a collection of recipes and swear words and maybe from the occasional visit of a grandparent who arrived in the United States as a sort of time traveler, stumbling about the apartment or the cul-de-sac in an old fedora, like my grandfather did when he came to visit us. When they had enough money they tried to enroll their children in tennis lessons, or Little League, or any other American institution that would let them get a foot in the door.

About halfway into the twentieth century, the Mexican writer Octavio Paz had wandered into a Los Angeles similar to the one my parents encountered on their arrival, the Los Angeles of the Pax Americana at its apex. In *The Labyrinth of Solitude*, his seminal treatise on Mexican identity, Paz describes the latent Mexican feel of the city then, a faint but discernible "delight in decorations, carelessness and pomp, negligence, passion and reserve." The city's Mexicanness "floats, never quite existing, never quite vanishing." Of the people of Mexican origin he encountered in Los Angeles he wrote, "They have lived in the city for many years wearing the same clothes as the other inhabitants, and they feel ashamed of their origin. . . . They act like persons who are wearing disguises, who are afraid of a stranger's look because it could strip them and leave them stark naked."

Unbeknownst to Octavio Paz, inside those withdrawn Angelenos there was a garrulous, self-confident Latin city waiting to be born. My father became a pioneer of this new city when he decreed that I would always speak to him in Spanish. At school, and in the Hollywood alleyways and side streets where I played with my friends, I did math, joked, and whined in English, but at home my father fought back against the Anglo-Saxon linguistic torrent with a steady stream of *castellano:* to this day he is always *papá.* At the same time, he would have been deeply upset if I didn't learn English, then as now the language of commerce and government. My undeniably accent-free English, with its native-speaker intonations and fluency in the peculiar vowel sounds no native Spanish-speaker can ever quite master, was in a sense a measure of his family's achievement. He admired American institutions, and his favorite class at Los Angeles City College was U.S. history, with its crimson-bound textbook, which he passed down to me as a kind of heirloom, telling me to pay particular attention to the chapters on the Civil War. My father was ambivalent about the United States, and in that, too, he was a pioneer: his ambivalence about WASP culture never faded, never surrendered to acceptance. He made learning English his own obsession too, taking night-school classes and making himself fluent enough to write business letters, but he also went to political meetings and seethed in Spanish about *imperialismo* in group discussions led by a Guatemalan leftist whose circle of would-be rebels later contemplated hijacking a plane to Cuba—it was a bit of a fad in those days. My father told me that Che had fought to free Cuba and that he was fighting for us too, for Guatemala, where our extended family lived under a blue sky and puffy tropical clouds I got to see every Christmas vacation. If we wanted to hear Che's voice, we could take our shortwave radio, string up a copper wire over our duplex apartment, and grab his words from the atmosphere. My father marked the frequency for Radio Habana Cuba on the glass face of the receiver with a piece of cellophane tape and a marker, a blue line that ran parallel to another one for TGW, Radio Nacional de Guatemala, a much weaker signal that came in only on certain summer evenings, when he and my mother would sit and listen to the sound of the Guatelinda marimba orchestra force its way through layers of static into our living room. I remember that music vivid, because it usually led my mother to quiet tears whenever she heard it. As for Che, to this day I can't tell you what his voice sounded like.

My father spoke to me about El Che in that earnest and gentle tone adults have when they speak to children about things like God and history. We are part of a bigger world, his voice said, full of beauty and horrors, where brave and smart men battle the forces of ignorance and darkness. Our history and our future cannot be contained within borders. This message, I believe, is essentially the same one communicated to new generations of Californians. Today, all of California, Latino and non-Latino, is increasingly immersed in the collective, cross-border narrative of its 11 million inhabitants of Latin American descent. In my own household, these stories have their starting point in my grandparents' villages, in places with names like Huehuetenango and Rincón Tigre ("Tiger's Corner"), and in a cluster of adobe buildings with plaster skins, set amidst the banana plantations of the United Fruit Company.

I grew up believing it was my destiny to advance this essentially Latin American story into new, northern territories. In the Los Angeles of today, however, the narrative traffic goes in two directions. It is not just the story of the peasant whose children follow the North Star to the California oasis of orange groves, rationality, and good wages; the story also flows southward, back down to the birthplace of the passionate, the chaotic, and the spiritual. If you grow up Latino in Los Angeles, you feel the pull of the south, of its pop singers, its revolutions, and its fads. If you can, you go to the south, in body or in mind. The frightened Mexican-Americans of Octavio Paz's day are a fading anachronism, because people feel free to dress, think, speak, or plan their futures thinking of the south.

I can remember standing and looking to the south—literally and figuratively—one day at about the turn of the millennium in the East Los Angeles neighborhood of City Terrace. I was standing on the deck of the family home of my *comadre*, which is what you call your child's godmother. The very fact that I was using such a term, "code-switching" it into my English (as a linguist would say), was itself a step backward in what should have been a steady march forward into North American assimilation. "*Hola, comadre*, how's it going? Such a long time, *qué no*?" My *comadre* María Cabildo and her husband Manuel Bernal, who was also my *compadre*, had invited a group of friends over for their annual New Year's Day tamale brunch, which we celebrated on a patio overlooking the Eastside on one of those rare days of crystalline skies that winter brings us in Southern California. In the distance you could see the Art Moderne tower of the seventy-five-year-old Sears building on Olympic Boulevard sticking up from the flat urban plain, and splashes of green palm fronds amid the gray and earth-toned cityscape of naked jacarandas and dormant maple trees, and stubby apartment buildings and warehouses. We filled the conversation with our southern obsessions. Our friend Evangeline Ordaz had been to Chiapas as a human-rights monitor, encountering Mexican soldiers and Mayan rebels outfitted with antique rifles; she had also met the famous guerrilla leader known as Subcomandante Marcos. María's brother Miguel talked about his work for the Mexico City investigative magazine *Proceso;* in recent days he had come under threat from the murderous Tijuana drug cartel. This was a conversation, like most others in the still small circles of the Latino Los Angeles upper middle class, that began in English and drifted frequently into Spanish, a language we speak with widely varying degrees of fluency. Another visitor told us the story of a recent visit to his family's Mexican village, a place deep in the dry valleys and windswept high plains made famous in the work of the writer Juan Rulfo. Our friend had wandered into the town square to find a man tied up on an enormous cross, hanging in the air with a crown of thorns on his head and just three nails short of an actual crucifixion.

"What are you doing up there?" he asked.

"I am showing my devotion to Jesus!"

"You should get down before you get a sunburn!"

We listened to this story and for a moment we were lost in the strangeness and wonder of it—a familiar sensation, because all of us have been to the places where such stories are born. Los Angeles is filled with people like us, people who have Latin American villages and peasants hovering around their lives. There are *campesinos* in our dreams, on our lawns cutting the grass, in the pickup trucks next to us on the freeway, in the picture frames on the walls of our living rooms. The peasants in the pictures might come from the age of the Mexican Revolution, or they might be twenty-first-century *campesinos* in villages connected to California by bus lines and extended family relationships. We can go down below María's family home and hear roosters crowing at sunrise from backyard chicken coops. In the newer Mexican suburbs of Watts and Compton, we can find stalks of corn growing in the front yards, a crop from the old country seemingly about to burst from its cage of wire fencing to populate all the other lawns, and a reminder to all that the gardener or the mechanic inside was once a *campesino,* and perhaps still longs to be one.

The peasant who looms over my own family is my late paternal grandfather, Francisco Tobar, a *campesino* from a province of rural Guatemala called Zacapa, notorious for producing men with a penchant for settling their differences with unsharpened machetes. Here an old rail line runs past the broad-leaved banana trees, and the train station where my grandparents first met is a forgotten, crumbling ruin marked GUALAN. My grandmother bore two of Francisco's children in Gualán and then left him, running away to Guatemala City with her oldest son. One morning she returned on the inbound steam train from the capital, kidnapped her younger son (my father), and escaped on the outbound train. They moved into an orphanage in downtown Guatemala City, where my grandmother was the cook for dozens of street urchins. Coincidentally, Che Guevara arrived in Guatemala City at about the same time, with just $3 in his pocket after having ridden his motorcycle and hitching car, bus, and boat rides to Chile, Peru, Panama, and other destinations. Guatemala City was a much smaller city then, and it is not beyond the realm of possibility that their paths crossed, Ernesto the revolutionary-to-be encountering Héctor Efraín the father-to-be in the doorway of the orphanage. I can imagine my father, then a scrawny boy of twelve or so, exchanging glances with the bohemian Argentine then in his mid-twenties, a clean-shaven man not yet sprouting the stubble that would become his famous beard, his hair short and nowhere near his collar.

Che went into hiding when Guatemala's leftist government was overthrown in a 1954 coup d'état, then took refuge in the Argentine embassy and prepared his escape to Mexico City, where he would meet Fidel Castro and board a small overcrowded boat with rebels headed for Cuba. My father, then thirteen years old, hid underneath his bed in the orphanage as bombs from American fighter planes exploded throughout the city. He would grow into a gangly teenager and meet my mother in the crowd drawn to the scene of a neighborhood car crash. After the drama of a shotgun wedding, they headed to California, where I was born a few months later at Los Angeles County General Hospital. In those days, few working people in Guatemala had telephones in their homes, and the news of my birth was communicated southward via the mail. In a similar fashion, the details of the family happenings from Guatemala arrived to us in Hollywood in envelopes with blue and red borders marked "Special Delivery." "They write that European-style seven over there," the mailman would say. My mother in turn gave him letters bound for Guatemala filled with snapshots of our visit to Sea World and the San Diego Zoo, or the bulbous used Chevrolet we had purchased, pictures that announced, "We have arrived in California."

These days the traffic in letters, cash, and gifts between Los Angeles and Latin America feeds an air freight industry whose final link is the motorcycle courier puttering up to the door of your relatives' home in a rural *pueblo* or an urban *colonia* neighborhood. The couriers deliver envelopes with pictures like the one I saw a young man posing for not long ago near the Harbor Freeway, across from the Financial District at the beginning of that neighborhood of tenements called Pico-Union. This man with skin the color of moist soil put his hands on his hips and smiled as he stood on one of the few spots in Los Angeles where you can line up the skyscrapers behind you for a Manhattanesque shot. The towers glowed in green and amber in the twilight. He had found a spot that said, "I am in the big city, I am at the center of everything." He is showing the family back home the new man he has become. This is what it means to be an immigrant. You undertake an adventure that is itself a process of reinvention. You send home the picture with a letter that tells the story of your tribulations in the new land. The snapshot is proof of your triumph and your transformation, and the act of placing it in the mail is a communion with the people back home and a celebration of the possible. Your letter home says: This is what *we* can become.

Ernesto Guevara sent letters home to Buenos Aires after he left, famously, on his motorcycle. Each bit of news was increasingly more fantastic and improbable. *I have seen Machu Picchu. . . . I have climbed to the crater of a volcano covered in snow. . . . I am leading a rebel army. . . .*

One day his adventures and his wandering ended in the mountains of southern Bolivia, where at thirty-nine he became a corpse displayed to the local villagers, his long locks of matted hair splayed across a table, his eyes still open. Sometime after Che died I learned my first acronym: CIA, which my father pronounced in Spanish as *see-ya*, the same as *silla*, which means "chair." My father had learned about the chair at Los Angeles City College. The chair, he told me in Spanish, had dropped the bombs he had heard exploding in Guatemala City, and the chair had killed Che, too—whether this news caused me to cry or feel whatever fleeting sense of mourning a small boy can conjure, I don't remember. The next year, 1968, I started kindergarten at Ulysses S. Grant Elementary. My father told me to conquer the alphabet and arithmetic as a prelude to the battles of my adulthood. I was picked best student in my class, which meant I got to carry the Stars and Stripes in the school parade.

I can remember standing at the blacktop of my school, the flagpole anchored to my belt, a nylon Old Glory catching the breeze. Being the youngest kid, I stood at the front, a line of progressively taller children behind me, boys and girls of various brown and peach hues, redheaded girls from the Midwest, curly-headed boys from Armenia, and some Filipinos and Mexicans too, the peculiar cultural kaleidoscope of East Hollywood then, each boy or girl carrying his or her own nylon Old Glory. We probably looked like all the other patriotic schoolchildren you see in documentaries of "silent majority" America in 1968, that year of the Tet Offensive in Vietnam and the Democratic Convention in Chicago. Each year, I studied harder and brought home new triumphs. I learned very quickly that being a good and studious *guatemalteco*, dedicated to honoring the memory of El Che, also happened to make me a good "American" in a traditional, Norman Rockwell sense of the word. I studied the map of the

United States that was in every classroom, and memorized all its state capitals. When my father brought home his government textbook from night school, I pored over the charts of how a bill becomes a law and the simple logic of the lines that linked boxes representing the House of Representatives, the Senate, and the Supreme Court. My sixth-grade teacher, a square-jawed Texan named Mr. Simmons, had us recite the Gettysburg Address for the school assembly that was to be our farewell to elementary school. He picked me to lead the class, and for a week I memorized those 270 words of Lincoln's that are like a civic prayer to democracy and its foundation in sacrifice, to "a new nation: conceived in liberty, and dedicated to the proposition that all men are created equal." On the afternoon of the assembly, we stood under a bank of hot lights, on a stage of polished hardwood, transforming Lincoln's words into a chorus song, until we got to the part that begins "the world will little note, nor long remember," at which point I suddenly didn't remember, and our speech turned into an incomprehensible mumble.

When I was five years old, when I was ten, even when I was a fifteen-year-old going to high school in the suburbs, I never saw any contradiction in the set of beliefs that swirled around me: that I should conduct my life according to the principles of equality and national honor of Che, who said America was an imperialist dragon feeding upon the entrails of the poor countries of the globe; and that I could also believe, as my father repeated again and again, that I lived in one of the freest territories on the face of the earth, an egalitarian democracy where I might become a congressman or some other kind of important person, simply by being the best student in the class. "You will be taller than me," my father told me, more than once, as I grew up into an average-sized American kid, two inches taller than my father and unusually tall for a *guatemalteco*. "Just like

I was taller than my father. And your son, when you have one, will be taller than you. In this country, people grow taller than they do in Guatemala."

Probably most sons and daughters of immigrants heard that speech in 1960s Los Angeles. The future was being born here, and even a skeptical Guatemalan like my father could be swept away in the feverish optimism and sense of limitless growth. We flocked to Disneyland to fly on the Rocket to the Moon ride and to stroll through the Monsanto House of the Future in Tomorrowland, a playground celebrating our own Space Age ambition as Californians and Americans. My mother wanted to embrace this modernism but also feared being consumed by it, so she prayed to St. Martin, San Martín de Porres in Spanish, to protect her against the evils that she feared came from too much future—ambition, coldness, godlessness. St. Martin was a seventeenth-century Peruvian friar, the mulatto son of a slave and a nobleman, and in our apartment he was also a four-inch-tall statue on the windowsill, a black man in a monk's robes holding a broom with a small dog at his feet. Proof of his powers was to be found in the events surrounding my birth and the miraculous intervention of a black stranger, Booker Wade. He knocked at the door of my parents' apartment offering my mother a ride to the hospital. He drove her to one emergency room in his convertible, and then a second one after she got turned down for lack of money and immigration papers. My mother said I owed my safe entry into this world to San Martín, who had sent his brother Booker to help us.

Eight years later, at about the time my parents were getting divorced, they took me to see an oracle in South-Central Los Angeles. Today, this moment is part family legend, part hazy memory: I remember only the dusty curtain that covered the doorway into the fortune-teller's room, and the smell of wet cement. My father tells me the oracle picked me out from the crowd of people waiting to see her: "Bring *that* boy to me." She stared at me for a bit before declaring, "This boy has a huge aura." Then she added, in a phrase that would resonate inside my head for the rest of my life, "This boy is going to help a lot of people one day."

Every time I came home with an A, every time I asked my parents about Che or Martin Luther King, every time a teacher sent home a note suggesting I might be "gifted," my father recounted that story. *This boy is going to help a lot of people one day.* Many years later, when I reached my mid-twenties and a somewhat delayed onset of full-blown adulthood, I would feel the burden of that prophecy and slip into a depression. But when I was still a child the prophecy only fed a strange kind of prepubescent ambition: a rampant desire to be the first to memorize all the multiplication tables, to read more books than any of my classmates, and to feed more American history into my brain. I imagined it was all a prelude to a future in which I would honor Che's memory, repay St. Martin for the ride to the hospital, *and* fulfill the prophecy of the oracle of South-Central Los Angeles.

Thus did the rational world of Yankee democracy become intertwined in my young mind with the antirational universe of Catholic saints, of ointments and murmured prayers. When I was young, I thought this world was mine alone, but now I see that the Latino supernatural hovers over most of the city. Los Angeles is roughly divided, in cultural and spiritual terms, by the multilaned byway called La Cienega Boulevard, a slight Anglicization of *la ciénaga,* "the swamp." Drive west across La Cienega and you are in the half of the city whose state of mind is exported to the rest of the world as the spirit of Los Angeles. Over there, mystique is something created by makeup artists and special-effects gurus, experts in the craft that is Los Angeles's best-known contribution to global culture. But on my side of the city we are ruled by the baroque, by angels who cure the sick, who relieve the suffering of wives with wayward husbands, and who sometimes take the souls of innocent children. My side of the metropolis is a round-the-clock Mass. The leaders of official, English-speaking Los Angeles might still try, as they have for more than two hundred years, to encourage the city's Spanish-speaking residents to shuffle along in good Protestant, moneymaking order, but they are working against the tide of history. They zone a corner of city territory for a business park, and then a Mexican woman passes one day and looks up at the office building that has risen there. She sees that the mirror glass of one of its windows has warped in such a way that the sunlight that shines on it is refracted into a swirl of primary colors, into the very image of the Virgin of Guadalupe. She tells all her friends and neighbors. Soon there are vast crowds of believers gathered in the building's parking lot, and police to keep the crowds in order, and English-speaking television crews to broadcast news of the crowds to English-speaking viewers: here we have hundreds of people with a strange and foreign faith, who see the pious face of a Mexican saint in the window of this non-descript office building. "Can you see it? *La virgen santísima*. Our mother. She is there."

Angelenos learned long ago that the Latin city in their midst is inescapable, and have come to terms with its permanence. Other cities and towns across the continent have undergone the same pattern of response to the creeping advance of Latinization: denial, anger, acceptance. In between those stages, or maybe after, comes curiosity. These days, it is an oft-repeated ritual of American journalism for the local newspaper to send one of its reporters down into Latin America so that its readers can better understand the brown-skinned people who have come to live among them. Over the years I have read such stories in newspapers from the Louisville (Kentucky) *Courier-Journal* to the Portland *Oregonian* and the *Press Herald* of Portland, Maine. "Oregon is more than just a name on the map to the 1,200 residents of San Juan Mixtepec," the *Oregonian* discovered when it went to Oaxaca, and the *Courier-Journal* tagged along with a tobacco farmer who visited the town in Nayarit where his field hands were born. The *Press-Herald* sent its correspondent to La Democracia, Guatemala, to tell the full story of a group of men who died working in Maine's North Woods. California newspapers are the pioneers of this form, which continues to be a staple. As I write these words, I read in the *Los Angeles Times* a columnist's description of his journey to a farm outside Mexico City in search of the long-lost brother of a woman from central Los Angeles, a single mother with a poignant story of separation and loss. "I was expecting you," the brother told the columnist, Steve Lopez, when Lopez found him; the brother had dreamed recently that a stranger would bring him news of his sister. The columnist and the brother talked as they walked through cornfields and past agave cactus plants. "Here on a mountain in Mexico," Lopez wrote, "I could feel the pulse of hearts split between two countries, and believed I had begun to know Los Angeles."

I made my first Mexico pilgrimage when I was twenty. I was also playing at Che, hoping that a faraway adventure in deepest Latin America would give me a raison d'être, and I reached the same destination he did—Mexico City. I stood before the murals Diego Rivera had painted at the National Palace, where portraits of centuries of presidents, rebels, and poets are crowded into a single composition, and decided immediately that this was the metropolis I should live in; I had arrived at a place explicitly connected to Latin American history. I hung out at Café La Habana in downtown Mexico City, the restaurant where Che and Fidel Castro had plotted their landing in Cuba. I sipped café con leche and ordered big bowls of the house specialty, cream of asparagus soup, delivered by indifferent wait-resses who seemed to have no idea they were treading on hallowed ground. I walked through old neighborhoods of quaint plazas with gazebos whose platforms were decorated with Spanish tile, where trees and grass struggled to survive in the carbon-laced air. I stayed there just long enough for it to begin to feel like home and to simul-taneously realize it could never be home.

"What *are* you?" the more inquisitive *mexicanos* I met would ask. "What do you consider yourself?" I didn't fit into the categories into which you placed brown-skinned people in Mexico: I was a U.S.-born young man with Mayan features who carried himself with a vaguely American air of entitlement and spoke a fluent but strange variant of Spanish. Much is made in Mexico of its multiethnic blend of Spanish and indigenous cultures, the *mestizaje,* or mixing, cele-brated in the paintings of Siqueiros and Rivera. But when it comes to the simpler notions of national identity, Mexico is a very homo-geneous place. To say "I am *mexicano*" implies an identifiable set of beliefs and customs; love for the tricolor flag, reverence for early-twentieth-century revolutionary icons like Pancho Villa, and shared grievances with respect to the United States. When I responded to the question *What are you?* with a perplexed knotting of my brow, my *mexicano* acquaintances would elaborate with "Are you *norte-americano?* Are you Guatemalan?" When I told them I was both, a "citizen of the Americas," this left them unsatisfied. Clearly, I had to be one or the other.

Eventually, I decided that Los Angeles was my *tierra,* as a *mexi-cano* would say, my land, a landscape seared into my memory the same way the banana leaves and the river in Gualán were seared into my father's: the green flesh of the succulents, the soot-covered urban palms, playing street baseball and bouncing line drives off parked cars; the scent of ash on fall days when brush fires burn on distant mountains. I went back home and got a job writing for my hometown newspaper, and began to explore how a new city was being fashioned on that familiar landscape.

I found myself drawn to the city's murkier recesses, to places like MacArthur Park, at the heart of a neighborhood of tenements and homeless camps. It was the late 1980s, near the peak of the great exodus of Salvadorans and Guatemalans to California, a process that had created a nineteenth-century kind of crowding and desperation clustered around the park itself, forty acres of lawns, palms, and lakes faced by old Deco hotels built for the swank clientele of the silent-film era. With its drug trade and immigrant street vendors selling mangoes covered with chili powder, its schizophrenics dressed in castaway rags, and its shoeshine men from San Salvador, MacArthur Park was a Dickensian candy store of melodrama; Oliver Twist had escaped from London and was now a Spanish-speaking Angeleno in the age of crack. One morning I walked on the park's muddy lawns, tracking the swirling scars cut into the grass the night before by patrol cars on the hunt for dealers. I was trying to speak to a cluster of blankets and old coats on a park bench that I believed to be a human being when I looked up and saw something halfway magical a few hundred feet away—a quetzal, a sparrow-sized bird with tail feathers two feet long, was flying across the top of a storefront. One of my father's countrymen had painted it there for the Mi Guatemala restaurant, because the quetzal was that country's national symbol. I wandered over and found the waiters and waitresses setting up for lunch, and a six-man marimba orchestra fussing over their instruments.

The *guatemaltecos* behind Mi Guatemala were people like my own parents, rallying around a symbol that announced the preservation and endurance of their identity. Their restaurant was a call to share in the nostalgic pleasures of a *tamal* prepared in the Central

American fashion, cornmeal and meat cooked inside the smooth, dark-green skin of a banana leaf. I had never seen a Guatemalan *tamal* quite as large as the ones prepared there: like young children, Guatemalan-American *tamales* seem to grow bigger stateside than they do back home. There were now enough Guatemalans in Los Angeles that you could find them congregating the way they did here, plump couples dancing between the tables to the kind of music that used to make my mother cry from homesickness, the slow waltz of "Luna de Xelajú" (Moon of Quetzaltenango) and the faster, polka-paced "Soy de Zacapa," I Am from Zacapa, which is the region my father was kidnapped from.

In the larger city, in those semi-suburban grids first cut into the orange groves and cabbage fields in the 1950s, the collective élan began to resemble that of the Mexican towns described by Octavio Paz in "The Day of the Dead," the third chapter of *The Labyrinth of Solitude*, in which the writer describes the village fiesta. If you drove slowly enough up and down those residential streets on a Saturday, you might see the streamers going up over a driveway for a *quinceañera*, the fifteenth-birthday celebration and coming-out party in which a young woman is dressed in waterfalls of white fabric and taken to the church for a Mass, and copious amounts of cash are spent on accordion bands, tuxedos, wedding-style cakes, and pots of food. In the late 1980s, upon learning that some lavish *quinceañeras* were setting Mexican families back as much as $10,000, the Los Angeles archdiocese issued an edict calling on the faithful to restrain themselves, but they were just shouting into the wind. The archdiocese didn't understand that, as Paz explained, "Wasting money and expending energy affirms the community's wealth in both." Paz also described how, on the night of the annual fiesta, Mexico's small, often grim villages exploded into a reverie of expressiveness. "This is the night when friends who have not exchanged courtesies for months get drunk together, trade confidences, weep over the same troubles, discover they are brothers, and sometimes, to prove it, kill each other." A half-century after he wrote those words, they are also an apt description of certain corners of Los Angeles on Saturday nights. Unable to contain their joy or their sense of abandon, people reach for their guns and begin to fire in the air. I can remember one New Year's Eve at my sister-in-law's house in the Eastside barrio of Lincoln Heights, when a bullet came falling through the window screen; it plopped harmlessly near the sink, an amusing brush with the unpredictable and the folkloric that brought chuckles of laughter from all the party-goers. Were he to be resurrected from his grave in Mexico and return to Los Angeles, Octavio Paz might smile knowingly at the explosions too, recognizing them as one more expression of a *mexicano*'s struggles with his inner demons. "And since we cannot or dare not confront our own selves, we resort to the fiesta. It fires us into the void; it is a drunken rapture that burns itself out, a pistol shot in the air, a skyrocket."

Another day I went to the MacArthur Park bandshell to find five hundred Salvadorans gathered for a political rally, listening to a short woman with vaguely Asian features speak: she was dating a friend of mine, an American-born son of Salvadoran immigrants. *China*, he called her. She had been a guerrilla fighter, and the story of how she became a rebel began in a village of Chalatenango. I had been told she could disassemble a FAL rifle and that she knew how to fire a mortar and I imagined her at the head of the columns of rebels you sometimes saw in the evening news in those days, the same ones who had taken the rich suburbs of San Salvador and then slipped back into the mountains, wizards with submachine guns. I wandered over to the front of the stage, past grandmothers with red banners, past home-sewn pennants with red stars, and saw that the official representative of the Farabundo Martí National Liberation

Front in California was standing on her tiptoes as she spoke. *"Hasta la victoria siempre,"* she shouted—Ever onward to victory, the phrase with which Che closed his letters. This was, explicitly, the world of Latin American radicalism brought home to the very center of Los Angeles.

The private world my own family had built two decades earlier in Hollywood—that childhood cocoon of hopes, ideals, and legends— was suddenly and inexplicably writ large across the entire metropolis. In the course of a generation, Los Angeles had become a Latin American city, the northernmost Spanish-speaking metropolis in the hemisphere, a sort of Mexico City Lite: crowded, but not so much as its southern twin; smoggy, but not as toxically polluted. I began to see my hometown near the top of an imaginary map, with California at the north, a sort of Yukon boomtown relative to the heartland of the Mexican states of Jalisco and Guanajuato. I would look at a map of the United States—that familiar outline with the funnel that was Texas and the pistol grip of Florida—and see a truncated, incomplete image. Those maps are dominated by the grid of the Interstate highway system, by the thick lines that run mostly east to west, across the Great Plains and the desert Southwest, linking the country that Lincoln and Jefferson knew to a country of saguaro cacti and suburban ranchettes. The Mexican highway system is rendered, at best, as a few thin lines running inconclusively off the map's southern edge. In my favorite map of all, the National Geographic map of the United States, California and Colorado shimmer in coral pink, Wisconsin and Nebraska in goldenrod, while Mexico falls off the bottom in a textureless pale yellow. To an Angeleno at the turn of the millennium, that map was inadequate to convey the shift that had taken place in the psychic geography of the city, the roads and highways people carried in their brains.

In this alternative geography, the great hub at the center of the map—the Chicago or the Kansas City, if you will—was Mexico City and its *centrales camioneras,* those massive bus terminals where travelers arrive from Oaxaca and Guatemala on their way to Brownsville or Denver, Georgia or San Francisco. I had passed through those same terminals on my way to Guatemala for a family vacation when I was twenty and they also brought millions of immigrants traveling in the opposite direction, to California, where I interviewed them for a newfound career as a community chronicler. I translated the tales of their crossings and arrivals into English, into stories that ran up and down and across the section of the newspaper called Metro.

I earned my first paychecks as a writer by tapping the thick vein of irony and absurdity produced by the sudden and massive arrival of so many peasants and provincial innocents into the world center of glamour capitalism. I met a Salvadoran immigrant grandfather named Fidel Chicas who fought a David-versus-Goliath battle with the man who had built the Hotel Hollywood, a black tower rising above the freeway of the same name. Fidel was one of the thousands of laborers then showing up at various Los Angeles street corners to look for work, their swarthy appearance causing consternation among certain native Californians who figured that a crowd of two hundred loitering "Mexicans" could only mean bad news. The hotel developer had hired Fidel to work at a construction site in a tony borough of Los Angeles called Los Feliz. He picked Fidel, then sixty-six years old, from a Santa Monica Boulevard street corner. After three weeks on the job under increasingly dangerous conditions, Fidel and a group of a dozen or so other men announced that they would no longer work past nightfall, because standing on scaffolding in the dark was an accident waiting to happen. The developer fired them on the spot without paying them for the work they had already done. All the workers except Fidel Chicas accepted this decision with nothing more than a few curse words muttered in Spanish.

Fidel Chicas decided to go to small-claims court, a highly unusual decision in the context of early 1990s Los Angeles. Most Latino immigrants then remained studiously distant from the institutions of American government, and especially courthouses, which were known as places where Spanish-speaking people went before they got carted off to jail. Much hand-wringing was taking place in English-speaking Los Angeles about this phenomenon—the so-called "Third World-ization" of the city—and the implications of living in a metropolis where millions didn't understand the rules of governance and civic life. Samuel Huntington was inspired to write an entire book about it. Most immigrants to the city, it seemed, had civic identities that were completely on the other side of the border; they hadn't read the Gettysburg Address or the Bill of Rights, and didn't know you should call your city councilman when the trash wasn't picked up or the street was full of potholes. Fidel was different. "He's trying to follow the system," Linda Mitchell, a representative from the refugee agency that was helping him, told me. "He's trying to be an American."

Fidel's campaign against the developer was part journey through American judicial bureaucracy and part Salvadoran peasant tenacity. He was a slightly younger version of my own grandfather, a dumpy man with a wispy mustache and a disheveled appearance. He fought back because getting cheated out of money he earned with muscle was a violation of the treatment he was expecting to find in the United States. You expected such corruption in Central America, where caste rules imposed themselves on government institutions, a state of affairs that had set off a revolution or two. After a legal-aid worker helped him fill out the small-claims paperwork, he showed up at the court alone and won his case. His trophy was one of those multiple-copy forms that American courts spit out by the pound, a pink sheet of paper that he carried around for a few months, supplemented by a second sheet after he won the appeal brought by the developer.

All by themselves, these court documents carried an aura of truth and power, Fidel Chicas vindicated by the authority of the California justice system—but of course the papers by themselves were powerless. The developer simply ignored the verdict, even after Fidel went back to court a third time to get something called "a writ of execution." It turns out that in Los Angeles County you have to pay the county marshals in advance to collect an unpaid judgment. Rather than give up and write off his loss, Fidel decided he would stake the developer out, showing up at his office, hoping that the physical presence of a persistent grandfather would provoke his debtor into paying. He had been at this for two years when I joined him on his stakeout.

We cornered the developer outside his condominium, Fidel with his court verdicts and me with my reporter's notebook and the sense I might help right a wrong. The developer looked at Fidel the way you might look at an unwanted piece of mail that someone slips under your door.

"I've never seen this man," the developer said. "I don't know who he is."

"You don't know me?" Fidel shot back angrily in Spanish. "What about there on the street corner? You knew me then."

My American-born readers liked that story because it suggested that all exotic, Spanish-speaking people living among them really were believers in "the system," that they wanted to be good "citizens," in the less literal sense of the word. I liked the story so much

I put it in the novel I wrote about immigrant Los Angeles a few years later. Except that in the book, the worker who's cheated never gets his money back: that is, after all, what usually happened in real life. Instead, he takes his revenge during the anarchy of the 1992 Los Angeles riots, the municipal day of settling accounts, a day to settle all vendettas, private and public. The riots were the other face to Fidel's patient wait for justice, the same frustration channeled outside the system. They began as a replay of the 1965 riots, an event that followed the historical logic of black-white race relations, but evolved into a parallel immigrant looting festival that would in a matter of hours become much bigger in breadth and scope than its African-American twin, spreading to places far from the conflagration's point of origin in South-Central Los Angeles, reaching even that Hollywood neighborhood where I had grown up and learned about Che a quarter of a century earlier.

Che would have disapproved of what I saw on the streets of Los Angeles that day. He was a notoriously stern disciplinarian, and in similar situations during the Cuban revolution he wasn't averse to restoring order with a summary execution or two. Still, he would have understood the collective desire to run down the street with ill-gotten canned goods, disposable diapers, imported beer, and other valuable objects as the predictable response of a people with a lesser legal and political status, a people who had come to believe, despite Fidel Chicas, that they lived outside the protective shelter of American democracy. In Los Angeles the one American legal term most immigrants are familiar with is also a double insult: "illegal alien." That phrase was not so much a part of the municipal vocabulary when I was growing up, an era when nearly anyone patient enough could paperwork his way into American residency and citizenship. Now it describes a way of thinking shared by millions of people in

California—"I belong here, you do not," and "They don't want me here, because I am not one of them."

On those blocks without burning buildings and shots being fired, the disorder took on a kind of playfulness: some guys rolling stolen tires down the middle of Pico Boulevard, for instance. This too was a fiesta, an expression of "the inflammable desires we carry within us," as Paz put it. For a fleeting moment, the city's stultifying sociological discipline was in ruins. At the end of the twentieth century, Southern California prospered, in large measure, because the Mexicans and Central Americans who made up the bulk of the low-wage labor force put in long hours and didn't complain as long as there was a little left over each month to send home. These same people now took over intersections that on any other day buzzed with orderly, low-budget commerce, and transformed them into frenzied spectacles of running crowds and exploding glass. It was the first Latin American–style class uprising in United States history, the same kind of visceral expression of rage that over the centuries had led peons to burn down the *hacendado*'s home, or villagers to turn up the cobblestones of their streets and throw them at marching soldiers.

With the *quemazones*, as they came to be known in Spanish ("the great burning"), a circle had closed in the life of the city. Two hundred fifty years earlier the U.S. flag was raised over Los Angeles for the first time, after the last Californio army surrendered to the forces of John Frémont at the Cahuenga Pass, a few miles up into the Hollywood Hills from the future site of Grant Elementary School. Ripped from Mexico by force, Los Angeles and the rest of California had been rejoined to the tragic, flamboyant arc of Latin American history, a narrative written by large crowds massed on streets, and peppered with dictators in epaulettes, messianic peasant leaders, and warrior priests. In the months and years that followed the riots, Latin America's mark on the city would be seen not only in the burned shells of liquor stores in South-Central Los Angeles, but also in the Mexican flags carried by protesting gardeners circling City Hall, and in the ideas and organizations of Central American émigrés, who quietly began asking what they could do to shape the future of the neighborhoods that had become their permanent homes. Because the city's legal and political forms were still those Colonel Frémont and the U.S. Army had brought across the Rockies in 1848, this activism gave rise to a hybrid civic culture, to bilingual banter at suburban city council meetings, and to neighborhood *comités de mejoras* (improvement committees) that met in garages to plot the unseating of unpopular mayors. The vocabulary of the Salvadoran and Mexican Left was being sprinkled into the city's civic discourse, a fact even now unknown to most of its English-speaking residents.

California had become so much like the places people came from that it too began to send off its more ambitious and restless sons and daughters to settle in newer places. News filtered back West of virgin lands to the East, where good wages were to be had and where the land was cheap and even a *jornalero* (a day worker) could own his own home. In North Carolina, the gossip went, there was so much work carving up chickens you could save up enough to buy up your own little *rancho,* and maybe even raise a few of your own birds for a good *caldo de gallina* soup. Go to this place called Maine, others said, way on the other edge of the map of the United States, and work in the forests and the gringos will treat you nicer than in California because there aren't as many of us *paisanos* over there. In that biggest of the big gringo cities, New York, there was work underneath the skyscrapers, well-paying jobs and big tips in restaurants and cafeterias and other places where the *gringuitas* smile at you because you look different. In the wake of the *paisanos* came various California entrepreneurs, and hucksters and artists, like corporations selling "traditional Mexican" radio programming by satellite, and the San Jose–based band, Los Tigres del Norte, whose songs would follow me as I tracked Latino culture across the United States.

The *paisanos* of Mexico, Guatemala, El Salvador, California, Texas, and other places where Spanish is spoken freely have pushed so far into the interior of North America that you could say a new Latin Republic of the United States is being born. About halfway into the United States, in places like Clay County, Alabama, the eastward push of the modern-day *paisano* pioneers meets the westward push of the Cubans and the Puerto Ricans, that other big, Caribbean strain of Latinness spreading across the country. In this new, Latin country, you can run a newspaper or run for office in Spanish, and save to send your children to Berkeley or Harvard while planning your retirement in a Salvadoran or Puerto Rican *pueblo*. A *ranchera* band's North American tour might begin in Monterrey, Mexico, and then make stops in Kearney, Nebraska, and Garden City, Kansas, before moving on to Salt Lake City. If you live on the Eastside of Los Angeles, you teach your daughter to be a good *mexicana,* which means passing on the conjugation of irregular Spanish verbs and an appreciation for *folklórico* dancing and for American-made Chevrolet Impalas that cruise down Cesar Chavez Avenue at twenty miles an hour. In Miami, you turn on the radio to "classic salsa" stations and Cuba lives in the Spanish-language rhetoric on the radio and in the cafés. All across this new country, people without a radical thought in their bodies are beginning to embrace, either consciously or subconsciously, that idea Che Guevara staked his life on in the last century: they believe they have a transnational identity, that their bodies and souls can live between two countries, that the physical border need not exist in the mind. I soon began wandering across this parallel nation being built inside the borders of the United States, to Rupert, Idaho, and Ashland, Alabama, to San Antonio and Little Havana in Miami. In all these places, people were practicing a new kind of Americanism, an *americanismo,* a dialogue about public life that takes place in both English and that language my mother and father kept alive in me by speaking it in the shelter of our home.

A certain Frenchman had made a similar journey two hundred years ago and chronicled the rise of a nation that was also then in its infancy, a democracy just unwrapped from the cellophane, its civic institutions raw and crisp. "The entire man is, so to speak, to be seen in the cradle of the child," Alexis de Tocqueville wrote in *Democracy in America,* which he began with a look at the "Origin of the Anglo-American." He believed that certain truths about American democratic culture had their root in the trauma of the crossing of the Atlantic, the harsh conditions endured by its settlers in those first, hardscrabble outposts. "The growth of nations bears something analogous to this; they all bear some marks of their origin. The circumstances that accompanied their birth and contributed to their development affected the whole term of their being."

My own examination of the values and beliefs of the recently born Latin Republic of the United States begins, then, in the crucible where its "new man" and "new citizen" is first shaped, during the horrors and tribulations of an often dangerous voyage. Like the Pilgrims, they've learned certain lessons about themselves and their future in their new homes from that crossing. For millions, the first step on this journey into a new Americanness takes place on the opposite end of the continent from Plymouth Rock, a two-hour drive south of Los Angeles, near the spot where a steel fence dips into the Pacific Ocean.

Chapter Two

WHERE GREEN CHILES ROAM
No es imposible

San Ysidro, California · Tijuana, Baja California, Mexico

The barrier rises and falls over gentle slopes and steep canyons until it finally reaches the ocean, dipping down along the sand and extending forty yards into the surf. It is a straight, man-made line imposing itself on the curves of the natural topography; seeing it for the first time, I was reminded of Christo's *Running Fence*, only this "sculpture" was rendered not in white fabric but in gray-black steel. Rising above the waterline, it cuts into the oncoming waves like a blunt, rusty knife.

Hardly anybody tries to jump over the fence during the day. Although it's past noon and the sun is out the first time I set eyes on the border, the beach is empty on both sides. The only living things are the seagulls perched along the top of the fence in a neat row, their beaks pointing south toward Baja, their backs turned to Alta California and the San Diego skyline far in the distance. The Border Patrol agents positioned in the park overlooking the beach spend eight-hour shifts sitting alone in their Ford Broncos, fighting the boredom and fatigue, passing uneventful hours looking out into the ocean for migrating dolphins or scanning the sky for the red-tailed hawks that circle overhead. They park between the stone picnic benches of Border Field State Park, a relic from the era when San Diego families on weekend outings could picnic here, before it became a battleground between competing national identities.

Farther inland, where the fence reaches a flat plain just north of downtown Tijuana, a handful of border crossers wait for nightfall on the Mexican side, defiant in the face of the innumerable obstacles before them—the new fence and the new Broncos and the new agents, who seem to have an uncanny knack for catching people, even in the dark. "I think that the border will disappear before we lose the desire to cross," a man will tell me later, in Spanish, on the other side. "Even if they catch us one hundred times, we're going to get in one day." There is little evidence here of the border these men expected to find, the one that still exists in the collective memory of a generation of immigrants. More than a million people stepped over that other border, across the estuary of the Tijuana River, the shortest route from Mexico into the gilded paradise that was Southern California. They were the arithmetic of the great demographic shift that transformed entire communities of Los Angeles and Orange counties into Latino barrios, who made Spanish the language of choice in suburbs like North Hollywood, Huntington Park, and Santa Ana. In the old days, the fence was a flimsy chain-link sieve, and the agents who guarded it were more than overmatched. At one popular crossing spot, the fence had been flattened, allowing crowds of immigrants to wander back and forth across the international frontier at will.

When I walked along the empty U.S. side of the border, I could still find footprints in the mud of the Tijuana estuary, pointing north toward the first suburban tract homes of San Ysidro, and bits of clothes and shoes scattered among the clumps of coastal sagebrush. But generally speaking, the open land north of this five-mile stretch of frontier had returned to a bucolic state. There were only the sounds of the ocean breeze rustling through the trees, blowing loose soil. A bean field grew without much difficulty just a few paces from the border, on a plateau where people walking north would have once trampled the seedlings underfoot. Standing on a hill on the U.S. side, looking down into Mexico, you no longer saw the crowds that used to gather along *la línea*. Instead, there was only the squat skyline of downtown Tijuana, the vacation homes of the Tijuana elite, the passing traffic along Calle Internacional, an urban organism pressing up against the fence, an unnaturally straight line laid out by surveyors fourteen decades earlier. The truncated cityscape before me gave no hint of people sleeping along the bottom of the fence on the other side, exhausted after waiting all night, in vain, for a chance to cross. It was possible to look into Mexico and not know that thousands of immigrants from places like Guerrero and Michoacán, Honduras and Guatemala, were milling about the city center, unable to cross after spending most of their savings just to get this far. It was possible to look into Mexico and not know that more than a few had given up and turned back, or were contemplating a death-defying trek into the white wilderness of the Arizona desert. It was possible to stand in the open, empty terrain of the United States and revel in the natural beauty of the Tijuana River estuary without knowing the dimensions of the drama unfolding just over there, on the other side of the fence.

The border had been transformed thanks to the cultural war taking place to the north, in California, for much of the twentieth century the preferred destination of the Mexican immigrant. Two years after I had witnessed that great Latino class uprising on the streets of Los Angeles, the voters of English-speaking California had taken their revenge by approving—by an overwhelming majority— an initiative called Proposition 187. It happened during a campaign season of xenophobia that also saw Pete Wilson get reelected governor of California by promising to stop the tide of brown-skinned people surging over the border. English-speaking California had demanded a last stand against the Mexicanization of the Southwest, that their leaders put an end to the mad dash for America taking place here, and the Border Patrol responded with Operation Gatekeeper. Intended as a series of temporary measures, Operation Gatekeeper became a permanent attempt to seal off the border to illegal crossings. The government had built the new fence, added about five hundred Border Patrol agents, and brought in the army for "logistical support." The Border Patrol was outfitted with new Ford Broncos and a lot of fancy equipment, much of it Pentagon hand-me-downs like motion detectors and thermal-imaging technology.

By all accounts, the strategy had been a resounding success, as was proved by the usual American barometer of bureaucratic achievement, a cascade of statistics. When I arrived, apprehension rates were up by 40 percent from the pre-Gatekeeper era: in the San Diego sector, from the ocean to the Imperial County line in the desert fifty miles away, the Border Patrol claimed to be rounding up 1,800 people every day; in a week they detained enough *mexicanos* and other immigrants to fill a smallish California town. In the suburban communities north of the border, residents complained less and less about people running through their property. "We can now sleep at night without being awakened by illegals congregating in our backyard," one grateful Imperial Beach resident said in a letter that the Border Patrol displayed in its San Ysidro field headquarters. The frontier had an orderly, official look to it, and as a visual reminder of how much they had achieved, the agents in the headquarters placed a collage of pictures of the old border in one of their offices. The pictures showed crowds of people, mostly men in jeans, standing around the spot where a fence sits now, but then only an open field of brown dirt with no barrier at all. The would-be immigrants looked like people milling around waiting for a modern-day Woodstock to get started.

Tijuana residents and human rights activists I talked to agreed that the five-mile stretch of border between San Ysidro and the Pacific Ocean had become more difficult to cross than ever before. Tijuana was full of stories of immigrants who had tried to cross into California over the traditional routes, only to be caught by the Border Patrol and sent back, again and again, in a hellish treadmill of detentions and deportations. The next-best place to cross farther east was over the Otay Mesa, north of the Baja California city of Tecate, but that route took thirty-five hours or longer to reach a safe spot in the north, something you could accomplish in as little as half an hour back at *el bordo*, the mile-long stretch of frontier just a few blocks from downtown Tijuana, or at the beach called Playas de Tijuana.

For Victor Clark Alfaro, a lifelong Tijuanense and founder of the Binational Center for Human Rights, it was the end of an era. I met him in his office, the usual activist's hovel of stacked pamphlets and denunciatory reports of rapes, robberies, and assorted acts of official corruption. His life had been threatened by Tijuana's notoriously violent and murderous drug cartels, but there was only a single, bored guard posted outside his office. In the long running list of offenses against humanity he kept in his head, the plight of the border crosser was the most repeated entry. "*El bordo* is no longer the traditional place to cross," he told me. "*El bordo* has passed to history. Playas de Tijuana belongs to the past." The consequences of this new reality, he said, were felt most strongly by the poorest immigrants, those who couldn't afford to pay the $300 to $700 a smuggler might charge them to make the crossing safely and without difficulty. "Imagine a group of people who arrived at the border without money in their pockets, or with money that is indispensable, with the minimum necessary to cross into the United States. And they find that there is this obstacle. They cross and they're deported. They cross, and they're deported again. And pretty soon their money runs out. Now we have people who've been deported eight, ten, fifteen times."

When I stood on the Mexican side of el *bordo* and talked to the people preparing to cross, there was one phrase I heard repeated again and again. "*No es imposible.*" It is not impossible. Every migrant I met held on to this hope. Yes, there were more agents, and yes, there was this new fence and rumors of other obstacles in the seemingly open territory beyond, but *no es imposible.* Some do make it. To hear people tell it, getting to the other side was becoming a lottery. The woman who sold candies and cookies and juices at a post on *el bordo* said that out of a hundred or so who tried, only two or three made it, though I suspected there was a touch of melodrama in that figure, because after all, how could she really know how many disappeared into California forever? But she said she watched people try every night, heading out past the lean-tos of scrap wood and tarpaulin that embraced the Mexican side of the fence. They set off sprinting northward in large groups, toward the massed Border Patrol agents, and got thrown back like cannon-fodder soldiers in a hopeless infantry charge. She was a witness to a nightly Gettysburg, and as in that famous battle the brave Southerners didn't have much of a chance against the well-outfitted Yankees. When her compatriots tried to cross in the rain, they would come back soaking wet, and she would give them a blanket to dry off and keep warm.

At first glance, it didn't seem that getting across could be that complicated. For all the talk of the "militarization of the border," the fence itself didn't present much of an obstacle. Although made of sturdy steel—"landing mats" used as temporary runways for military aircraft during the first Iraq war—it was still only ten feet high and did not have any barbed wire on top. There were wide grooves in the steel that were like the steps on a ladder. Getting back into your apartment after you've lost your keys would present a greater challenge. The phrase "Tortilla Curtain" captured the apparently makeshift nature of this new border, especially when compared with its much older and now-vanquished cousin, the Iron Curtain. This is no Berlin Wall. There are no guard towers, no machine-gun nests, no moats or attack dogs.

There are even a few narrow spots in Tijuana where, thanks to small accidents of topography, there is no fence at all. Standing in the rain one night on the dirt shoulder of Calle Internacional, I interviewed two men at one such spot, a twenty-yard-wide fenceless stretch. Here, U.S. territory drops off the edge of a ridge, while the Mexican side stays up, rising over the imaginary line of the frontier, over the top of where the fence would be. For Ignacio Ayala and Raúl Rodríguez, crossing the border would be as simple as taking one step and dropping four or five feet down an embankment. One step, and they would plop down out of Mexico.

They sat waiting, soaking wet in the cold rain. It was still early in the evening, and their vigil had only begun. At the moment, crossing was impossible thanks to the Ford Bronco parked about fifty yards away, its windshield wipers going and engine running. Under the tall lampposts, rain fell in white sheets against the black sky. Their great hope was that the large group of border crossers in the canyon about a half-mile to the west would make a run for it and draw the Bronco in their direction, thus opening a path for the two of them. "It's harder than last year, but *no es imposible*," Rodríguez told me. "The thing is to jump, and the rest is easy. Once you get to San Ysidro, it's a piece of cake. But you have to get past them," he said, gesturing toward the Bronco. "You cross, and they see you hidden someplace, but you can't tell they see you. You can hear them calling out. 'How many do you have? I've got this many!'" Rodríguez was able to rattle off a list of what he was up against: agents in Broncos, agents in helicopters, agents on bicycles. They also have "*cámaras infrarrojas*," he said, and this was clearly unsettling, to know that the heat of his body might give him away. "You can't see the cameras. We don't know where they are. We jump and think no one saw us, but then, before we know it, there's the Immigration."

At the new border, the obstacles are in what you can't see. The heat-sensing equipment, the agents hiding in the dark. This is the Border Patrol's great accomplishment: to have constructed a barrier as innocuous-looking as the fence around a high school, yet nearly as effective as anything Erich Honecker built.

T he average immigrant at Tijuana those days was feeling a bit defrauded. *I left the bosom of my family for this? I should be in Long Beach by now, but instead I am here, in this nowhere, limbo place.* Or maybe he thought he waited too long, that he had missed his chance to walk through the open door his more punctual countrymen had stepped through without much difficulty or trauma. People in the town of Tlalchapa, in the southern Mexican state of Guerrero, would have heard crossing tales such as the one told by Flocelo Aguirre, a onetime *bracero* (a seasonal worker granted temporary permission to work in the fields of American farmers) and *fútbol* fanatic who lived with his family in an expansive adobe home with a sturdy tile roof. Flocelo made his permanent and first illegal crossing into the United States in 1968, the year of the Olympics in Mexico

City. He arrived at the border by bus, with a wad of cash and a fake credential as a schoolteacher given to him by a friend at Mexico's Secretariat of Public Education. With the money, the document, and the courage to tell a necessary lie, he gave the American immigration official at the Calexico, California, border crossing his cover story: *I am a Mexican professional, a teacher on vacation, who is going to see this place called Disneyland that everyone is talking about.* These days, such a transparent deception would probably earn you a howl of laughter and a finger pointing firmly southward. But back then, Flocelo's brief, pleasant border interview resulted in the agent handing over a 100-day tourist visa. Flocelo stepped onto a northbound Greyhound and headed to Los Angeles for the next quarter-century or so, and then later to Dalton, Georgia, where he would become the unstoppable organizing force behind the largest Latino organization in that part of the Deep South, the Dalton International Soccer League. The most uncomfortable thing about his 1968 journey was that he had to hold his bladder a few hours from the border all the way to the town of Indio, California, where he finally had a chance to go to the bathroom.

Leopoldo Avalos, whose daughter Carmen would one day help rescue democracy in the working-class Los Angeles suburb called South Gate, had a slightly more difficult time of it, heading out on foot across the mountains at dusk, entering the United States under a starry sky and then stepping toward the earthly constellation of lights of an American city, ready to begin a life of hard work and reinvention. Like most immigrants of his generation, after he had settled down in California he sent back word for his family to come join him. His two-year-old daughter Carmen crossed in the arms of a relative, dressed to look like a boy because her fake document was a boy cousin's birth certificate. That's the way it was when no one in the English-speaking United States imagined that the hundreds of people coming to see Disneyland, or the baby boys who weren't boys, were in fact packages of culture who would one day change their country forever. The immigrants had all passed through Tijuana, Mexicali, Laredo, and other border towns without much incident, leaving behind villages in the Mexican heartland that became a little emptier with each passing year, like those one-stoplight towns in the Great Plains where so many young people have left that there aren't enough beefy kids to put together a football team anymore.

A gent Scott Marvin was a member of what he calls "the new Border Patrol." The old Border Patrol wasn't adequately funded, and it suffered from public-relations nightmares, including a few agents who reportedly beat and raped the immigrants who came into their custody. The new Border Patrol, he told me, is better trained and better educated. Marvin himself had been to graduate school, and as he guided me on the standard press tour of the new border, he seemed to be dictating phrases to me, including the occasional attempt at a poetic turn. "At night the lights of Tijuana shine like jewels, and the lights of San Diego are equally radiant." He was a tall, fit, mustachioed man, and as we drove about the border in the mount of his Bronco, along the American side of the fence, across mudflats and up and down canyons, with me playing the skeptic as he made triumphant pronouncements, I felt like a shortish Sancho Panza to his Don Quixote. Morale was up, Agent Marvin told me, the battle against the disorder and anarchy was being won. Agent Marvin was a knight in a brand new Border Patrol army whose troops beamed with the can-do spirit Americans get when their budgets are increased, when they've been outfitted with the latest technologies.

"This is the human element," Marvin told me as we looked at yet another agent inside yet another Ford Bronco. "And then there's the sensors in the ground." Seismic sensors, he explained, about 450 of them buried in the soil of his "sector," pick up the tiny earthquakes caused by a migrant's footsteps. Raúl Rodríguez did not know that not only the heat of his body but even his footsteps and the weight of his body would give him away. "With the helicopters and the people up on high points with the nightscopes, you've got it all in one package. The sensor is triggered, dispatch tells you the sensor went off. The scope operator looks over to see—was it possibly an animal that set it off? They say, 'No, someone's jumped the fence, there's four people that are headed along the creek bed.' The scope operator watches this in pitch-black. You'll go to the north end of the creek bed, and [someone else] will wait for them. And maybe your partner in another vehicle can come around to the south and sandwich them, and you'll have an effortless and painless apprehension."

High on a mesa, not far from the bean field, we parked near the fence and took a walk around. Agent Marvin found a hole underneath the fence, just big enough for a person to crawl under. I couldn't help but make the observation that "it looks like they found a way through Agent Marvin." The hole was next to a spot where concrete had been poured under the fence to patch up yet another hole. "It doesn't matter how deep you go down," Agent Marvin conceded, "they'll dig under it." To all my questions about the new technology, Agent Marvin gave quick, precise responses. What about the infrared binoculars? No, he said, what they use is called "thermal-imaging equipment." It's a large lens on a telescoping tower, operated by an agent in the vehicle below, who moves it around with a joystick: "It's almost like playing a computer game." The helicopter, called Foxtrot, is a Vietnam War survivor with metal patches over the holes caused by the Viet Cong's AK rounds. There's new fingerprinting equipment (the IDENT system, an acronym no one was able to decipher for me), which allows each illegal immigrant caught to be entered into a computerized database. The Army helped build the fence and, even more important, helped build and improve the all-weather access roads that allow the Border Patrol agents to drive right up to the edge of the border, acting as a visual deterrent to potential crossers.

"The vehicles are newer and in good condition. There's more agents in the field, the fence is there. It's a clear line," Marvin says. In the California I knew, the lines were blurry. But here the Border Patrol and its allies in the Army had taken the equivalent of a giant black Magic Marker and made sure everyone could still see that that line was still there, that it hadn't dissolved into the desert sand. The message to everyone on both sides was clear: "We're here and you're there and you need to stay there. And we're going to help you stay there. And if you don't stay there, we're going to help you back across, after we've taken your fingerprints, taken your picture, and taken your biographical data. If you come back again, no matter what name you use, we'll know you crossed."

We proceeded to the communications center. Four men sat at computer consoles, wearing headsets and microphones, watching the computer track "hits" on the motion sensors planted out in the field. Place names flash on the computer screen: SPRING CANYON . . . NORTH AMBUSH ALLEY . . . GOAT CANYON. One of the technicians clicked a mouse, making graphs of seismic tremors appear. At his feet, there was a copy of *Wired* magazine.

One night, not far from the bank of the Tijuana River, I interviewed a man I could not see. I was standing on the American side of the frontier, on a bare patch of mud illuminated by a single, powerful sodium lamp; my interviewee was inside Mexico, a pair of lips puckering through a seam between the metal plates of the border fence. I had stopped here after spotting two Ford Broncos parked nearby, keeping watch over an especially popular crossing point. I placed my palm against the steel, and then listened to dozens of Spanish speaking voices, an unseen chorus of anxious and angry people trapped on the other side. The man I was talking to was a coyote nicknamed "El Cochi Crazy," and he was one of the men in charge of the people waiting to dash into the United States.

El Cochi Crazy said he was going to cross five of his *pollos*, "chickens." He wouldn't let the photographer I was with, a roly-poly Serb named Slobodan, take his picture through the fence, because he'd already been in two U.S. jails and he didn't need any more hassles. He served six months for one smuggling sentence, he said, and a year for the second. El Cochi Crazy wanted to know if I would do him a favor. Would I go over to the Border Patrol agents and ask them to move back, just a little? If the agents moved back, he would send his *pollos* over the fence and Slobodan and I would be treated to the show we'd come to see: actual humans sprinting under the lights in an all-or-nothing dash for the safety of the darkness that began a hundred or so yards into the United States. The desperation in his voice suggested this was not intended as a joke. I looked back at the Broncos, imagined the gruff American agents inside, and already knew what the answer would be: and besides, did I really want to be responsible for setting off such a sickening spectacle? So I declined the request, and for the moment the stalemate persisted.

The smuggler said he charges his *pollos* $350. For this, he'd get them to the airport in Los Angeles, a gateway to the continent beyond, the jobs busing tables in Las Vegas, picking apples in Washington State, construction in Phoenix. Although he didn't say so, it soon became clear El Cochi Crazy was part of a larger smuggling outfit, the kind that had been described to me by people on both sides of the border: a mini-corporation with an elaborate division of labor that includes recruiters at the Tijuana airport and bus stations, guides at the border, drivers waiting in San Ysidro, and safe houses beyond.

"Ten of us jump, and the *migra* only catches two," El Cochi Crazy's lips yelled through the fence. The longer he talked, the more macho the inflection of his voice. "There's only one *migra*. There's hundreds of us, but the *migra* has just one brain."

"Do you jump with them?" I asked in Spanish.

"We go just a little. They don't catch us, they just catch the people. If they catch me, I'll go back to jail."

"When will your *pollos* cross?"

"When these agents leave, that's when we jump. We just run. We can't fly, so we run." His bravado started to infect the would-be immigrants with him, people I could not see, voices behind the fence. "The more *migra* they put in," one man yelled, "the more we'll massacre them."

"We hit them with rocks," another said. "If they hit one of us, we throw rocks."

I felt I had stumbled upon a tiny riot in a bottle. I felt the tension of certain overcrowded and underpaid neighborhoods of Los Angeles standing there. Tijuana was a Los Angeles without good-paying jobs or enforceable laws. Both places were filled with the desperately poor of Mesoamerica and white English-speakers being served by those poor people. The men behind the fence wanted to fight, they wanted to let loose with violence against the Ford Broncos and the agents frustrating their ambitions and plans. For months after the L.A. riots, I had a nightmare in which a mob of young men pulled people from their cars and beat them, and at moments like this the old demons of my subconscious stir to life again; I wanted to leave and drive back through the dirt roads across the estuary to my relatively comfortable hotel in San Ysidro. Or maybe I would walk over to Tijuana and have a margarita to relax and forget this craziness: for me, crossing back and forth across the border presented no difficulty whatsoever, even though I looked as "Mexican" as the men hanging on to the top of this fence. I didn't even need a passport to cross back and forth: the perfect English with which I answered the immigration agent's curt questions was enough to establish my citizenship. My voice was the document my parents had bequeathed to me by ensuring I was born in the United States, and if any of the men on the fence before me made it across, they would surely bequeath it to their children too.

Agent Marvin told me that Border Patrol agents call this stretch of fence Memo Lane, because when they drive their Broncos here they get rocks through their windshields, thus requiring a memo to their supervisor. That's the way it is on the border: one man's odyssey is another man's bureaucracy, one man's life-defining drama is another's routine. One of the *pollos* climbed the fence. Straddling the top, he leaned over and spat into the United States. Then, suddenly, a man in blue sweatpants plopped over onto the U.S. side, but he was just taunting the agents. He quickly rescaled the fence and jumped back into Mexico even before Slobodan could snap his picture.

"Is it harder to cross?" I asked the smuggler.

"No, it's the same," he said.

"But I've talked to people who keep on trying and can't make it."

"It's because they don't want to pay!"

Then in English, he yelled, "Don't pay, no crossing!"

. . .

Of course, not even the East Germans could create a hermetic seal around their country, despite motion detectors, dogs, barbed wire, and guards with shoot-to-kill orders. The larger, inevitable truth at the U.S.–Mexican border was that all the technology in the world would not hold back the tens of thousands of men, women, and children who headed northward because they believed their lives would be better there. In Latin America, you were born to a station in life. Class mobility was something that existed only in the *telenovela* soap operas, with their deus ex machina endings in which the maid becomes a millionaire. The only sure way to give your life a *telenovela* ending was to head northward.

José Antonio Gutiérrez, a future United States Marine who was among the first troops to enter Saddam Hussein's Iraq in 2003, was born into the lowest rungs of Guatemala's social ladder. He was an "untouchable" whose toddler years were spent on the streets and in the hovels of the city of Escuintla, an existence dominated by the turbid waters of the stream that ran through his *colonia* and the vultures who fed there. His baby sister drowned in a puddle of water on the street, his mother died of tuberculosis and his father's liver was destroyed by cirrhosis, and much of his boyhood was spent in orphanages and detention centers, until he graduated from all that to become a migrant, crossing the border at about the same time I visited there. He traveled overland from Guatemala across Mexico, was detained twice by the Mexican authorities, but had still made it over the final obstacle, the U.S. border itself, by hiding "underneath a freight train," or by stowing away inside the train, according to the various accounts he later provided to foster parents, juvenile court judges, and immigration officials. Like an earlier generation of immigrants, he had resorted to a quick-witted deception, telling the social workers who finally caught up with him in California that he was sixteen years old (he was in fact twenty-two), because he knew that undocumented immigrants who were "unaccompanied minors" were often declared wards of the court and would be allowed stay in the United States. Thus he became a poet and a high-school soccer star—in short, he achieved a fuller expression of his humanity—and lived to see himself crowned with the white dress hat and gold shield of the Marine Corps.

It was precisely this kind of miraculous reinvention that inspired people in the modern-day cities and towns of Latin America to take their chances against Operation Gatekeeper. They gathered their meager resources and assembled in groups for what could be called Operation Sahara, a desperate detour around the new obstacles put up by Agent Marvin and his colleagues, a trek across the desert that in the early years of the twenty-first century became a human drama of Cecil B. DeMille proportions (a drama that remains mostly invisible to Americans because it unfolds far from cities and television cameras). Some 2,000 people died trying to cross the U.S.-Mexico border between 1998 and 2003, and every summer the stories of their deaths peppered American newspapers. They walked in circles under the sun and died face-down on the Arizona soil, seeking the nonexistent shade of the mesquite brush; they died with empty milk jugs at their side or after dropping unused diapers and phone books with telephone numbers in North Carolina. They died cooked inside railroad cars, or suffocated inside the stainless-steel containers of tractor-trailers. They died trying to cross the Barry Goldwater Bombing Range and within sight of the runway at the Bisbee, Arizona, airport.

Two daughters of Marisol Romero (not her real name) crossed this desert on their way from Chiapas, Mexico, to Ashland, Alabama, in the company of a coyote smuggler. They were the last of

Marisol's ten children to cross, all hoping for work in the chicken plants and furniture factories in that orderly landscape of Baptist churches and fenced-off pastures in the foothills of the Cumberland Mountains, a landscape green in the winter and green in the humid summer. Ashland was a verdant Eden to keep in mind as they walked across the brown Arizona desert, wondering if they would make it to the van waiting for them on the highway the smuggler told them was just a few miles up ahead, even though they saw nothing in front of them but wilderness. Marisol's daughters were stopped not far from the border by a band of robbers, men who pointed guns and knives at them. But *"gracias a Dios, nada más eso,"* her mother tells me, "thanks be to God, they did only that": in other words, her daughters were not raped. They were simply relieved of all their cash, and the coyote leading them was ordered to strip naked: the thieves punished the coyote because he had denied being a smuggler and tried to blend in with his "chickens," which was an insult to the intelligence of the thieves, who knew a fellow delinquent when they saw one. Marisol's daughters survived and arrived in Ashland to begin to look for work and to plant roots in a place where their father already worked for a utility company, a dream job for a man from the hills of Chiapas. Probably they will spend the rest of their lives in the Deep American South, long enough to tell their grandchildren the story of the naked smuggler.

Perhaps in the distant future the travails of the desert crossers will become the institutionalized and mythologized narrative that the Underground Railroad is today, a story told to schoolchildren in history textbooks illustrated with idealized drawings like those of Harriet Tubman leading escaped slaves toward a bright North Star. Or maybe their story will enter the canon of American literature, like the tale of the Joads in *The Grapes of Wrath*, who cross the California desert after playing a small deception on the officials manning the Inspection Station at the Arizona-California line, Ma Joad explaining, in her Oklahoma accent, "The fambly hadda get acrost." The long arc of American history can perform startling feats of transformation: it can make the lawbreakers and despised Okies of one epoch into the heroic icons of another.

Every week, the Border Patrol in San Ysidro was tossing hundreds of lawbreakers back across the border. The most unfortunate of these crossers would end up at La Casa del Migrante, a motel-like complex of 220 bunk beds where daily meals were served. I stopped by there one afternoon and found a courtyard crowded with a sad cross section of men from every corner of Mexico and Central America, men with baseball caps and the mud of the Tijuana estuary on their pants. Many looked pale and exhausted, as if they had walked here from Mexico City and been tossed over the fence and back a hundred times, and could not carry the plastic bags and backpacks that contained their possessions a day longer.

Sitting on a bench in the courtyard was a man who looked especially forlorn. Ramón Gonzales García stood out because of the cast on his leg and the crutches at his side. Nine days earlier, he had tried to jump the border's steel fence for the first time. He was a dignified *campesino* with coffee-colored skin and a droopy mustache who bore a strong resemblance, except for his baseball cap, to the late revolutionary Emiliano Zapata. Gonzales had arrived in Tijuana after a two-day bus trip from his hometown of Morelia, Michoacán, expecting to cross when night fell, only to find the situation was "hotter" (*más caliente*) than he expected. When he finally saw a gap in the Border Patrol's line, a moment when no Ford Broncos patrolled the other side, he made a run for it, hoping to get past the row of sodium lamps on the U.S. side. He was about fifty yards into California when an agent stepped out of the darkness and yelled, "Hey you! *Prieto!* [dark-skinned man] Go back!" So he did. But when the agent turned his attention to another group of border crossers, Gonzales hid in the bushes. "I thought that as soon as he left, I'd be able to slip by." Gonzales lay there, flat on his stomach on the sandy soil, until this same Border Patrol agent surprised him from behind. In a moment, the agent pulled his arms behind his back and handcuffed him. Then the agent lifted him up, the way a rodeo cowboy lifts up a calf, and stomped down on his leg.

"Ay!" Gonzales said faintly as he recounted this part of the story. Reaching down his pants leg toward the broken limb, now in a cast, he gritted his teeth, pantomiming the pain. He tried to tell the Border Patrol man he was hurt, but all the agent did was yell at him in Spanish, "We told you, *cabrón!* We told you to go back! Why didn't you go back?" Gonzales asked for a doctor or an ambulance, but instead the agent led him, limping, back toward the fence. The pain was blinding, and before he knew it Gonzales was sitting in an office. Only when a Mexican policeman entered the room did he know he was back in Tijuana.

All this had happened nine days earlier, but Gonzales still looked shaken. He'd been caught breaking the law and had been treated like a criminal and the idea of this was like being forced to wear a set of clothes that belonged to another man. He did not think of himself as a criminal, of course. He thought what he was doing was an act of nobility and self-sacrifice: he had risked arrest and injury to bring his family a better life. Now the handcuffs had caused his wrists to swell and he had been thoroughly humiliated, but the worst part of it was that the agent was a Latino, one of "our people." He spoke perfect Spanish, without even the trace of an accent.

I asked him how long his leg would be in a cast.

The doctor said four weeks. Maybe longer. The way his luck had been going lately, longer seemed more likely.

"I'm going to go back to my *tierra*. It doesn't make any sense anymore to cross. You start to think about a lot of things. I'm going through one of the most difficult moments of my life. I didn't expect this. I had a plan, but it didn't work." We talked a little more and he struck a reflective note. "I lived better back home," he said, taking a look at the shelter around him, at its concrete floors and spare rooms. In his hometown he'd been a shoemaker, a waiter, and a gardener. He'd just turned thirty-four and thought he deserved something better. If Michoacán was a place where everything and everyone seemed to be stuck in the same place, California represented the possibility of "reaching a goal." Now that he'd broken his leg, Gonzales seemed to think he should be more humble, accept his station in life. "Sometimes ambition, your dreams, the desire to live better puts you in a bad spot. You fall to this level." It was as if he believed his broken leg and empty wallet were a kind of divine punishment for having overreached in his ambition.

Statistically speaking, Gonzales and the other men inside that refuge were an anomaly: every year the Border Patrol detained about one million people crossing the border, but the most conservative estimate placed the number of successful illegal crossers at three times that figure. Three million people entered the country each year, because not even the United States was wealthy enough to put motion detectors and Ford Broncos along a border that was two thousand miles long. Instead, those millions who did make it across would carry the memory of their passages through the border purgatory, a region staffed by English- and Spanish-speaking agents of retribution, some uniformed, others not, men who assembled to inflict modern humiliations and archaic torments on those who passed through their desert gauntlet. To the south of the line there were the venal Mexican police officers who mined the busloads of migrants of the wads of cash they carried, tossing the moneyless into concrete holding cells. To the north there were the Americans, the Border Patrol and their computers waiting to catalogue the detained before shipping them southward, and the vigilantes—ranchers and storekeepers armed with shotguns and a sense of violated entitlement—itching to round up the trespassing hordes.

Tocqueville said that the traumatic circumstances of the seventeenth-century pilgrims' crossing of the Atlantic and arrival in Massachusetts—"a hideous and desolate wilderness, full of wilde beasts, and wilde men"—defined "the whole term of their being" as Americans. Their austere Puritan faith and egalitarian beliefs saw them through, leaving a mark on the Anglo-American republic that endures to this day. Eventually, the migrants of the twentieth and twenty-first centuries will become de facto Americans, too, settling permanently in the United States, sending their children to public schools and paying a variety of taxes to keep the roads paved and the hospitals in good working order. But their crossing story is often one of violence and powerlessness. More than likely, on this journey the migrant has encountered, or entrusted his fate to, professional criminals like *El Cochi Crazy*. The migrant who succeeds in entering the United States under these circumstances does so with a degraded sense of self.

There is another group of people in U.S. history who endured a similarly violent and troubled path into Americanness. In *The Souls of Black Folk*, W. E. B. DuBois explores how African-American identity was shaped by Reconstruction, the beginning of the long purgatory between slavery and the flowering of freedom that came in the second half of the twentieth century. The post–Civil War South was "an armed camp for intimidating black people," he wrote, with its roving bands of Klansmen, racist judges, and police stripping Southern black people of the notion of themselves as citizens, in the broadest sense of the word. *The Souls of Black Folk,* written in 1903, was a spiritual and moral snapshot of a people not yet free, and as I read its pages a hundred years later I can't help but see parallels to the Spanish-speaking people I've met who have undertaken a crossing, a birth into a new country. The black man strives to be "a coworker in the kingdom of culture, to escape both death and isolation, to husband and use his best powers and his latent genius," DuBois writes. But he discovers that "to be a poor race is hard, but to be a poor race in a land of dollars is the very bottom of hardships."

I wandered from the administrator's office back to the shelter's courtyard. Gonzales had risen with his crutches and joined the line of men waiting to step into the dining room for their dinner: a plate of beans, beef, and vegetables. When the meal was served, they sat down at long tables, dozens of men bowing their heads to say the Our Father, the room and its concrete walls filling with a chorus of whispers. To be undocumented—or illegal, if you don't like euphemisms—is to live continuously in a mental state similar to the one I saw among those men in Tijuana, the state of not quite being at your destination, of not quite having arrived. Because even after you get past the border, when you are sitting in the relative safety of your apartment in Los Angeles, or a trailer in Kentucky, you know you can step outside and fall into the arms of the authorities, who will have every right to deport you forthwith. I have a Guatemalan relative, a computer technician, currently living in the greater Los Angeles area who lives in precisely this set of circumstances, the possibility of detention and expulsion from his new home hovering over the routine of his daily existence. He knows that one day he could step out from his San Fernando Valley apartment and never return, the food in the refrigerator left to grow stale and rot. The people at his job who rely on him to keep their computers working will wonder what happened to him, and probably have an inkling of what did. They will not be surprised when he finally makes it to a Mexican telephone and calls to deliver the news: No, I will not be there tomorrow to help clean the latest worm from the boss's hard drive. Probably he has thought through precisely this scenario, he has imagined himself erased from the picture of his California life as cleanly and thoroughly as if he were a digital image on the office computer screen, wiped out with a few clicks of a mouse.

The officers of El Operativo Beta are the "untouchables" of Mexican law enforcement. Recruited from local, state, and federal agencies, their mission is to patrol the border area and protect the immigrants not only from smugglers and the *bajapollos* (loose translation: chicken hawks) but also from the corrupt police officials who, for decades, have made ripping off migrants a lucrative business. While the U.S. Border Patrol is outfitted with new Ford Broncos, their Mexican counterparts in Beta make do with a variety of battered jalopies. The black LTD Crown Victoria driven by Officer Cuauhtemoc Montesinos could have been a refugee from a demolition derby or a relic from the *Adam 12* era of police work; its passenger-side door opened barely enough for me to squeeze inside.

Officer Montesinos wore a California Angels baseball cap, which turned out to be quite appropriate, as he spent most of his patrol shift acting like a guardian angel to the migrants who sleep and live along *el bordo*. He told them where they could go for a hot meal and which number to call if any smuggler or police officer tried to shake them down for cash. In El Cañon del Muerto ("Dead Man's Canyon"), known as Smuggler's Canyon on the U.S. side, Montesinos talked to a group of wiry men who live in tents hidden in a cluster of bushes. They said they preferred to live amid the scrub of the canyon, because when they would go downtown, *cholos* harassed them and tried to steal their belongings. Montesinos noticed that one of the men carried an inhaler for asthma medicine and gave him the number for the Red Cross.

Still, there were not many migrants for Montesinos to talk to on this shift, not as many as there were, say, a year earlier. "This was a place where a lot of people used to come," Montesinos said as we drove along the bank of the Tijuana River at the point where its concrete spillway runs diagonally across the border. Just a half-dozen or so men were standing around, waiting for nightfall. "There used to be a lot of people here," he said a few minutes later, about a place where the border fence cut across a ravine in the working-class neighborhood of Colonia Libertad. "It's very slow here today," he said as we stopped by the beach. At each spot, we looked over the fence and saw the ubiquitous Ford Broncos of the U.S. Border Patrol. At some places, there were almost as many agents waiting on the other side as there were migrants on this side.

Tijuana is a maze of twisting streets and diagonals and traffic circles that occupies nearly every square foot of terrain right up to the edge of the fence. Where the border runs past Colonia Libertad, the lonely Border Patrol agents parked high on a rocky ridge in the United States could look down into a crowded Mexican neighborhood and watch boys and girls in navy uniforms walking home from school, women hanging their laundry, and street vendors pushing their carts up and down the steep streets. The agents in the Broncos on the U.S. side of the fence watched as Officer Montesinos and I interviewed a group of men gathered near *el bordo* about a mile from the ocean. Enrique López, a thirty-year-old warehouse worker from Mazatlán, told us he had left his hometown three days after his wife gave birth to their daughter—he'd been in Tijuana for twenty-two days, about twenty-one longer than he'd expected. He left Mazatlán because he and his wife were having a hard time making ends meet, and it wasn't going to get any easier with the new baby. With what he made at the warehouse, sometimes he had only $14 a week to give his wife for groceries. Deported after his first two failed crossings, he found a construction job in Tijuana for a few weeks, hoping to save enough for another attempt. But he soon discovered that "everything here in Tijuana is too expensive" and that saving was impossible. "Any little meal you get, a breakfast, a lunch, is going to cost you fifteen, twenty pesos. So you end up paying forty-five, fifty pesos a day to eat. And then there's clothes. You buy some pants, and that costs ten, fifteen pesos. And you don't have anything left." He's developed a new appreciation, he says, for how his wife took the little money he gave her and made it last a whole week. "I don't know how she does it. She just takes that hundred pesos," he says, using his hands to mimic pulling a rubber band, "and stretches it and stretches it."

My tour ended in a cotton field on the edge of town. "This is as far as we go," Montesinos announced.

"What's up there?" I asked, pointing toward a series of hills rising in the east. "Don't people try to cross over there?"

"Yes, but we don't go there. It's too dangerous." The coyotes and the drug cartels who operated in those parts were heavily armed. They would probably kill a policeman if he was stupid enough to wander around there alone. This is something I had never experienced before: a place where police authority meant nothing. It was a first hint of the larger institutional breakdown that reached in patches across the length and breadth of Latin America. The drug cartels and the smugglers were a secret, parallel power in Tijuana, and beyond the immigrant purgatory of Tijuana they were centaurs inflicting tortures on the shades in the first and second circles of hell, a landscape of spindly yucca and prickly pears where not even a policeman with an Angels cap could protect you, where you were at the mercy of the sun and men with automatic weaponry.

Sergio Medina and Victor Ley had walked through this inferno and had the sunburns to show for it. In Tijuana, where it had been rainy for several days, they stood out with their red faces. I met them at La Casa del Migrante. They told me they had tried crossing the border about 350 miles to the east, walking for days under the winter sun in the Sonora Desert north of Nogales. They hoped to make it first to Tucson and then to Phoenix—where Medina once lived for three years—but ran up against a thick line of tall Border Patrol agents in olive-colored uniforms, who Medina calls "the green chiles."

"The green chiles chased us," Medina said. There was something of the jester in him, and he embellished his storytelling with lavish gestures. "Some real tall green chiles on bicycles, in shorts. You try to run, but they're really fast and big. Nobody gets past them." He pumped his arms to imitate the agents' muscular pedaling, showing how their dirt bikes sped over the desert brush. "One of them stepped on me with his shoes. Really big shoes, size twelve."

Medina spent a couple of days detained in Arizona. They kept him in a bus, and he had a lot of time to think. Clearly, it had been a mistake to leave the United States in the first place. A lot of other people living north of the border would come to a similar realization. Over the long run, Operation Gatekeeper and all the other military-style crackdowns would have an unexpected long-term consequence for the people who lived north of the border. They would start giving up on the practice of slipping back over the border once a year to see their relatives, lest they get stuck like all these people I was meeting in Tijuana. In trying to close down the border, the American government had made the Mexicans living in the United States a more sedentary, less nomadic people. When he lived in Phoenix, he had worked two jobs—as a helper on a horse ranch and as a cook— and had a *"gringa"* girlfriend. "I was going to get married with this *gringuita*. But she wanted to have me locked up in the house like I was a little doll. She didn't like me spending time with my friends." Now that he was stuck in Tijuana, he realized how good he had had it. "If I find another *gringuita*, I'm going to stay with her," he said with a sardonic smile. "I'm going to say, 'Let's go for it!'"

Medina said he and his friend Ley would stay in Tijuana for a while. They had already found one job—at a car wash just a few blocks from the shelter. Soon they would try to find better jobs (as cooks, perhaps) and rent an apartment. "We're going to wait for the green chiles to leave. I don't think they'll be there for long. In about six months they'll leave, and then we'll try again." But of course the green chiles never did go away, nor were there any plans to mothball all those new Ford Broncos and motion detectors and dirt bikes.

Just before leaving Tijuana, I agreed to help a couple of the stranded migrants at La Casa del Migrante. Rosalino Montero, a thirty-nine-year-old owner of a small business in Mexico City, asked me if I could write a postcard to his wife. He told me he left home "to forget." What, I asked. Family problems, he said, giving me a maudlin expression that suggested either tragedy or betrayal or both. He had been deported once already and had been stuck in Tijuana for five days.

In the postcard, I wrote in Spanish:

Your husband wanted you to know he arrived safely in Tijuana. He was a little sick with the flu when I saw him, but it wasn't anything serious. He was in good spirits [a lie, I know, but only a small one] *and promised to write as soon as he gets across. He asked that you take good care of the store.*

I gave Montero my number and told him to call when he made it to the United States. I never heard from him.

But I would speak again to another migrant I met that day, a tall, skinny man with Moorish eyes who told me his name was Miguel Ángel Gonzales. He said he had been living in Los Angeles when the INS showed up at the bar where he was having a few drinks. The agents plucked him out of his daily routine and deposited him in Baja California, and now he was desperate to get back to his new wife and son on "the other side." On a piece of paper, he scribbled the name and address of said wife and a friend in Los Angeles, a man who could help him escape Tijuana and La Casa del Migrante. Could I visit this person, he asked, and pass on a message? Of course, I said, *con mucho gusto*, it would be my pleasure.

A few days later, I was standing in a doorway of a home in Watts, a neighborhood that was surrendering its claim as the heart of black Los Angeles and becoming a Mexican neighborhood. I had reached the address on the slip of paper I carried from Tijuana. Over the next few hours, the man I met there would unravel the lies Miguel Ángel Gonzales had told me.

Chapter Three

BROTHER CITIZEN, BROTHER ALIEN
Sin fronteras

Watts, California · Ameca, Jalisco, Mexico

The man I met at Watts was a shorter, chunkier version of the man I had spoken with at La Casa del Migrante a few days earlier, although at first I didn't see much resemblance. He lived in a plain stucco box set behind a big 1930s Craftsman with a pitched roof and an ample front porch. I had knocked on his front door by tapping my pen on a wrought-iron security screen, which was apparently a de rigueur accessory in that neighborhood, a barrier suggesting brushes with forced entry, or that gunfire might erupt at any second, that you might have to take cover from fifteen-year-olds firing Uzis in butterfly patterns at other fifteen-year-olds. José García studied me through the pinholes, then opened the door. He said he didn't know anyone named Miguel Ángel Gonzales, and he didn't know anyone who would have any reason to be stuck at the border. I showed him the address I had scribbled down in my notebook and the name of Miguel Ángel Gonzales's wife, one Imelda López. Did he know her?

"That's this address," he told me in Spanish. "But I don't know anyone named Miguel Ángel Gonzales or any Imelda López."

I shrugged my shoulders and gave a polite smile: I could have walked away at that moment and gone back home, but the memory of the man stuck at the border made me try one more thing. "Well, I interviewed him on tape. Let me play it for you, and maybe you'll recognize his voice."

José unlocked the door, stepped out, and took my tape recorder to his ear, looking a bit irritated and suspicious about who I might be and what this was all about. His door faced a driveway with an old, electric-blue Buick parked in front, and I leaned against the car while he listened. On the tape, Miguel Ángel Gonzales described his plight in Spanish, the story of how he had been caught by the agents and sent to Tijuana, the tinny echo of voices and closing doors at La Casa del Migrante in the background. *If you could do me the favor of calling this person,* the voice on the tape said in Spanish, *I would be muy agradecido.* After a few moments, José García's eyes became startled circles of befuddlement, as if he were watching a movie that had taken an unexpected and disturbing turn.

"That's my brother," he said. "The voice is unmistakable. But he's supposed to be in jail."

He turned to say something to a person inside his home. "It's Pedro. He's out of prison."

"Pedro's here?" a woman's voice called back.

"No."

José gestured for me to follow him inside, and together we sat at the table of a room that functioned as kitchen, dining room, and living room all at once. I gave José a business card from one of the priests at the Casa shelter and he sat at the table quietly for a moment and examined it, contemplating what he should do next. A boy watched cartoons on a television nearby, the volume turned low in deference to his father. José's wife stood by the sink, having been caught halfway through a pile of dishes, and looked relieved to see I was not Pedro. I had the feeling this table was the place where José sat to make important decisions, to pay off bills and balance checkbooks, to sit and consider the letter a teacher might send home with his son. I would soon learn that he was an auto mechanic who often worked two jobs simultaneously, and that the little house we were sitting in, as well as the big bungalow in front, were his property, and that he was somehow paying off the mortgage and all his family's bills without making more than $8 an hour.

"It doesn't surprise me," José said. "It's always a new problem with him. Right from the first day he got here."

Over the next few days, I would learn a lot about the man who had introduced himself to me as Miguel Ángel Gonzales. He was the younger brother of José: both had been born and raised in a place called Ameca, in the Mexican state of Jalisco, and both had come to Los Angeles as young men to play out their ambitions. Each had an entirely different notion of what the United States stood for and how he fit in his new home. On the day that I met him, José García was just a month or so away from taking the oath to become a U.S. citizen. His brother Pedro had been deported a week earlier as a "criminal alien." Pedro's face could very easily have featured in the grainy television spots of the Proposition 187 campaign, with their xenophobic stereotypes of the Latin American immigrant as gangster and scoundrel. He had come to Los Angeles to start a life of petty crime that would merit the attention of various sheriff's deputies, prosecutors, and DEA agents, leaving behind a thick file in the archives of the Los Angeles County Criminal Court for me to peruse, and a plowed field of worry wrinkles across his older brother's forehead. José was his only adult relative in California, which made him a surrogate father figure, which meant he had spent many hours before at this table, in precisely this same pose, pondering how to rescue his brother from disaster.

Not knowing any of that then, I said the first, banal thing that came to mind, to fill the uncomfortable silence of sitting next to a stranger to whom I had apparently brought some bad news. "He seemed to be in good spirits when I saw him in Tijuana," I said in Spanish. "He looked healthy. I mean, he didn't look like he'd been hurt or anything trying to cross the border. A lot of people get hurt. I talked to one man with a broken leg . . ."

"I'm going to go and get him," José said abruptly. "It's not too late to help him. If he comes back here, he's just going to get in more trouble." His plan was to reach Pedro before he tried again to jump over the fence, and somehow force his younger brother to stay in Mexico.

About an hour later, José had fired up the Buick in the driveway and was headed south to the border, to that barrier of recycled metal and motion detectors that was keeping his brother over on the other side. José was a legal U.S. resident and could cross the border freely. That line drawn across the map of North America divided the family history in two: between a Mexican half of stern parents, low wages, and small-town plazas where boys and girls eyed each other but never touched; and a parentless American half of opportunity and licentiousness, where a man's wealth might multiply into absurdly large numbers, but at the cost of his soul. By chance, I had stumbled into this fable at the moment when its moral was being revealed, when each brother would choose—or be forced to choose—a national identity; to say, My life will be on this side and not the other.

José García had left his hometown at the age of eighteen, on March 2, 1979, a date he remembers because it was right after the biannual town carnival. Ameca was a provincial town of 56,000 whose municipal slogan was "nobility, progress, work"; life there revolved around the sugar mills and one of Mexico's largest Coca-Cola bottling plants. José's little brother was still an obedient thirteen-year-old in 1979 and stayed behind, with parents who kept order in their home with the occasional blow from a belt. "I came alone, on an adventure, because I had an aunt here, in the United States," José told me. As a very young woman, this aunt had eloped with her boyfriend and future husband, running off to a life first in Tijuana and later in Los Angeles. Like countless other California Latino families, this one had a story that straddled the border.

If you dig deep enough into the family history of even second- or third-generation Mexican Americans, you will probably find a border story. My wife's grandmother, Guadalupe Chavira, tells one of growing up in Ciudad Juárez, and the wintry day she took a walk across the bridge spanning the Rio Grande: in those days, people on both sides of the river crossed freely, and there were streetcars linking Ciudad Juárez to El Paso. Suddenly, the already swollen waters of the Rio Grande below her began to rise higher, covering part of the bridge and leaving her stranded in the middle: it was there that she met her future husband, while she and hundreds of others stood and waited for the floodwaters to recede, stuck halfway between the United States and Mexico.

José's two cousins had been born in Tijuana before "jumping over" (*brincando*) into the United States. They had exactly the same first and middle name, Juan Manuel, thanks to a typically Latin confusion at the hospital. "My aunt was unconscious for a long time after the younger one was born. They had to give him a name and the nurses decided to do all the paperwork and give him the name Juan Manuel too. And that's how it stayed." Later, when the cousins grew up, "one would get into trouble and the other one would get punished for it, because they had the same exact name, only their birth dates were different." José had never met his aunt or the two Juan

Manuels before the day he showed up in Tijuana, wondering how he might cross the border. He found her thanks to a *comadre* who lived near her old address in a rundown corner of Tijuana. From the *comadre*'s Tijuana home he called his aunt, and she came from Los Angeles to get him: in Mexican families, a blood bond that's been dormant for decades can count as much as any other. After spending a few hours with José catching up on family history, she put him in a taxi with one of the Juan Manuels. So permeable was the border in those days that all he had to do was sit in the back seat of the taxi and wait through a seemingly interminable traffic jam, until he finally turned to his cousin to ask, "When are we going to cross?"

"We already did."

From the first day in Los Angeles, he was in a hurry to get to work. His cousin told him he might be able to find him a job at the car-painting shop where he worked. "You can come with me—but later. Maybe next week. Now you should rest."

"What would I need to rest for? When you haven't been doing anything, you don't need any rest."

The next day he started working, alongside one of the Juan Manuels and a lot of other *mexicanos.* He had arrived in California on the cusp of its big ethnic transformation. In the years to come, he noticed that whenever a Latino showed up at a company looking for a low-wage job, he seemed to get it right away. To a sociologist, this phenomenon spoke to a new class order in California, with immigrants at the bottom. But from José's perspective, all those Latinos getting paid $5 or $6 an hour were *privileged*: it seemed as though the bosses favored hiring Spanish-speaking people at the expense of others. His first day at his first job, his cousin gave him a lecture about how work was different in this country, advice that sounded a lot like my Guatemalan father's: "I'm just going to tell you one thing," José's cousin said. "I want you to do the job well, or don't do it at all. I don't want someone to say tomorrow, 'What sort of shit is this work you did?' [*qué cochinada hiciste*] and then have you say it was me who showed you how to do it." My father's variant of this advice would go along the lines of, "Whatever you decide to do in life, be the best at it." What is it, I wonder, about small towns like Ameca and Gualán that they produce people who believe they can conquer the world?

José remembered his cousin's little speech because its tone and spirit matched the ambition that had brought him to the United States in the first place. If he didn't have any ambition, he would have stayed in Ameca, walking around the plaza on Sunday afternoons, smiling shyly at the girls until he found one to marry him. Instead, he came to Los Angeles and made himself into this other man, who was now educating himself on the finer points of home mortgages and property ownership by clipping out articles from *La Opinión*, Los Angeles's Spanish-language daily newspaper. A *La Opinión* article about saving on realtor fees sat on the table of his tiny kitchen-dining room–living room as we sat to talk a second time, after the drama of his brother's appearance at the border had been resolved. On the table, too, there was an envelope with a letter from the Immigration and Naturalization Service inside: José was just one step away from becoming a U.S. citizen. All of this put him in a reflective mood.

"I had my rough times too. I liked to drink, to spend a lot of time in bars and party. But I've never let my work suffer for it. On top of that, I've always had a desire to progress, to get ahead. I'm not a person who's satisfied with what he has. I always like to find something new—to change for the better. If I have a car and I decide to get another one, the next one has to at least have a nice paint job, or one other thing about it that's better than the last one."

Not long after arriving in California, José García learned that the

United States is a country of such abundance and wealth—especially next to poor Ameca—that you could succeed in a field in which you had no formal training. He taught himself how to be an auto mechanic. At first he would hold the oil filters and carburetors and fan belts like a child trying to figure out how a toy works, but eventually he learned how to make it all hum and spark and whirl. In Mexico, he had been a delivery driver at the Coca-Cola warehouse, "but if a car broke down on me, I didn't know what to do. I learned here by working on my own cars, because I didn't have the money to pay for repairs." Eventually, fixing cars became a side job that would earn him thousands of dollars and help pay the down payment on the house with the bulletproof door and the Buick parked in front. In Los Angeles, José was surprised to learn, people treated cars as disposable objects. They were sitting around everywhere—you could buy a serviceable car for $50 and, with just a little bit of work, make some money off it. The Buick out front was another of his purchases; it had just gotten him down to Tijuana and back in time to make it to his latest job, as a mechanic at a respectable American corporation, United Parcel Service. "Without exaggerating, I've bought and sold two hundred cars. I've fixed them up and sold them all, sometimes in the same day. I never took a professional course on how to be a mechanic. It was pure experience, of having cars break down on me and finding ways to fix them."

José had been in Los Angeles for a few years when his younger brother decided that he too wanted to try his luck in the United States. Pedro set off on his own, like José. By this time, José had a small apartment in Lynwood, a working-class suburb built for white families during Southern California's 1950s boom. Lynwood had started to go to seed in the 1980s, when the state Department of Transportation cut a big swath through the middle of town to build the very last in its famous multilane network of freeways. Unbeknownst to José, Pedro, and most of the other *mexicanos* landing there, that freeway had severed Lynwood from its *Leave It to Beaver* past, sending most of its old-time residents packing, making it a more transient, meaner place. It created dead-end streets and shadowy blocks of condemned buildings where manic young men sold magic potions that could make anyone feel like a king for twenty minutes, baggies and vials that the neighborhood's broken and wounded residents would pay anything to get their hands on. Those manic dealers and the rolls of bills in their pockets pulled Pedro in—just as the discipline and steady pay of the American workplace, and the business potential of its cheap automobiles, had pulled José in.

Pedro found in Lynwood a fertile ground for his unfulfilled ambitions, which were shaped by his vision of himself as a hard man prepared to outfight or outwit the many people and forces bent on destroying him. To Pedro, California was a stratified society that white people dominated in some ways and that Latinos dominated in others, with blacks pitted against both groups in a Darwinian race war. "In Huntington Park, Lynwood, South Gate, it's all people from the Latino race; the Americans tend toward Santa Monica, Long Beach, and those places that are more fixed up, where the Latino isn't really involved," he told me in Spanish. "Los Angeles to me is a place where you have to be very alert and ready, you have to be prepared when you go there, because it's dangerous. . . . I never had any problems with the blacks; maybe because of my color they confused me with a black person. I had problems with the infamous cholos, the gang members, who say they're from over there [the United States] but who are more Mexican than I am."

José would go off to work, leaving Pedro at home, though soon enough Pedro seemed to be making money. It didn't take long for José to figure out what was going on. "He would try to hide it from me. He wouldn't sell in front of me." To José, the money seemed piddling next to the danger involved. "He was helping bigger people. What could he make? Ten, twenty, one hundred, two hundred dollars a day? And for that, he's marked for life." While José was considering getting married and beginning to plot out a future of property ownership, savings accounts, and medical plans for the kids, Pedro was already accumulating his own status symbols. "He was always well dressed, with chains and watches and what have you. Sometimes he'd even had bodyguards, two or three guys who were always at his side. But all of that was just a passing thing. Whatever riches you get that way don't last for very long."

Within a few days of their respective arrivals in the United States, José and Pedro García had both studied the moral landscape this country presented to them and reached completely opposite conclusions about how they should proceed in their new American lives. Ever the idealist, José saw opportunity in the vacuum created by the absence of English-speaking workers in California's dustier, sweatier, and smellier workplaces; like Simon Rodia, the Italian immigrant from an earlier era who built the Watts Towers a few blocks from José's American home, he had found a form of self-expression in the things Americans threw away. Rodia built his towers from discarded fragments of plates and bottles; José sent junk cars rolling again, each a moving monument to his work ethic and his belief in the possible, an apt metaphor for the constructive contributions immigrants make, in otherwise abandoned neighborhoods and marginal professions, to the continuing advance of American history. Pedro, on the other hand, looked at the same California neighborhoods and saw decay and inequity, and believed he had been dropped into an arena of struggle in which only the cynical survived. The dichotomy in the García family was the dichotomy in immigrant America, a dichotomy you found also in middle-class and affluent families, and among city councilmen and entrepreneurs. Pedro saw barbarism around him and responded with a dark faith whose chief tenant was an unwavering belief in his own strength and courage. It is the same religion shared by tattooed and armed young men you find across the country in those places that Latinos call home. Like them, Pedro sought out a villainous and ultimately self-destructive heroism. This is an oft-repeated barrio narrative, cast with groups like the Mara Salvatrucha gang in Washington, D.C., and rural Maryland, or by the 18th Street gang in Los Angeles and small-town Kansas. If you listen carefully enough, you will hear Shakespearean brio and melodrama in their stories, the tragedies of young men headed into battle and death, and the comedies of young men who overreach in their street ambition. In Pedro's case, the details that embellish the story include flying bullets and falling bar stools, neighborhood gossips and semi-miraculous resurrections from the dead.

In March 1988 Pedro was arrested and charged with possession of marijuana for sale and got ninety days in the county jail and three years' probation. He was twenty-one years old and just beginning a career in delinquency: other crimes would follow, his life becoming a jumble of dates and penal-code numbers and assorted aliases that county prosecutors would have to sort out each time he was arrested. There were fights in bars and arrests for providing false identification to police officers. He was convicted of an attempted burglary that went awry one night in Huntington Park because one of the residents of the apartment he was breaking into happened to be asleep in the living room and saw him moving the curtain on the front window; the burglary-victim-to-be got up from the couch, chased Pedro down the street half a block, tackled him, and held him for the police.

Then there was the time Pedro died.

It happened over Christmas, when José was back in Ameca for the holidays, enjoying the familial warmth of shots of locally produced rum and the hymns the neighborhood children sing during Nativity processions. The phone rang: it was one of José's neighbors in Los Angeles.

"They shot Pedro," the neighbor said. "He's dead."

José rushed back to Los Angeles and placed a call to the local police, who answered his queries about his dead brother with the wry humor police use when dealing with "knuckleheads" and their families. "Oh, no, he's not dead. He's safe and sound. We've got him right here in one of our cells." Pedro's explanation of what happened was this: He had been working in a bar, covering for a man who had just left to try his luck in Georgia, when he came to the defense of a customer and friend who was being harassed by another customer. Yes, there had been gunfire, but no, he was not hit. The story of his death was spread by *"unas personas embusteras,"* people who were, according to the varying shades of meanings of the word *embustero*, liars, gossips, and hypocrites.

After one of his many jail stints, José sent Pedro down to Ameca, hoping that being in the company of the family's *jefes* (in Mexico the word for "boss" is also slang for "parent") would help straighten him out. But the exposure to the tough love of the *jefes* and the simpler life of Ameca only strengthened Pedro's resolve that he was meant for the adrenaline rush of the North. He headed back to California after promising the *jefes* he would be more like his older brother, and that he would stick close to him and his protection.

Inevitably, José came home for work one afternoon to find a festival of law enforcement being staged on his block, clusters of patrol cars and vans parked here and there, with their attendant officers in windbreakers marked SWAT, LASD, and other acronyms, a helicopter circling overhead. Inside one of those patrol cars, his hands cuffed behind his back, was Pedro. Court files record the observations of officers who saw Pedro selling rather large quantities of marijuana. The probation officer assigned to the case listed his primary source of income as "criminal activity" and added something that everyone in Pedro's family already knew: "He does not learn from prior mistakes." In his presentencing interview, Pedro was still denying that he had ever been arrested before. He was off to the Big House for a while, drawing a two-year state prison term.

José, meanwhile, had applied to become a legal and permanent U.S. resident through the 1986 amnesty program. The law was a two-pronged approach to the growing number of "illegals" like José in the American workforce. In exchange for tougher penalties against employers who knowingly hired workers without immigration documents, the Reagan administration offered those *mexicanos* and other immigrants already here legal status, as long as they could prove they had been living and working in the United States for several years. José had to go about collecting the documents from his play-by-the-rules life in the United States, the check stubs and the house bills he had dutifully paid. "The oldest kid I have helped a lot, because he's always been in school, for many years. So I legalized my situation. And the whole time I was thinking about becoming a citizen. The person who helped me with the amnesty told me I had to wait five years. The five years passed and I went to apply. I saw a table in a park with some materials and I went to check it out. I filled out the application and everything. It was a week before I started working at UPS. About two months ago, they [the naturalization office] answered to say everything was ready. And two weeks ago, I went to the office and they made me take a test, which I passed, and then they told me all I needed was the certificate from the police." At about the same time he was waiting for that certificate—proof of the clean record he would need to become a citizen—I showed up at the front door with my tape recorder.

As far as José knew, his brother was then behind bars in the high desert north of Los Angeles, in a place called Lancaster, about two hours' drive from Watts. Pedro the inmate was being bused regularly from the prison to a local slaughterhouse, where he beheaded chickens for 49 cents an hour, working alongside other inmates as the bland carcasses whirred past on a chain. He took some pride in the fact that his jailers considered him trustworthy enough to hold the ten-inch knife he used. But to Pedro prison was the outside world in miniature, a place where your status was determined by skin color. "The Latinos do the hardest work. The hardest. The lighter work is done by the Americans—or the gringos, as they're called. And a little harder than what the gringos do, there's the Afro-Americans." Pedro managed to navigate through prison life without getting stabbed or shot, no small feat considering the race war inside most California prisons—blacks, Latinos, and whites organized into "brotherhoods" and "mafias."

When his release date came, he did not get his old clothes back; he didn't get a bus ticket and some spending money, or a guard escorting him to the front gate, or a chance to stand in the sunlight outside the prison fence, or any of the things he might have expected. Instead, the State of California handed him over to an agent of the federal government, who delivered him to the fluorescent-lit room called an Immigration Court, where he was duly ordered deported from the United States of America. "They deported me because there's a law that you have to give each prisoner two hundred dollars per year . . . for having completed your sentence and for having behaved well, for good conduct. But these people keep your money when they deport you. This is what happens with the Latinos, no matter if they're Mexicans, Central Americans, or South Americans. If you're not an American, they send you back to the place you were born. I think that's wrong. It's like a mafia. I won that money by my forced labor, by my good conduct—they didn't have any complaints about me."

They shipped Pedro to Tijuana, where he became just another of the multitude of people on the other side of the fence, hoping to get back across. He tried more than once but was caught each time by the green chiles. Finally, he ended up at the shelter, where he told his story into my tape recorder. Not being completely trusting of me, he gave me a false name, but the right address for his brother. Pedro would say later he didn't expect me to deliver his message. It caught him by surprise when, a few days later, his brother showed up at La Casa del Migrante.

I had given José the shelter's address, from the business card of one of the Scalabrian brothers there. José introduced himself to one of the caretakers, and then called out his brother's name. When no one answered, he tried calling out the pseudonym, "Miguel Ángel Gonzales!" Still, no one answered. So José poked his head around into several of the rooms and eventually saw a tall, thin, cinnamon-skinned man mopping the floor.

"What happened to you?" José asked. *¿Qué te pasó?*

For a moment, Pedro wouldn't look up at his brother. "It was like he wanted to hide," José would tell me later.

"What are you going to do now?" José insisted.

Pedro looked up. "I'm getting some money together to go back," he said, as if he had known his brother was there all along, as if years hadn't passed since they had last seen each other.

"To Los Angeles?"

"No . . . to Ameca."

"You're not thinking of jumping over the fence?"

"No, I don't want to have anything to do with that place," he said, meaning the United States. "I've already been there. I just want to get some money together and go back home."

Pedro said he wanted to stay in Tijuana a few more days to get the money an "engineer" owed him for some work he had done. But José said he would give him the money. "Get your things and tell these people who helped you thank you." They got in José's Buick and went to the airport, where José bought Pedro a ticket on a flight to Guadalajara. The *jefes* picked Pedro up at the airport there and took him to Ameca, where he's still living today.

"I feel *tranquilo*, here in the company of my family, who've had to suffer so much at my expense," Pedro said when I talked to him again, this time on the phone, long-distance from Los Angeles to Ameca.

I had called Pedro up to sort out his side of the story, now that I knew his real name and the details of his stay in the United States and his deportation. I went back to Watts too, and talked to José again. I asked him what he would do when he became a citizen. Would he feel any different? Would he feel like an *americano*?

His response to the first question was straight out of a word-association test: after he became a citizen, he'd like to visit the Statue of Liberty in New York: "For what it says, for what it stands for, for its history." In response to the second question, he told me to listen to a favorite song of his, "América," by the Mexican *ranchera* group Los Tigres del Norte. The song is on the Tigres' album *Gracias América: Sin Fronteras* (Thank You America: Without Borders), and is an extended riff on the meanings of "America" and "American."

I was born the color of earth
And my inheritance was Spanish
Those from the north say I am Latino

They don't want to call me American.
I am the gaucho galloping on the Pampas
I am charrua [Uruguayan], I am a jibaro [Puerto Rican]
I am chapin [Guatemalan], Eskimo, a Mayan prince.
I am a guajiro [Cuban], a Mexican charro.
If he who is born in Europe is a European
And he who his born in Africa is African
I was born in America and I don't see
Why I can't be called American
Because America is the whole continent
And he who is born here is American.

The song was written by a band of Mexican-born musicians to claim the term "American" for those born south of the border. Now José had turned the meaning of the song on its head: even though he had taken the oath to become an "American," that didn't make him any different from before, because both the United States and Mexico are in America. In other words, faced with a choice between national identities, José believed in that broader notion of *americanismo* that I had first tried to embrace when I was a student in Mexico City.

Like my leftist friends in Mexico, Pedro was confused by what he saw as his brother's desire to be two things at once. Why, he asked, would any Mexican want to embrace a system that is designed to keep brown-skinned people down, where they will always be second-class citizens?

"I was never interested in those things," he told me on the phone from Ameca. "It's like throwing money away for me. Because I'm never going to stop being *mexicano*, even if I change my name, if I call myself Peter instead of Pedro, I'm never going to stop being *mexicano*, because the color of my skin will still be brown."

"So for you, it's like denying your . . ."

". . . the place where I was born," Pedro said.

"So you never applied for residency or anything like that?"

"No, never. My brother would tell me, 'Go get that fixed because one day you're going to need that.' And I told him, 'That's just throwing money away.' Because jobs are always easy to find and it's never a problem to get fake documents. Over there, all that matters to them is that you work—and if you're a Latino, that you work hard."

"You and your brother are different that way," I said. "He didn't care about having to wait in line and spending his money, which is how he got amnesty. And now he's going to be a citizen of the United States."

"I think he's very close to doing it. I hope that he keeps being lucky. I wish him the best, if that's what he wants, good for him."

"So you and your brother are going to be citizens of different countries."

"Yeah. He wants to be an *americano*."

"But he's also proud of being *mexicano*. I think it's more of a practical thing to him than anything else."

"He keeps it inside that he's a *mexicano*. Sometimes you have to be that way. You have to show two faces. One for the *americanos* and your own to the *mexicanos,* to your race. You tell the *americano* you're on his side, to get what you need, that same way they've always done, and they keep on doing."

Pedro never returned to the United States. He's still in Ameca, working for the city for a modest wage. He had gotten California out of his system. José took the oath to become an American citizen, along with hundreds of other people at the Los Angeles Convention Center. In those days, in the late 1990s, more people were becoming naturalized than ever before, with California especially swept up by a citizenship mania. It was thanks, mostly, to the fallout over Proposition 187, which barred immigrants without documents from public schools and hospitals. Many people in José's position thought Proposition 187 was only the beginning of a movement meant to marginalize them, that even their status as "legal aliens" might be revoked. Deportation could mean losing the property and savings they had worked so hard for. In those days, people who had been living as "legal aliens" for decades were becoming citizens. Citizenship was for them an idea tied up with their sense of personal achievement and the idea that they needed a form of protection. Above all, citizenship meant security. For the same reason, José had agreed to make a little less money in his job at UPS than he could buying and selling cars, because after a few months at UPS they gave you the trophy of full medical and retirement benefits.

At about the same time José García was being naturalized, Los Tigres del Norte recorded another song, "Mis Dos Patrias" (My Two Fatherlands). It opens with a recording of an American official leading a roomful of people in the Pledge of Allegiance, then announcing "Congratulations, you are now all American citizens."

"To those who say I am a *malinchista*, and that I've betrayed my flag and my nation . . . ," the song begins, using a word that means two-face and traitor, slang spun from the name of La Malinche, the Indian woman who helped Hernán Cortés defeat the Aztecs and claim Mexico for Spain. "So that my song can break borders, I will open my heart to the fullest." Los Tigres del Norte then go on to describe a man with a life like José García's, a *mexicano* who comes to the United States in search of work, and whose children are born there.

> I worked, my children were growing up,
> they were all born in this great nation.

My rights have been stepped on
because they keep writing laws from the Constitution. . . .

What does it matter if I'm a new citizen
I'm still mexicano like pulque *and the* nopal.
So that they respect the rights of my race,
two Fatherlands can fit in the same heart. . . .

The judge stood up in the courtroom
the afternoon of the oath.
From my heart came a salty tear that burned me inside.
Two flags shook me
one green, white and red with the seal of an eagle,
the other deep blue
with stars, red and white stripes, the flag of my sons,
who looked at me with joy.
Don't call me a traitor
because I love both of my fatherlands.
In mine, I left my dead
here, here my sons were born. . . .

Like the man in the song, the Mexican brothers of Los Tigres del Norte all made their lives permanently in the United States and have children born on the northern side of the border—they live in a suburb of San Jose, California, perhaps the leading troubadours of America's new binational identity. The Hernández brothers, born in Sinaloa, Mexico, crossed over to the United States during those early days of the Latino immigrant tide, in 1968, having been hired to play at a Mexican Independence Day parade in San Jose. They overstayed their visas and in 1972 they recorded the first *narcocorrido*, ballads about the adventures of quasi-heroic cross-border drug dealers, men who smuggle bundles of marijuana and get shot in alleyways and barrooms. Recorded in the United States, *narcocorridos* became big hits south of the border, a kind of reverse crossover hit, and made the brothers millionaires. Eventually, the genre would become the staple of Los Angeles radio stations like KBUE, "Que Buena," taking them to the top tier of the Southern California ratings. Movies based on their songs would fill cinemas on both sides of the border. *Narco-corridos* are songs that revel in the daring and tragedy of people like Pedro García. Los Tigres del Norte, like the García family, had found themselves trying to accommodate all the contradictions that come with being a Mexican north of the border, the tension between belonging to the system and throwing yourself against it with violent pride and recklessness.

Part Two

PIONEERS AND PILGRIMS

Chapter Four

THE WANDERERS
El destierro

Ashland, Alabama · McAllen, Texas · Piedras Negras, Coahuila, Mexico

Gregorio was a Mexican goatherd who had always wanted to go north, but his mother, his beloved *jefecita*, had wanted him to stay home. He resisted the temptation for decades, long after goatherding became a fool's errand because nobody ate goat meat anymore, they preferred beef or chicken. "People started to think of goat meat as something common. I don't know why. It's just one of those things that changed." It took years, but eventually chicken wiped out most of the goat herds. Gregorio raised horses and worked in farms across the arid plains and mountains of Tamaulipas and Sonora. He worked for others, to the rhythm of the business clock, toiling six days a week for that moment of satisfaction when the boss slapped money into his palm. None of those jobs was ever quite as fulfilling as those weeklong journeys he first took with his father across the desert, on horseback under the open sky, when he guided the braying goats to market across a landscape of gray rocks, prickly pears, and chaparral grasses, looking out for wolves and sleeping under the stars.

So, at the advanced age of fifty, when most of his friends were starting to worry about their grandchildren and their miserly pensions, Gregorio pretended he was a young man again and undertook a great adventure, a long trip like those treks across the desert. He hauled his big beer belly north, over the border, with the help of some Texas relatives who got his papers fixed. He worked milk farms in Wisconsin, apple orchards in the state of Washington, then tobacco in Kentucky, where a devious, tattooed man stole a week of his earnings. Eventually, his wanderings took him to Alabama.

It was there that I met him, in the quiet of a trailer park planted precariously on the red soil of Clay County, Alabama. He was a big burly man with a booming laugh who loved to spend hours watching nature programs on television—migrating geese, snow leopards, the wild dogs of the African savanna. The Discovery Channel was his last treat before stepping out of the trailer and onto the company bus to the plant, where he dismembered poultry for $6.45 an hour. Chickens had done in the goatherding life, and now Gregorio tended to their moist, freshly killed bodies during long nights inside the metal roar of the plant, thousands of birds floating past him on a serpentine line of stainless-steel hooks.

When I met Gregorio I was in disguise. I was undercover as a down-and-out *guatemalteco*, hoping to see America through the innocent eyes of the wandering migrant. This transformation required only the shedding of my middle-class mind-set, the embrace of my brownness and its natural camouflage. All I had to do was put on a pair of jeans, toss my résumé in the trash, and forget the pretensions my father had inculcated in me since I could talk: the idea that I, his only son, was meant for something better than the life of hard work he had been forced to endure since the age of twelve, that I should earn my living with my brain and keep my palms respectably soft.

I set off from Los Angeles for the Rio Grande Valley in Southern Texas, to join the stream of *mexicanos* and *centroamericanos* who gather there before heading north, to become a *jornalero* guided by labor contractors and fate to some unknown place in the interior of the United States. My first stop would be at one of the manpower recruiters along the U.S.-Mexico border, small outfits that hired handfuls or dozens of workers at a time for food-processing plants from Kansas to the Carolinas. I arrived in McAllen, Texas, and roamed through its faded downtown shopping district, where *mexicanos* make up the bulk of the clientele in faded LBJ-era department stores now home to storefronts with discount merchandise where the Asian merchants rattle off cash-register totals in Spanish. Sometimes I felt several butterflies hovering around my head, floating past my field of vision, and I wondered if this was some sort of symptom of my feeling anxious about the journey I was going to undertake. But no, the headlines in the local newspapers confirmed that millions of Monarch butterflies had arrived in town at about the same time as me, fluttering southward on their annual migration. They drifted over the town square, landing by the gazebo, pausing momentarily on the mailboxes and park benches. Butterflies, unlike birds, do not migrate in flocks. Each one makes its way forward alone on its own spiraling route, floating from this flower to that tree, from this man's shoulder to that rooftop until they've traveled thousands of miles, from Oklahoma and Texas to their destination, the lush highland mountains of Michoacán in southern Mexico.

The migration of people through Texas mimics this behavior. Having somehow conquered the barrier at the border, the Mexicans and immigrants from other countries to the south travel alone for the most part—or at least in very small groups—in unpredictable patterns that, taken together, add up to a massive flow of people and hopes northward. I would join them at a moment in their lives when they first tested that oversized, gassed-up car that is American individualism, rolling out onto the freedom of the open road, embracing a social ethic where packing up and leaving your family and friends behind to seek your fortune is considered normal behavior.

What Mexico exports over the bridges and through the river smuggling routes across the Rio Grande is a chunk of its restlessness, the surplus ambition left over from the declining way of life of Gregorio the goatherd, a life centered on the rhythms of the soil and small-town life. The labor recruiters of the border played an active role in the dismantling of this culture. Like the pitch for some magical elixir sold by an old-time carnival huckster, their promises were so fantastic they had to be true. They made their case not on soapboxes, or from a wagon parked on a roadside, but via the airwaves. In one town in the northern Mexican state of Durango, a young man named Román turned on his radio and heard a commercial that in less than sixty seconds had visions of dollars dancing before his eyes. *"Señoras y señores,"* the voice on the radio began, "it is communicated to you that in the employment office of Eagle Pass, Texas, we are accepting job applications. Six dollars and forty-five cents an hour. For the Tyson chicken factory in Alabama." The ad promised overtime. Román started to do the arithmetic. The labor contractor was offering almost $7 an hour, plus free transportation to Alabama and $200 for a housing deposit once he got there. Maybe it could work for him. Forty hours a week meant $280, or more than a thousand a month. Subtract a little for food: Román had always been frugal when it came to food. He wasn't afraid to pick up a skillet or open the oven and save money by cooking for himself. Maybe in a few months he could save a couple of thousand dollars, enough to pay off that debt, fix this pickup. He would do it for two or three months and then come back home to the shelter and goodness of his family in Durango. Overtime made the offer irresistible. The equations in his head bulged with fat numbers; he could even imagine $400 in a single week.

The tale of the migrant pulled forward by a gilded vision of what awaits him at a new destination is, of course, an old one in American history. "I seen the han'bills fellas pass out, an' how much work they is, an' high wages an' all; and I seen in the paper how they want folks to come an' pick grapes an' oranges and peaches," Ma Joad tells her son Tom as they prepare to set out for California in John Steinbeck's *The Grapes of Wrath*. "An' it'd be under the trees, workin' in the shade. I'm scared of stuff so nice. I ain't got faith." Eventually, the fictional Ma Joad embraced the hope she saw in the Oklahoma multitudes headed west, just as Román was swept up in the "Northward, ho!" fever gripping Durango. He packed up some clothes, his boom box, and his collection of *ranchera* tapes, a little Tigres del Norte to get him through the bus trip, kissed his wife goodbye, and headed to the United States for the first time ever. If not now, when? He was twenty-five years old, married just three years and not yet a father: later, with children, it would be harder to leave. He would confront the obstacles that might face him with a sense of humor. If things went wrong, there would always be Durango and his wife to come home to. He wasn't the type to have too much pride to admit that things didn't quite work out the way he planned them.

In an office in the McAllen suburb of Pharr, I heard a pitch that was just as elaborate and appealing. The recruiter showed me and a *mexicano* named Rafael a video of a futuristic world of white factories with smiling workers dressed in white, tending to chickens with flesh washed white, working happily on factory lines that were the antithesis of what you would expect a slaughterhouse to look like; bloodless, sparkling, gleaming. Indeed, I might have imagined I was signing up to work at a place where chickens were put back together again instead of dismembered, where they entered as chicken nuggets and returned to the world as living, feathered birds. Rafael and I were invited to become part of the Tyson corporate family. Rafael seemed genuinely moved, even though it was in English and he didn't understand much of the narration. Besides the video, the recruiter didn't put much effort into getting us to sign up. It seemed like a foregone conclusion that both of us would fill out applications and show up a few days later for the bus ride north.

"So where is this job?" I asked in English.

The recruiter took a second to size me up when I said this, as if I had violated a certain boundary. Much later, I found out that the chicken company that had paid this man to hire me was implicated in a complex scheme to bring undocumented Mexican workers to its plants in the Deep South, charges that would be outlined in a 36-count federal indictment. The company and the recruiters were alleged to have provided forged documents, with one recruiter from Tennessee helping smuggle workers over the border. Perhaps the recruiter sitting before me smelled a narc, even though there was nothing illegal about his hiring me, since I had signed up with my actual name and Social Security number.

"Alabama," he answered after a brief pause.

"Where in Alabama?"

Now he seemed a bit peeved, and maybe curious too about who I might really be. I had embellished my blue jeans disguise with a loose-fitting T-shirt and a baseball cap purchased from a Korean man in McAllen, embroidered in the Old English script favored by Chicano homeboys: *HECTOR*

"Not sure," he said. "Don't know yet. Don't care."

F rankie and Linda were recently married and the parents of an infant boy. For them, the journey began on the Texas side of the Rio Grande Valley, in the bus station in Eagle Pass, a slice of the United States that is more like Mexico. Here people speak a strange Spanglish that can be impossible for outsiders to decipher, what linguists call pidgin, a language meshing English and Spanish grammar and border slang. Frankie and Linda are like me, American by birth but with a good chunk of their souls connected to a place that is, culturally speaking, in Latin America. Just a few years beyond high school, they too were drawn in by the pitch of the labor contractors and the promise of a new beginning in a secret corner of America. The pull is so strong, and the Rio Grande Valley so needy, that dozens of Frankie and Linda's Eagle Pass friends jump into the stream along with the *mexicanos,* filling up trailers on a red patch of Alabama soil, hidden from the highway that runs past it by a strand of trees.

Frankie and Linda were pulled away from the only home they had ever known by the hope you hear on people's lips when they speak of the jobs that await them, by the exclamation points on flyers attached to the walls of the bus stations in McAllen, Harlingen, and Brownsville, and that pass from one needy hand to another, back and forth across the border. "Attention! Laborers needed for field work in Kentucky, Tennessee, Mississippi, North Carolina and Louisiana! Travel and expenses paid!" Often, only one requirement is listed: *"Ser hombre."* The jobs are available if you are "a man." You read this and feel the echoes of the full *mexicano* understanding of the word. *Un hombre.* For Frankie the word is like a challenge. It asks if he is someone who will not shirk from his responsibilities, someone not afraid to sweat and labor to feed his family, someone who won't complain or whine if the work is hard.

A stout street fighter not much past twenty, Frankie had little doubt how much *hombre* he had in him. Gregorio, the aging goatherd, felt a bit the same way, though for entirely different reasons. Román, a skinny twenty-five-year-old, seemed happily free of anything to prove. Linda was just nineteen. They all ended up in an Alabama trailer with me, a writer just along for the ride.

There were no butterflies in the air the cold morning I arrived at the bus station, dropped off by a cabdriver after checking out of the McAllen Doubletree Hotel. There were two other men waiting for the bus, both workers recruited by the company in Pharr, though neither was Rafael, the man I had met in the office. These two men and I would spend the next thirty-six hours on the bus, scrambling to find something to eat during fifteen- and thirty-minute stops and transfers in bus stations in Houston and Baton Rouge, cast amidst single mothers, young backpackers, and the lumpenproletariat drifters of middle America, the drug dealers and the babbling psychotics. I berated myself for not packing a map, because not knowing exactly where I was made the trip all the longer and never-ending, and because I'd never heard of the destination printed on the ticket the contractor gave us when he met us at the station: Anniston, Ala.

Gregorio told me later that he never carries a map with him when he travels. He is dependent on the kindness of bus drivers and station clerks and the cleverness of his fellow *jornaleros* to get him to the right destination, which always seems to happen. He said the journey north is a trip you take alone, surrendering all links to family and friends. For them, your absence will be a temporary death, months will pass without a word from you. You are like those ancient, seafaring explorers that people watched from shore, disappearing over the horizon, unsure if they would ever return. Gregorio had learned, on his first trip north, that this was a price he had to pay for his newfound freedom. He had left for a Wisconsin dairy farm, two thousand miles away from home, half a continent away, after finally persuading his mother Tomasita to put aside her fears. "My *jefecita* was one of those traditional old ladies, a true believer from way back." She was eighty-six years old the day he first left, the mother of ten, and thought that if her sons left for the United States a curse would fall on them, that evil forces would spirit them away, but in the end she had relented.

"'Go, son. Go. But if you leave, you might not catch up with me again. I'm very sick.'

"'No, don't say that. I'll be calling. I won't be gone more than two months. In six weeks I'll be back.'"

Once in Wisconsin, he had tried phoning home, but the call wouldn't go through—a recorded voice on the line kept repeating something about the area code being wrong. For several months he was cut off completely from Mexico, in a cold place that could not have been more different from Sonora, tending to rows of cows in a long shed. He had no way of knowing what had happened back at his mother's *rancho*. "It wasn't until I got back, when I arrived in Piedras Negras, where one of my daughters lives. She told me, 'Haven't you called the *rancho, papá*?' I told her no. 'So you don't know what happened at the *rancho*?' she said. 'What happened?' I said. She couldn't find a way to tell me. But I already knew more or less what she was going to say."

Gregorio had lost his mother. She had died eight days earlier; he'd even missed the funeral. "I left Piedras Negras and I got ill. I was sick for something like twelve days. When these things happen I get very bad diarrhea, from my nerves. When my father died I was sick for eight days, when my mother died it was twelve. Twice they had to take me to the hospital at night. They would sit me down, and I would feel very small, like I was shrinking. And then I'd get chills. They had to hold me up when I went to the bathroom. Those were twelve humbling days for me. Finally a lady doctor at Francisco I. Madero [a town in Coahuila] gave me medicine and I got better. I took the medicine at eleven in the morning and didn't go to the bathroom again until four or five that afternoon.

"That's how I found out about my mother. My brothers said, 'We wanted to tell you, but we didn't have any way to reach you.' I was in Wisconsin."

For the young Gregorio goats were the chief source of his family's limited wealth, each animal an investment watched over and tallied, the humble capital of people trying to subsist off the land. Goats were valuable because they fed people; even though they were scrawny little mammals, the culinary resourcefulness of the *norteños* had found several tasty uses for them. You could slaughter one and use the meat to make tacos *al pastor* (shepherd-style), or milk the nanny goat and make goat cheese to sprinkle on top of your beans and rice. The older Gregorio worked to feed people too, though now it was in an industry. Steinbeck had witnessed the birth of the food factory that came to be known as "agribusiness." The term first appeared in American English some fifteen years after *The Grapes of Wrath*, a novel that is in part a description of that industry's birth. The food business of California helped set loose that first migration of white peasants (if I may be allowed to call them that) east to west on the old U.S. Highway 66. Steinbeck described a California where "some of the farms grew so large that one man could not even conceive of them any more, so large that it took batteries of bookkeepers to keep track of interest and gain and loss; chemists to test the soil, to replenish; straw bosses to see that the stooping men were moving along as swiftly as the material of their bodies could stand." Agribusiness conquered the rural United States, and in the decades to come it required enough labor to empty out Oklahoma a dozen times. Agribusiness took the small chicken coop behind the Alabama farmer's house and made it into a mechanized shed the length of a football field where 10,000 birds or more clucked before computerized feeders. Agribusiness was the reason Gregorio the Mexican goatherd would travel to Washington State to pick the apples that became apple pie, to Wisconsin to work machines attached to cow udders, and to Alabama to slice chickens into neat little pieces that fit inside cellophane packages. For Steinbeck it was an industry built upon the desperation and the ambition of the dispossessed farmer of the land, and today its factories are still being fed with the muscle of such men and women, though hardly any of them still speak in the Oklahoma lilt he labored to capture on the page. Instead, they talk in the assorted regional varieties of Latin American Spanish, telling tales of the abundance of unseen California valleys, of the wages that await them in dreamlike Dixie towns.

W hen the sun had risen in the sky and warmed the air inside my bus, the butterflies returned, beating against my window as our bus ground northward through Texas, stopping at a dozen little towns with Spanish names, rolling past El Loco Tattoo and La Feria Farm Supply and the Raging Bull Gentleman's

Club. The ten-gallon hats of a half-dozen *mexicanos* bounced over the tops of the seats. Next to me one of the other recruits told me he had worked at a chicken factory in Kentucky a year earlier. "They had the KKK there. There was a part of town where you weren't supposed to go because the KKK was there and they don't like Mexicans." The other recruit didn't take such stories seriously. He was in Alabama just a few months ago. "They told me the same thing . . . that the KKK was there. They got me real scared. On the bus, on the way over, I kept on thinking I saw the KKK in the window at night, with their hoods *y todo*. Like ghosts."

We left the plains of brambles and yucca plants behind, speeding past the neon affluence of Houston and one roadside mall after another, watching most of the ten-gallon hats disappear by the time we reached Louisiana. There was a sudden foreignness to the landscape— gone were the familiar *nopales* of Texas. We were deeper into the United States, and hardly a soul on the bus spoke Spanish besides the three of us recruited in McAllen. Suddenly, half the people on the bus were black—there are hardly any blacks in northern Mexico and the Texas border towns—boisterous young men and women who couldn't be more different from the good ol' boys of Corpus Christi and Laredo. We passed through Mobile, on the Gulf Coast, where I spent thirty seconds inside what has to be one of the most fetid bathrooms in the Greyhound's North American empire. I stopped by the magazine stand and picked up the new issue of *People* magazine. I had posed for a *People* photo shoot a few weeks earlier—the magazine was going to review my novel—and sure enough there I was, a Guatemalan-American author leaning against a wall in Los Angeles. My first moment of national celebrity—"I am a People," I told myself—arrived at precisely the moment I was trying to be a nobody.

Our bus headed north through Alabama, past green fields littered with thousands of tiny white balls of cotton. For a moment I wondered if, in fact, hooded men really did prowl these roads in search of Mexicans. We left the flatlands and climbed into the forested north, toward the Cumberland Mountains. Finally, we arrived at the bus station in Anniston, exiting to an empty lobby with two vending machines and no company representative there to greet us. It was a spartan little terminal, with no benches; much later, I learned the station was infamous as the place where a mob of white people attacked a group of Freedom Riders in 1961, setting their bus on fire in the name of the South and segregation. If I had known where I stood—in historical terms—I surely would have taken a look around and studied the place for those old ghosts. Instead, I wandered out to the parking lot, examining the empty bays that suggested a past filled with bus fleets and hordes of passengers. Finally, a pickup truck pulled up. A Mexican-American man who spoke perfect English and Spanish stepped out, introducing himself as Franco, the guy from Tyson. He drove us to our new home.

We arrived at a cluster of trailers on Alabama State Highway 9, planted on the Mars-orange dirt that covers everything in that part of the country. Franco introduced me to Frankie and Linda, who stood guard at the door of their trailer, sizing me up like concerned property owners worried that I might disrupt their suburban idyll.

"Do you drink?" Linda asked, in a disarmingly direct way for a nineteen-year-old. Behind her, Frankie peered out through the screen door, an ironic smile on his face.

"No," I said.

"Okay. You can stay with us, then."

Frankie made it clear they wanted theirs to be a "good" trailer. Some forty people, nearly all of them Tyson employees, lived in this camp, in a half-dozen mobile homes parked not far from the highway. Frankie and Linda wanted none of the smoking or drinking or late-night parties that went on in their neighbors' trailers. They had come from Eagle Pass and Crystal City for a new beginning and had made a great sacrifice to do so, the biggest a mother and father can make: they left their son, eighteen-month-old Frankie Jr., at home with his grandmother. All they had to remind them that they were parents was a photograph of an infant boy sitting in a room in Eagle Pass. They couldn't hear his voice, because even though his grandmother reported that he had become a precocious little chatterbox, he wouldn't talk when his grandmother raised the phone to his ear. There was only a light static on the line when Linda, a thousand miles away, called to him, "Hi, Frankie! Hi, it's your mommy!" Frankie Jr. was at the age when you see a boy grow from one week to the next, learning to walk and then run, to point at things and name them. His parents weren't sure when, exactly, they would see him again.

Frankie and Linda told me they had traveled to Alabama, leaving their son behind, because it was the best and fastest way to escape their old life, what some people call *the* life. Frankie didn't talk about his past much, but others were more than happy to fill in the picture. "Frankie was craaaazy," Fonzi, another young man in the camp, told me. Fonzi knew Frankie growing up in Crystal City—he was a hard-fighting, mean dude. When I looked at Frankie—a stocky, gentle young man—I had trouble believing this. His wife, Linda, wore braces and had a girl's squeaky laugh. Frankie told me about going to church in Texas, how different it was from Alabama. In Crystal City his neighbors looked at him funny, as if to ask, What is this tattooed gangster doing in God's house? "They stare at me because everyone knows I was in *malías*," border slang for badness. The people in Alabama didn't treat him that way, not Mr. Bob, from the Church of Christ in Lineville, who gave him a Bible to read and a collection of study materials, filled with questions about salvation, sin, and the apostles.

The Bible sat on a nightstand in a corner of the living room, for the most part unread. At night, the television was a bigger draw, especially Monday, when Frankie insisted on watching *Monday Night Nitro* wrestling, an hour of men strutting about a ring in spandex. He leaned forward on his chair, taking in the action with a kid's grin on his face. The Bible would sit on the nightstand until Sunday, when Frankie picked it up and took it with him to church, Linda at his side, Gregorio tagging along. The Bible was a symbol of the new people they were becoming, its very presence an antidote to the past, a power it retained even though they were usually too tired to read it.

If Frankie and Linda worked at Tyson long enough, Tyson would give them health insurance, which they needed for their growing family. But before Frankie Jr. came they would have to find a decent place to live, because this rickety trailer wouldn't do for raising their little boy. They were trying to filter out the bad influences from their life, a dark cloud that had, in a certain sense, tried to follow them to Alabama. The trailer park was filled with people who knew them in the Rio Grande Valley, hard-drinking young men who liked to fight and were already on a first-name basis with the local state trooper. Linda fought back against the past with a soothing tonic of domestic normality; she taped a cleaning schedule to the refrigerator, and one Sunday afternoon I watched her transform one of the tall black rubber boots that Tyson gave us at the factory into a vase, filling it with wildflowers picked from the side of the highway.

The bus from Tyson arrived at our trailer park at about 8:30 P.M. I couldn't work yet because my company-required drug test wasn't back, so I could only watch as Gregorio and the others slipped on their boots inside their trailer, their steps pounding out a drum roll on the rickety floor. Through the window I watched them line up, puffing little vapor clouds into the cold night air, and then climbing into the bus, which rolled away, leaving me to admire the moon and the bright star of Jupiter rising over the ridge of pine trees in the distance. Ten hours later, after the sun had taken the moon's place above the ridge, they were back, pulling at the tight muscles in their fingers, waving their arms in windmill circles to shake out the soreness. Gregorio raised his shirt and rubbed the globe of his belly, the way large men do. A quick breakfast and then to bed, Gregorio plopping into a lower bunk, Román the top, Gregorio's snores causing the thin walls of the trailer to tremble.

Waking up one afternoon, Román told me that in his sleep he had traveled to Mexico. He dreamt he was caught up in a *pleito*, a quarrel with some people in his hometown. That's the way it is when you find yourself in a new and strange place: even your nightmares are tinged with a longing for home.

Gregorio had a dream too: he saw a bowl of soup, tasty and rich, like the ones his *jefecita* used to make.

After a few days, I started to pace. Unable to work, I spent lonely days walking in circles around my trailer, hours and hours wondering where the hell I was, exactly, on the great map of the United States. Someone told me it was a mile walk to the nearest telephone. Once a week, another person told me, a bus would come to the trailers to pick me up and take me to town (for a fee, of course) so that I could shop at the local Piggly Wiggly. Well, that's something to look forward to, I thought. The Piggly Wiggly motto, I learned later, is "Down Home, Down the Street." When I got tired of pacing, I studied the highway traffic, sitting on a bench in front of an abandoned gas station, counting the trucks carrying birds to the plant. *One hundred chicken dinners; five hundred chicken dinners; one thousand chicken dinners.* Once I was joined in this activity by a young man who looked even more bored than I was. He had the swarthy handsomeness, the good grooming, and denim wardrobe of an actor in *West Side Story* or *Giant*. He told me he had come to the plant to earn enough money to get the transmission fixed on his car back home but now he was regretting that decision.

"I'm not used to living in a *ranchito* like this," he told me.

"Me neither," I said. "I'm from the city."

"Me too."

"Where?"

"Eagle Pass," he said. By the longing look on his face, Eagle Pass was a booming metropolis next to this lonely stretch of Alabama State Highway 9 on which we found ourselves marooned. "There's nothing here."

"You have to walk a mile just to make a phone call," I said.

He rolled his eyes in agreement and exasperation. "I think I made a mistake coming here," he said.

He was an Eagle Pass tough guy who had inadvertently exiled himself to the Alabama countryside. Who would have thought, his eyes said, that you could have traveled so deep into the United States to wind up in a place that's just like those *ranchitos* in Sonora and Durango that everyone with any sense is trying to get away from? We were living in an Alabama *ranchito* like the one Gregorio had left a generation ago, with caged chickens in place of braying goats, and kindhearted evangelicals carrying Bibles instead of old ladies with rosary beads praying for their sons to return safely home.

In the late twentieth century, the United States had become a country with a peasantry—a *campesinado,* as they say in Mexico. It was filling with people like Gregorio, whose sense of themselves is tied to the rhythms of life of the earth and the soil. They were the characters who filled Juan Rulfo's *El Llano en Llamas*, The Burning Plain, a collection of short stories that transport you to Mexican *ranchitos*, at the mercy of the weather and abandonment. In Rulfo, it never rains, or else it rains too much all at once and the floodwaters take away the farm animals and ruin the crops. The old, abandoned churches crumble into ruins before your eyes, and the boys drink goats' milk and go to the ponds to listen to the frogs croak. In Rulfo, mystery and superstition impose themselves on the natural order; the crickets chirp day and night, "without stopping even to breathe, so that you can't hear the screams of the souls suffering in Purgatory." In Clay County there are no crickets, but you don't hear the screaming from Purgatory either, perhaps because the Latino faithful have not resided here long enough to leave a chorus of tormented souls.

Gregorio had done tougher work in Mexico and didn't think the work at the chicken plant was especially hard. He didn't have many complaints against Tyson either, or against the labor contractor who brought him to Alabama, even though the contractor did lie when he said Tyson would pay him overtime and give him some money to look for an apartment once he got to Alabama. He'd seen worse. "I worked in Wisconsin for eight months, at a dairy farm. I left because I had a problem with my boss. He owed me two weeks salary. But I didn't complain, because there were two *muchachos* there who had paid a coyote $3,000 to bring their families from Mexico. I didn't want the authorities to come and start peeking around and get those guys in trouble."

It is a measure of Gregorio's work ethic that not much time passed between the moment he heard his mother died and his decision to hit the road again. This time he went to Kentucky, where he spent six weeks in the tobacco warehouses. He came home with about $2,000, which is a lot of money in Piedras Negras or anywhere else. He liked the feeling that earned money brings, which was why he almost never turned down a good-paying job, no matter how nasty it might seem to others. "In Mexico I worked in the countryside. . . . I had jobs slaughtering pigs, barbecuing pork, making *chicharrón,* slaughtering cattle. Whatever, anything. I was a *milusos,*" a jack-of-all-trades.

On the night I first went to the plant, after my drug test cleared, I joined Gregorio, Román, Frankie and Linda, and about twenty other workers waiting along the side of the two-lane road. We clustered together in the darkness, our hands in our pockets, shoulders hunched together against the cold. We were dressed in street clothes, with only our black rubber boots and our collective Latinoness announcing to the world that we were laborers. Our bus followed the same route that Tyson's trucks used to deliver chickens to the plant. The birds arrived scrunched in stacked metal cages, which opened automatically, dumping the birds down a chute. I had been taken to see this during my plant orientation a few days earlier, watching with fascination and dread as the fattened hens gave a few, last, and desperate flaps of their wings and slid into the machinery. I had seen the Dantesque tableau in the dark room where the birds are electronically put to their deaths, a single *mexicano* manning a machine that gave off an electric-blue glow, watching as a line of bodies, already mechanically stripped of feathers, emerged from the other side on a passing line of metal hooks. The plant had an insatiable, round-the-clock appetite for chicken, swallowing double tractor-trailers full of birds every fifteen minutes or so. My friends from the border and I had been brought in to make sure this machinery ran at night too, that there were enough hands to tend to the flesh in a section of the plant known as "live processing"—a misnomer, because every chicken there was as dead as when you see it at the grocery store.

The birds drifted through the refrigerated air, past the attentive hands of Gregorio, Román, Frankie, Linda, and me, wings drooping from necks and shoulders, winding their way through the plant on metal riders that circled from one crew to the next, thousands of birds made to look identical, as if they had never been living things at all, as if they had been designed by an engineer and spat out by a mold. Gregorio cut wings, one of the more difficult jobs in the plant, work that can turn your arms into lead. I was assigned to a section where I grabbed a chicken off a hook, placed it on a metal cone, and sheared off the flesh around the neck. To perform this task safely I was outfitted with several layers of protective clothing, including safety glasses and a steel-mesh glove on my left hand that resembled a piece of medieval armor. For eight hours I assaulted chicken flesh with my knife, becoming more intimate with their chicken lives with each bird that passed through my hands. Some were healthy, buxom creatures that rarely passed up a meal, apparently, because even in death yellow grains of feed lingered in their throats. Others were puny, pathetic hens who suffered during their short lives, arriving at my work station with broken limbs and shriveled skin. From time to time an older black man with kind eyes (the only part of his face I could see clearly) walked over, inspected my chickens, and gave me a thumbs-up sign. That little child of the meritocracy inside of me who is always eager to please my superiors felt a twinge of accomplishment.

We worked for eight hours, wrapped inside layers of cotton and plastic, hardly talking to one another, because the roar of a dozen machines working simultaneously wiped out conversations. With our earplugs in, we felt the noise as a deep, rhythmic vibration, as if we were small parts inside a single, grinding engine straining to lift an impossibly heavy load. This was the kind of work that erases portions of your memory if you do it too long. Another supervisor drifted by and shouted in my ear, "You're going too slow! It doesn't have to be perfect!" No, I wanted to shout back, these are my chickens, Héctor's chickens, and they *will* be perfect, because being a perfectionist got me where I am today. I sliced open a big cavity around each bird's neck, while across the room other people sliced off their limbs and tossed them in buckets and packed them in dry ice, washing the blood on the floor into drains.

Halfway through the shift, it suddenly began to rain, water falling from the ceiling in drops and then in a thick stream; a pipe had burst over our heads. An alarm went off, the serpentine line of chickens stopped. Low-level supervisors in khaki smocks began to shout into radios attached to their uniforms, gesturing to us line workers to step away from the chicken flesh. Work crews with hoses appeared to spray the cadavers with a foamy, sterilizing substance. A group of engineers and mechanics arrived, men with clipboards and take-charge attitudes, their smart eyes gazing up at the ceiling. Every single one of them was white. They were the only white men in sight—office personnel, members of a higher company caste apparently. I began to feel very dark in their presence, to feel the full weight of the word "Alabama." There is no other way to say it: I felt I was on a plantation. I had spotted the leak and felt another twinge of satisfaction at being able to point it out to the technicians, but they completely ignored me, as if I were some babbling, gesturing idiot. Several minutes later, after finding the leak themselves and fixing it, they barked a command over the grind of the machines, which had started again. "Back to work!" Just as suddenly as they had arrived, they were gone, to the quiet shelter of their offices in another corner of the plant.

Gregorio, Román, Frankie, Linda, and I worked until sunrise. That was why we had been brought here from Mexico and Texas, along with the black workers recruited from Selma: to fill the night shift, jobs no local would take.

Don Pablo was sixty-five years old, which made him the oldest worker in the trailers on Highway 9. He was a slight man from Nueva Rosita, Coahuila, with a fringe of gray hair around the bronze dome of his bald head, and lived in the trailer next to ours. Don Pablo was said to be the father of fifteen children, and looking at him you might have guessed that the effort of so much procreation had sapped him of all his strength—he was hunched over, frail and thin. One night, while working on the line hanging chickens, Don Pablo had a stroke. Franco, the Tyson man who had picked me and my fellow Texas recruits up at the bus station, arrived at the trailer camp the next morning to deliver the news. "It looks like he's going to be okay." He had come to tell Pablo's roommates, so they could pass on word to his family. "He's getting a little feeling back in his arm. He's lucky he didn't fall and hit his head on the machinery." No, Don Pablo did not tumble into the grinding metal robots and the hooks of the evisceration section. Nor did he fall into the open drains of fast-flowing water that carry away defective chicken parts to some secret receptacle, like that worker at the slaughterhouse who falls into the vat in Upton Sinclair's novel *The Jungle*, to be boiled and boiled until he became broth. Instead Don Pablo fell out of harm's way. He was lucky. He was at Clay County Hospital, on his back, resting.

Don Pablo's accident left us all in a reflective mood, reminded us of our vulnerability and the safety videos Tyson had shown us during orientation, the testimonials of workers maimed in split-second accidents, the macabre close-ups of hands with severed pinkies and index fingers. Only Frankie, who was burly and strong, didn't seem bothered or worried. "I know where Don Pablo works," he said, his voice betraying a bit of contempt for the older man. "What he's doing isn't hard." Later, Gregorio, who wasn't that much younger than Don Pablo, would hear the news and wonder how much longer his own fifty-something body could stand up to the lifting and strain of factory work and other jobs like it. "Don Pablo told them the line was going too fast, but they didn't listen to him." Gregorio told me he would work as long as he could walk, until his heart started to give out, like Don Pablo's, at which point he would finally stop his own wandering across North America and return to that patch of land in Luchana, Coahuila, that would always be home, his *tierra*. "My kids don't want me to come over anymore, but I will until I get my Social Security."

"I tell my sons that wherever you go, you have to do what you can to find a job, because if you don't work, if you don't have money in your pocket, you start to rub people the wrong way. You have to get a job, even if it's just washing the neighbor's car. If you just sit around saying 'I want this, I want that,' and you don't have any money, people start to get sick of you very fast." For the time being, no one would look at Gregorio and see a lazy man, no one would hear him complain about not having money. He remained an *hombre*, down to the tips of his *mexicano* toes.

T he five trailers on State Highway 9 were not a place people stayed for very long. After I'd just started to get used to the peculiarities of the Piggly Wiggly grocery store and the stares of Alabamans uncertain whether I would understand them if they spoke to me in English, after I'd finally gotten used to sleeping on a bunk bed, all my new friends were gone. I came back from working at the plant one frosty morning, on a later bus than my roommates, and was surprised to discover that Gregorio and Román had moved out the night before, to an apartment in Ashland. Román's boom box and *ranchera* tapes were gone, as were Gregorio's enormous jockey shorts hanging in the closet. Frankie and Linda were upset with them, because they had taken most of the food out of the cabinets, even boxes of cereal all five of us had bought together. "They were all nice, and then they take off with the food like that. They didn't want to leave us anything." Soon afterward, Frankie and Linda moved out too, headed for the public housing in Ashland, Frankie making plans to fly back to Texas and drive back to Alabama with his son and mother-in-law, the family reunited again.

Before saying good-bye, I decided to let Frankie and Linda in on my secret: I'm a writer, not a chicken worker, I told them, tapping the moment for whatever drama it was worth. I came here to write about Alabama and the trailers, "to tell the world what's happening here."

"You see, I told you!" Linda said, beaming. "I told Frankie, 'This guy Héctor, I just have this feeling about him. That he's an important person.'" I mused about this later. Of course, what gave me away to Linda was my aloof demeanor. She saw me moping about the trailer, riding off on a borrowed bike to the public telephone to call California and New York, and figured: this guy doesn't belong here. Once I liberated myself from the idea that I was pretending to be someone I wasn't, I could feel the distance between us evaporating. I could feel I was a teenager again, living in a Southern California barrio populated with girls in braces who looked like Linda, and burly tough guys like Frankie. I could feel I was that Guatemalan boy in Hollywood, listening to his mother tell him to be humble.

That sense of belonging, of having embraced my inner *jornalero*, of stepping closer to the hardscrabble world my parents knew, lasted for about a day. Then, deciding I could not live in the trailer-jail a day longer, telling myself that my wife and toddler son in California must be frantic to have me back, I did something only the most desperate *mexicano* would do: I scurried back home without even waiting to collect my paycheck. I hitched a ride to the bus station in Anniston, where I bought a ticket for the relatively short ride to Birmingham. I checked into a luxury hotel, made a plane reservation to fly back to Los Angeles, and ordered a burger and a glass of wine from room service. When the food arrived and I left the bellhop a tip, my conversion back to the privileged classes was complete.

The counters of the Census 2000 arrived in Ashland and the surrounding towns a year after I left: they tallied 253 people of "Hispanic" heritage in Clay County (a severe undercount, by my reckoning), about 2 percent of the total population. Even that small number was significant, representing the very first anomaly in a rather rigid ethnic status quo that had reigned in Alabama since the early nineteenth century, when Tocqueville had wandered through its forests. In *Democracy in America,* the Frenchman reports an 1831 encounter in which he saw representatives of "the three races which inhabit the territory of the United States," sitting together by a spring in the Alabama forest: a Creek Indian woman dressed in the "barbarous luxury" of ear and nose rings; a white child of about six, whose gestures displayed "a consciousness of superiority"; and a black woman, "dressed in squalid European garments," tending to the child. The Creeks were marched off to Oklahoma soon after. Since then, nearly everyone in Alabama could be counted in the groups known as black and white, two American identities with a history of conflict and coexistence. The arrival of my trailermates on Highway 9 marked the beginning of a new epoch: a modern-day

Tocqueville would have added my round Mesoamerican face to Alabama's ethnic tableau had he stopped by the week that I lived there. Across the rural South—in Siler City, North Carolina; Bentonville, Arkansas; and another town I would soon visit, Dalton, Georgia—newspapers and city fathers were taking note of the arrival of people who were from exotic places that straddled the Tropic of Cancer. It was a demographic explosion brought forth by the swing shifts at the chicken plants, by the need for busboys and construction workers in Memphis and Atlanta, and by the spinning yarn mills at Georgia carpet factories. In the 2000 census, 75,830 Latino people had stopped in their wanderings long enough to be counted in Alabama, 378,963 in North Carolina, and 435,227 in Georgia. They were beginning to plant roots, slowly and inexorably changing the character of Dixie.

But others would continue wandering. Román was upset that the promised overtime never materialized, and I suspect he returned to Durango with a wad of cash that was not quite as thick and green as he had hoped. Gregorio, for his part, had always said he never expected to stay for more than a few months anyway, moving on in search of something better, something different. "I'm thinking of going to North Carolina. To Raleigh. My niece lives there." Before he left, we opened up a map of the Southeastern United States I'd recently bought at the Piggly Wiggly and spread it across the trailer's kitchen table, examining the potential routes: a few hundred miles across Georgia and over the Appalachians, a bit longer than he expected but still enticing. We talked about how long the trip would be and how much the bus fare. He said he would check in with the labor contractors to see what was available. "I like working through the offices, because with them everything is set up, guaranteed. If you get to the new place and there isn't a job waiting for you, you just call back the contractor and he pays for your bus ticket back. Once I went to Washington on my own to work the apples and I got stuck there without any money."

This is why Gregorio never stayed at one job for very long, and why he left Tyson even though the company would have been glad to keep him for a while longer: the challenge of the journey, the conquest of something new, was as important as the money. Gregorio's reward was the letter he sent home, the envelope with the money order, proof to his sons that the old man can still do any job they can. That's how I will remember Gregorio: about to undertake yet another journey across the United States, the goatherd on the Greyhound, unafraid of the perils that might befall him. Once he was a boy who guided his *chivos* to market along timeworn footpaths in the deserts of Coahuila, past sandstone vistas; today the mini-marts and truck stops of the Interstate serve as the mileposts to his travels. He will keep coming to the United States because each year he spends here is a shining medal on the uniform of his life, battles won against tobacco in Kentucky, cows in Minnesota, and slippery chickens in the icy air of an Alabama factory. He will cross into new cities and counties that for now exist only in his mind's eye.

F our years later I returned to Alabama, this time liberated of all disguises, in a rental car, to see the place where I had lived. Entering Clay County from the north on State Highway 9, I saw a verdant landscape I had been too worried to notice before, a bucolic oil painting of rolling pastureland, hay bales, and Baptist churches with marquees engaged in holy conversation with those who drove past: ARE WE FAITHFUL? one asked. I drove up to the trailer park where I had lived with Frankie and Linda and the others, but most of the trailers had been towed away, and wild grass and shrubs were swallowing up the others. The lot where I had sat talking to the lonely young man from Eagle Pass, and where I had waited in my boots for the bus to take me to the plant, was filled with junked cars. The Latino community was living in more permanent abodes now; those who decided their wandering would stop here had settled into the neighborhoods of Lineville and Ashland. I tried to track down preacher Bob at the Church of Christ but was not successful. Instead, I headed for the new Catholic Church the Latinos had built, Saint Mark's, in Ashland.

The church was more the size of a chapel, inhabiting a smallish replica of a white plantation-style home, high on a hill overlooking the Clay County Country Club, the cornerstone proclaiming, "SAINT MARK'S, FOUNDED FEB. 2000." Inside, three dozen or so families filled the small space, each a family portrait of immigrant humility, only their babies dressed in new, Sunday-best clothes. The main crucifix was a simple wooden affair not more than two feet tall, and to the right of the altar there was a framed poster of the Virgin of Guadalupe, the kind you can buy at any religious store in Los Angeles. Infants gurgled and dropped rattles that rolled in the aisles, and the older children played peekaboo over the tops of the pews, but no one seemed to mind, least of all the goateed Colombian priest standing before the altar. His sermon was a straightforward retelling of Old Testament allegories of migration and displacement that most obviously applied to the families before him. "The Israelites were enslaved, subjugated to forced labor," he said in Spanish, "but they never lost their faith. And they returned to Jerusalem. They returned to the Temple. . . . They kept their faith while they lived among the Babylonians, during the exile [*el destierro*], even when they were invited to worship idols, they kept faith in the one God."

Through the windows, you could see golfers on the fairways and Country Club Road winding toward the Talladega forest in the distance; this was the Babylon where the Latino pilgrims were challenged in their faith, challenged by the money they yearned for and needed, challenged by the great distance from those places and values that had anchored them, challenged by the burly cops who threw them in jail when they dared to drive without Alabama licenses. Marisela Ibarra sat near the back with the same Bible she would consult during a meeting of catechists I attended later; it was the same Bible she had crossed the border with, and the same Bible she had carried when she first stepped off the bus in Alabama. "It helped me," she would tell me. Her children were healthy and her husband had not drifted off to join the Babylonians, like many other men who go north and lose their souls; in fact, he was at the back of the church playing guitar and singing "You take away the sins of the world."

I tossed a bill into a collection basket filled almost entirely with wrinkled one-dollar bills, and clapped with the church band, a quartet that included a tambourine, a conga drum, and an electric keyboard. The time came to take Communion and the families filed into the center aisle, lining up before the priest and his altar boys. I brought up the rear of this procession, deciding I would take Communion with them. After two decades, I'd started going to church when my oldest boy turned seven because we'd enrolled him in First Communion classes, something I would have never expected to find myself doing; when you become a parent tradition has a way of sneaking up on you. One by one the Ashland parishioners opened their mouths to accept the Communal wafer, and the priest delicately placed it on their tongues. There was something visceral and crude about this ritual, I decided, to allow a stranger to plop something in your mouth like that. After all, even if he is a priest, who can really say where his hands have been? Similar concerns among hoity-toity Catholics led Rome to approve "Communion-by-hand" years ago as a more hygienic, though less reverent alternative.

At the church I attended in Buenos Aires, half the congregation received the host in their palms, lifting it into their own mouths, but here in Alabama no one seemed to have heard of such proprieties: mothers, fathers, girls, and boys were all flashing their moist tongues at the priest. As my turn approached, I faced a moment of decision: would I surrender, again, to my middle-class squeamishness and be the only person in church to hold out my palm and clamp my mouth shut? Or would I be a real *hombre* and stick out my tongue like all the Latinos before me?

I opened my mouth.

Chapter Five

IN THE LAND OF THE NEW

En la tierra de lo nuevo

Dalton, Georgia · Nuevo Laredo, Tamaulipas, Mexico · Memphis, Tennessee

Whten I was in the fourth grade at Grant Elementary School, our teacher introduced us to the word "ecology" and to that alternative version of the American flag that flew sporadically in the 1970s, the one with green and white stripes and a lowercase yellow *e* in a green field in place of the fifty stars. We couldn't raise our ecology flag in front of the school where Old Glory flew, but our teacher claimed that space in the name of Mother Earth with a class project to put a planter box at the base of the flagpole. We raised the money for the material to build the box, learned about compost and mulch, and debated whether we should plant daisies or roses or drought-hardy jade plants with fleshy, oval leaves. In the end, we filled the box with shovelfuls of moist black soil and planted marigolds, whose deep orange sunbursts are seared into my memory.

Thirty years later our planter box is still there. I see it whenever I return to my old neighborhood, which has suffered the many insults of recent California history. A few years after my sixth-grade graduation, a gadfly named Howard Jarvis led a middle-class rebellion against California's high property-tax rates, and the wellspring of money that had funded the Golden Age of California public education dried up. With each passing year, my old elementary school looks more like an exhausted old ship; its windows are sealed off with steel bars, and the blacktop where I once played touch football and baseball was wiped out long ago to make room for a flock of trailer-bungalows, "temporary classrooms" that have been fixed in place for decades. No one bothers much with the old planter box anymore, other than to repeatedly add layers of paint over the old redwood to erase the latest graffito. The building is sealed off most of the day, the better to protect the children inside against any outbreaks of unexpected violence, because in modern Los Angeles you just never know what kind of lunatic stalker might be out there. No one bothers or dares to lead groups of green-thumbed children to plant marigolds or roses or anything else in what has become a forgotten box of dirt.

Other Los Angeles schools have fared worse. At the Eastside elementary school where my wife once worked, teachers have resurrected the old "duck and cover" drills from the Atomic Age as an emergency response to the poorly aimed gunplay of local gang members; when bullets explode outside, the children know to dive under their desks, making a game out of it, giggling while their teachers cast worried eyes toward the windows. When I became a reporter at the *Times*, I inherited the thankless job foisted on all rookies: rolling out to the scenes of campus homicides to interview grieving classmates and stunned principals, and to reconstruct the path of bullets that somehow ended up in the torsos and skulls of children. For many years, it was hard for me to think of being a mother or a father without remembering the convulsive agony and sorrow of those parents I'd interviewed an hour or a day after they'd lost a son or daughter. One day an editor handed me a three-line dispatch from a wire service called City News. "URGENT: SCHOOL SHOOTING, COMPTON . . ." A few hours later I sat down in the newsroom to type a story that began with this sentence: "The stray bullet struck and killed 11-year-old Alejandro Vargas as he stood at the heart of his school campus—on the front lawn beneath the flagpole. . . ."

Alejandro had been waiting for his mother to pick him up at Ralph Bunche Middle School when a gang member opened fire on the school's security guard, not noticing or caring that there was a young boy standing nearby. His family gave me a copy of his last school photograph; here was a young man with a Mona Lisa smile and a neat part in his hair, standing against the obligatory blue-gray wash background, a lifetime of portraits seemingly awaiting him. My newspaper ran that picture and also a front-page, full-color photograph of his mother, Elisa Vargas, weeping not far from the spot where he fell, grabbing a chain-link fence in a moment of utter despair, a scene I had witnessed from just a few feet away, close enough to hear what she was repeating between sobs: *"¿Por qué? ¿Por qué te fuiste?"* Why? Why did you go? I had just finished scribbling those words in my notebook when a group of Latino parents corralled me and pulled me away. At first I thought they wanted me to leave Elisa alone, but no, they wanted to show me something, a more mundane injustice, but one that nevertheless helped explain how it had come to pass that an eleven-year-old boy would be shot down at his school's flagpole. They took me to see a small concrete block some thirty paces from where Alejandro died: it was the girls' bathroom. The toilets were backed up with a fetid stew of human waste, a putrefaction that hinted at the greater plague of decay that had swept through the school and the society and government responsible for it. "You see?" the parents said. "You see what kind of school this is?" How is this possible, their Mexican eyes asked, in this wealthy country? Why is it that *our* children suffer this daily indignity, and now death from random bullets?

At that moment I thought: *The public schools are dead, like the body of that boy at the bottom of the flagpole.* The idea that the California public schools might be a cocoon of learning and safety for immigrants like the Vargas family had passed into history. Across Southern California, uncounted thousands of immigrant families were reaching similar conclusions about the place they had come to with so many hopes and dreams. They expected a California where their children would build planter boxes and fill them with marigolds, where they might find work planting gardens for Americans, but instead there was this other, meaner place. Socorro Ibarra had gone to Los Angeles at the age of fifteen, but after a few disappointing and exhausting years in California—"what we found there was lies and abuse"—she joined her family in an eastward exodus. Socorro ended up in Ashland, Alabama, pioneering the route followed later by her brother Martín, who came directly from Jalisco, Mexico, and who now plays guitar in the Ashland church band. Flocelo Aguirre, who had arrived in California from Mexico with fake teacher's credentials in 1968, settled near the old railroad yards in central Los Angeles and lived there until things turned sour in the early 1990s, at which point he decided to set out for a town in northwestern Georgia called Dalton.

Many years after that day of horrors in Compton, I visited a school in Dalton, thirty miles or so down Interstate 75 from Chattanooga, Tennessee, and the Civil War battlefield of Chickamauga. Dalton had undergone a stunning demographic transformation similar to the one that had swept through California a generation earlier. The small seed of Latinoness that I had seen planted in my trailer park in Clay County, Alabama, had become a forest of Mexicanness in north Georgia, a place thick with *taquerías* and *fútbol* and *rancheras.* In Dalton, Latinos made up more than half the school-age population, and I wondered what lessons those children were learning, and if they had to interrupt their studies to practice how to "duck and cover."

I arrived at Roan Street Elementary School late one morning, after all the students had filed into their classes, driving up to the low-slung and clean administration building, taking a seat outside the office of the principal, with whom I had scheduled an interview. The usual school-office clientele wandered in and out as I waited— children with runny noses, mothers trying to sort out a midterm admission. They were all Spanish-speaking children and parents, communicating with staff through an interpreter who patiently translated their questions into the local, Blue Ridge variant of English, which sashayed along as patiently as the rural Spanish of the people settling here. The parents spoke in low voices, as if they might be afraid to disrupt the sense of order and calm that permeated that place. I thought I might have wandered into a seminary tucked in the pine woods that enveloped the town, and not a school for six hundred boisterous five-, six-, and seven-year-olds. You didn't hear the usual patter of footsteps in the nearby hallways and corridors, because every square foot of the building was carpeted. Even the boy with the runny nose had a fresh part in his hair.

Finally, the principal appeared, Dr. Frankie Beard, a petite no-nonsense administrator with short salt-and-pepper hair. She recounted the story of her arrival in Roan, which coincided with the arrival of all the Mexicans. They had seemed to sneak up on the district and the school, she told me. A decade earlier, there were only a handful of Latino students; now they made up 80 percent of the student body. "A few years ago, we were all running around in circles. The teachers couldn't communicate with the students. Our staff couldn't communicate with the parents. We were like that episode of *I Love Lucy* where Lucy and Ethel are working at the candy factory, and the line keeps moving faster and faster and pretty soon all the candy is falling on the floor. We just didn't have a clue." The district had tried to recruit bilingual teachers, but it's hard to lure people from places like Miami or Houston to a little Southern burg where a night out on the town requires an hour-long drive to Chattanooga. So for several years now, the district was paying to send small groups of its veteran staff each summer to Monterrey, Mexico, to study Spanish, and to become acquainted with the education system that had first taught their new Dalton charges about the alphabet, numbers, and the story of Benito Juárez, the father of the Mexican republic.

"Isn't that incredibly expensive?" I asked.

"Of course it is," Dr. Beard said. "But the people here think it's important." Dalton's team of newly bilingual teachers presided over most of the classrooms I saw during a tour of the schoolhouse. Each was leading his or her charges with equal measures of *"por favor"* and please, and "What do you think, Joaquín?" and *"¡Muy bien, niños!"* A white-haired specialist in language problems floated from class to class to help the small groups of children straggling behind the rest. In Los Angeles, it seemed every other teacher was someone just out of college, working with "emergency" credentials. Here in Dalton the teachers averaged thirteen years' experience.

After local administrators had discovered that most of Roan's students came from the Mexican state of Zacatecas, Principal Beard had decided she needed to go there too. She recalled visiting rural schoolhouses with dirt floors where the teachers ran short of basics like pencils and chalk, a vision that had violated her notions of human dignity and justice. "If I were living in those conditions and I were pregnant, I'd crawl across the border to get here."

Like all schools in Dalton, Roan Street was spending more than

$7,400 per student each year: few of the Spanish-speaking parents in Dalton knew of this figure, though they surely would have considered it extravagant if they did. It was among the highest in Georgia and significantly higher than the state average in California, then $5,414. The schools were funded by the property taxes paid by the more than one hundred local carpet factories, where Mexicans filled jobs as "roll-up wrappers" and "spinners" and in "yarn mills." The factories of the "Carpet Capital of the World" threw in the rugs for the local schools too, persuaded by local leaders like Erwin Mitchell, a World War II veteran and local attorney who a generation earlier had been one of the first local Democrats to suggest it was time to embrace the demands of the civil rights movement. That role had made him the target of some withering cartoons in the local, segregationist media, which were displayed as trophies in his office in downtown Dalton when I visited him later that day. A new set of clippings was gathering on his desk, nearly all of them upbeat articles about the Georgia Project, founded by Mitchell and other local leaders who wanted to ease the adaptation of the new arrivals to the state. "The factories need the workers, and the workers come with families," he told me. Without good schools for the workers' children, the county would leave itself open to a whole host of social problems down the road. Giving Dalton's Mexican kids a decent education was the sensible thing to do, "pure self-interest," he said.

In the person of Dr. Beard, such pragmatism had been translated into the compassionate idealism with which a certain breed of American has always greeted the arrival of downtrodden newcomers, be they nineteenth-century Irish or twentieth-century Italians. "We're trying to build on the strong family values of the Mexican people," she told me. "It's just phenomenal to us how quickly these children can learn."

Word of Dalton's good teachers and the carpeted hallways at the schoolhouse had quickly spread through the Mexican community, reaching by international mail and long-distance telephone to Zacatecas and also to San Luis Potosí and Oaxaca. "When I first got here and started working in the carpet factories, they told me the schools were good," a former factory worker named Rafael Huerta told me. But when you leave for the States, your ears are filled with "land of milk and honey" stories, and Rafael was skeptical. In the case of Dalton, however, those stories turned out to be true. Inside the din of Dalton's factories, *mexicano* workers could daydream about the quiet classrooms where their children were turning their ears toward their teachers, trying to catch the difference in sound between a "sh" and a "th," neither of which exists in Spanish. Huerta's daughter had learned to speak English in just six months of kindergarten at Roan Street. In California, the majority of the electorate had just voted to keep illegal immigrants out of schools. But here in Georgia, the locals' honeymoon with all things Latin American was just beginning.

At Roan Elementary, there were love and money at work in the way the teachers rounded up their charges into neat lines in the hallways, in the maintenance crews and janitors who roamed the campus to keep the water streaming in sturdy arcs from the fountains and the bathrooms stocked with paper towels, and in the smile of the boy with the runny nose who was now emerging from the nurse's office with a box of tissues. For a moment, I felt the strange sensation that I had been transported back in time to the California of my childhood to cast my eyes once more on that age of optimism and innocence. Suddenly, I understood the pain that had been lurking behind those old memories of playgrounds and schoolyard parades. My parents were divorced at about the same time I left elementary school: the crowding and neglect of my old school felt like a kind of rejection too; it said that neither I nor any other son of an immigrant was worthy of the largesse of a Grant or a Roan Elementary. And yet here in Georgia there were people who wanted to embrace us, who believed we could be geniuses and good citizens. When the bell sounded, the hallways were filled with brown-skinned boys and girls taking silent steps on the carpeted hallways toward the classrooms. I could look into the faces of those *mexicano* boys and imagine one of them was Alejandro, the martyred boy of Compton. If Alejandro had been resurrected from his resting place at the base of the flagpole and carried across the continent to be reborn that very same day in Dalton, he would have been seven years old the day I visited. He'd be growing up in this nurturing cocoon of *el nuevo* South, learning to speak English with the drawl of his second-grade teacher.

After I'd said my good-byes to principal Beard, I drove through Dalton listening to *rancheras* on WDAL radio and three ads in a row each commercial break for jobs in carpet factories. "More than seven dollars an hour and overtime for those who want it!" They were like those ads in Mexico that enticed people north, with an important difference: here you could go to the prospective employer and check things out, and if you didn't like one job you could easily switch to another. This is what it was like for my father in 1960s California, I thought: you could arrive somewhere in the morning and by the afternoon find a job falling into your hands like overripe fruit from a tree. I couldn't remember ever being surrounded by so much optimistic *latinidad*. With Southern California no longer a welcoming Eden for Latin American immigrants, those people were transporting their ambition and their sense of industry to the Midwest, the Great Plains, and the Deep South. The first pioneers arrived in these towns alone, disoriented by the strange surroundings, as I had been at that bus station in Anniston, Alabama. But those who were resettled Californians and Texans brought a deeper Latino way of living with them, a strain of Latinoness toughened by time spent in those teeming Spanish-speaking places. Eventually, they moved out of their trailer parks, then placed phone calls to brothers and sisters, friends and cousins in central Mexico, El Salvador, and Orange County, California, announcing the discovery of a bountiful new American place: *"Vengan, y pronto, porque sólo Dios sabe cuánto tiempo dure esto."* Come, and be quick about it, because God knows how long this is going to last.

In Georgia, the second, third, and fourth wave of new arrivals stepped off the Greyhound to be greeted by neat, clean little towns where cupolas rise over the old government buildings and stone Confederate soldiers stand guard over the town squares. A Latino person here encountered both the familiar and the unfamiliar: a practiced eye could see a new Latin American townscape emerging inside the old one. In Gainesville, northeast of Atlanta, I examined the statue of Johnny Reb keeping watch atop a tall pillar in the central plaza, and the plaque placed by the Daughters of the Confederacy when the monument was dedicated a century or so earlier. Johnny Reb patrolled a town square of brick storefront houses, antique shops, and unpretentious cafés, but if you walked a block or so from the monument, following the very faint scent of cooked corn tortillas and mole poblano, you wound up at the Taquería Los Rayos. I toasted the Confederacy with a beer and a chicken burrito at Los Rayos (the Lightning Bolt), admiring the collage of pictures underneath the glass of the front counter: snapshots from the owners' visit to Birmingham, Alabama, to see the Mexican national soccer team play. Stepping out the front door with a belly full of beans, I almost got run over by a car from Taxi Mexico, which sped past with two women in the back seat.

The *mexicanos* fit in because at heart they were country people like the locals, puttering around north Georgia in beat-up pickups. They wore embroidered leather boots that, while more ornate than the footware of the locals, suggested the same down-home outlook. Flocelo Aguirre saw Dalton as a Dixified version of that small pueblo in rural Guerrero, Mexico, he had left many years earlier. Life was slower here; you took time for the little courtesies. You might even reach for the brim of your hat and tip it slightly when a lady walked past. I was sitting on Aguirre's front porch underneath the shade of pine and dogwood trees not far from Roan Elementary, talking about his all-abiding passion—the Dalton International Soccer League—when a good ol' boy in a pickup truck drove past and gave a long and friendly wave.

"Do you know him?" I asked.

"I think he's one of my neighbors, but I'm not sure." Seeing that I was a bit confused, he added, "Sometimes, I'm out here working on the yard and white people, strangers, drive by and wave hello. In my *pueblo* people do that. But in Los Angeles, they're more likely to give you the finger."

In Aguirre's Dalton neighborhood, the scents of grits and goat-meat taquitos, of barbecued ribs and pork rind *chicharrones* were beginning to intermingle, creating a cross-border, cross-cultural stew of heartland flavors. Bitsy McFarland, a volunteer on the Georgia Project and fourth-generation Dalton resident, told me she had already surrendered to the aroma of freshly baked bread wafting from the local *panadería*. "It smells so good, I can't resist going in there." Like McFarland, most of the natives in Dalton were hopeful that this new Latino or Mexican thing or whatever you wanted to call it would work out. After the strife and the ugliness of Georgia's previous encounters with race relations, the state had been given a second chance to prove that its people are as friendly and welcoming as they believe themselves to be. This spirit infected other corners of the South I visited, where community leaders were falling over themselves to make the newcomers feel welcome.

In Memphis, Mayor Willie Herenton had created an Office for Multicultural and Religious Affairs, in which local Latino and Asian leaders rubbed elbows with the police chief and other top city officials to discuss issues like racial profiling, community development, and the upcoming census. Herenton was the city's first black mayor. A generation earlier, in those days before Martin Luther King, Jr., was killed in Memphis, he had marched with the striking garbage workers wearing the "I Am a Man" sandwich boards. The site of Dr. King's assassination, the Lorraine Motel, is a museum now, and on the day I visited, its gallery space was devoted to "Americanos," a traveling photo exhibit of Latino immigrant America. Throughout the United States, the poorest Spanish-speaking immigrants tend to settle in black neighborhoods. Mayor Herenton was reaching out to the Latino community: perhaps he saw in them what W. E. B. DuBois saw in his own people at the turn of the previous century: people whose "weak wings beat against their barriers," people who might one day believe in "the struggle for another and juster world." The meetings of Mayor Herenton's Multicultural Office were rarely conflictive, in part because the Latinos and Asians in the city were a manageably small minority, and even the most assertive among them were people who had been in the city less than a decade. They didn't feel a sense of entitlement, were cautious about pressuring the city fathers much, and were happy just to be listened to. "You don't have a lot of second- and third-generation Latinos here," Narquenta Sims, the head of the Mayor's Multicultural Office, told me. "We haven't had any time to build expectations. Everything is brand-new. Let's keep it brand-new."

The prevailing stereotype about Mexican immigrants in the

South was that they were industrious people with large families. They might produce a black sheep or two, but you could deal with the occasional troublemaker because of all the work that got done when a dozen of them were around. José Velásquez, a Mexican activist at the Latino-Memphis Conexion, told me he was disgusted to learn that some white people in town insisted on seeing Latinos through the old lenses of paternalism and intolerance for which the South was famous. "You know, we have our problems with black people here," they would tell him in whispers. "But you Mexicans are different. You're hardworking people, family people. You don't give us much problems." About a dozen Klansmen protested against Mexican immigration in Gainesville, Georgia, in 1998, and about a dozen or so Nazis in 2001, though each time they were outnumbered by several hundred counterprotesters. In 2000, David Duke made a much-publicized appearance in Siler City, North Carolina, his supporters carrying signs that read "NO WAY JOSE" and "THE MELTING POT IS BOILING OVER" and later on his website he decried "the minoritization of Whites" in that community. But mostly, Southerners seemed to simply marvel at the changes, at the new culture and customs sprouting up around them. In Memphis, Los Tigres del Norte filled up a thousand-seat auditorium at up to $50 a seat, which caught the attention of Judy Peiser at the city's Center for Southern Folklore. Like Bitsy McFarland in Dalton, Peiser found herself wandering over to see what this Mexican music was all about, what men in wide-brimmed hats with accordions could add to a city that had already seen Elvis, Otis Redding, and Jerry Lee Lewis pass through. "They have these mammoth dances. All these kids come in, young people working in construction," Peiser told me. "They all have money in their pockets. It's an amazing scene. They take over entire warehouses." One day, perhaps, what Americans mean when they say "Memphis" and "music" will have to be redefined. "It's not New

York or L.A., and it's never going to be, because it's hot and humid and it's still the South. But it's a more cosmopolitan place than it used to be."

In a strange way, both black and white Southerners greeted the arrival and settling in of the Latinos as a kind of coming of age, a symbol of the beginning of a new era. Shortly after opening the mayor's multicultural office, Narquenta Sims placed a call to the Mexican consul in New Orleans and proposed that the Republic of Mexico establish a consulate in Memphis. Atlanta had a Mexican consulate and so did Omaha. Why not Memphis? She was excited by the possibility of the city having its first diplomat—the word itself carried a certain cachet. After months of waiting, she got a letter from the foreign ministry in Mexico City. Unfortunately, no one in Sims's office could read it because it was in Spanish. So she ran it through a computer translation program: no consulate yet, the letter said, but maybe soon.

The longer I spent in the South, and the more visits I made, the more familiar it resembled a slice of Spanish-speaking California. I sat and talked with a group of Latino teenagers at Gainesville High School, in a chicken-processing town and bedroom suburb northeast of Atlanta. We gathered around a table in the school library and they told me their arrival stories. Erika Venegas said she cried for days: her parents were always gone, off at the chicken plant, and when they came home all they would do was sleep. But these days she ran into friends at every corner, on the bus, and downtown; she couldn't imagine living anywhere else. Erika and her friends showed me the most recent issue of their Spanish-language school newsletter, *Onda Latina* (loose translation: Latin Groove), which reported the football team's 40–3 loss to a cross-county rival and concluded, *"No comieron frijoles!"* They didn't eat their beans! Alejandrina Duran told me the story of an uncle of hers who had announced to everyone he knew in Gainesville that he was going home to Mexico City—he was through with the gringos and with Georgia. He departed after a week of elaborate, heartfelt good-byes but a few months later he was back in town and back at work, trying to look the other way when he ran into people he knew, hoping that no one would remember he had made such an *escándalo* about leaving. "People in Mexico say Gainesville has a curse," Alejandrina told me. "Once you come here, you can never leave."

In the new Latin Republic of the United States, once you get your hands on that precious document that classifies you as a "lawful permanent resident," you can migrate to a Georgia town, work for a year or two, then change your mind and go back home to Mexico, then change your mind again and return to Georgia. The proximity between the United States, Mexico, and Central America, and the roads and highways and air corridors that link the region, make this possible. This simple fact is what makes the newest wave of immigration different from all the others in American history and what will probably change the course of American history itself in our current century. The mythical Vito Corleone, for example, could not travel back and forth from New York to Sicily so easily. He could not hit the road and hitch a cheap ride back home to Corleone every Christmas, the way tens of thousands of people from Nebraska, Oklahoma, California, North Carolina, New York, and other states do, packing up their belongings in the back of a GMC truck, or an old Econoline van, heading south to escape the cold, for a winter vacation with the *jefes* and brothers and sisters, and nephews and nieces next to the nopal in a village outside Guadalajara, or even all the way to Central America. When I was six, my mother and father and I plopped into a Volkswagen and drove from East Hollywood to Guatemala, my mother surprising her sister by showing up at her door in Guatemala City and giving their secret whistle, which caused my aunt to scream my mother's name in joy—"¡Mercediiiiitas!"—as she ran to open the door.

To be able to make the journey easily, without having to try to outrun *los chiles verdes,* you have to spend years getting your immigration status straightened out. This is an arduous but by no means impossible task. Even now, with the rules stricter than in years past, you can get legal residency if you have a child, parent, or sibling who is a U.S. citizen. Thus, as the millions of Mexicans and other Latinos living legally in the United States gradually become naturalized citizens, the number of undocumented *mexicanos* eligible to apply for legal residency increases too. Once you sort out your *"papeles,"* driving across the border becomes a mere bureaucratic hassle— when you enter Mexico, you have to register your car and leave a security bond, a daylong interruption in what is otherwise open driving along U.S. Interstate 35 and Mexico's Ruta Nacional 85, the main highways linking the southern United States to the Mexican heartland. At the border metropolis of Laredo, Texas–Nuevo Laredo, Tamaulipas, I encountered one Tennessean-Mexican halfway in a journey between the towns of Franklin, Tennessee, and La Piedad in Michoacán, the same state in which the monarch butterflies end their return, southward migration. I had heard about the Christmas rush through these towns and decided I needed to see it for myself, and I arrived one morning at the parking lot on the Mexican side of the border, a strip of asphalt facing the Rio Grande. Here I found license plates from the aforementioned U.S. states, including the green and white "VOLUNTEER STATE" plates attached to the tan van of Francisco Guzmán.

Guzmán was driving in a caravan with his brother, who also lived in Franklin, and with a guy they had met along the way who was from Georgia. "Ever since I got my work permit fixed, I come back every eight or nine months for the holidays," he told me. He was thirty-six years old and sported a long mullet and bugged-out eyes from a couple of days of round-the-clock driving. He told me he worked at a Ford dealership detailing used cars in Franklin, just outside Nashville. "This year, I wasn't going to come, because sometimes an extra job falls for you in Tennessee if you stay there, but my brother said he didn't want to drive alone, so I came with him." His brother was following behind in a pickup that was towing a small tarpaulin-covered trailer, which was filled with TV sets, toys, and kitchen appliances. "I've been trying to get my wife and daughter to come and live in Tennessee with me, but they're always finding excuses for not coming."

Francisco had resigned himself to the idea of driving south from the American South into the deeper Latin south of Mexico once or twice a year, "until the family could be in one place," although he was not sure which place that would be. Since he was on the road, traveling between the two poles of his current existence, I asked him a question I rarely ask, because I found it so annoying when people asked it of me: "Do you still feel *mexicano* when you go back home? Or do you feel a part of you has changed from living in the United States?"

"Well, yes, you start to feel different," he said. "You're living more time over there in the United States than you are here. To be honest, you can say that when we come here, it's really just to vacation." He was going to help out at his parents' farm, which was just outside of town, and that labor helped him reconnect with the core of his soul that had come from that rustic place, but with each year it faded a bit. "I do what I can to help the family and keep busy, because they're not used to seeing you sit around and do nothing. I'll paint the house. I'll help out at the rancho with the cattle, the harvest and the planting. More than anything, I'll tend to the cattle." But after just a few weeks at most he would be back in his van, driving north to Tennessee and his job detailing cars, because the money was too good.

The U.S. census numbers, the school enrollment figures in Georgia, Tennessee, and elsewhere offered proof that when faced with the choice, Spanish-speaking people kept coming back to the states of the old Confederacy.

In Dalton, Georgia, the 2000 Census counted 11,291 Latino residents, some 40 percent of the city population. By then, a new event was well established in the city's annual cultural calendar: the Mexican Independence Day celebration. Each year, low-rider Chevy Impalas and old Ford pickups with bulbous front hoods cruised past the old downtown, followed by convertibles filled with girls dressed in the jerseys of the soccer teams Chivas of Guadalajara and Club America of Mexico City. At the fifth annual parade, queen Veronica Salazar waved to the crowd from a convertible that cruised down the same streets General Braxton Bragg retreated to after the Confederate defeat at the "Battle Above the Clouds" outside Chattanooga. General Bragg built trenches on the outskirts of town, but eventually surrendered Dalton to the Union forever in 1864. More than thirteen decades later, the guest of honor at the Mexican Independence Day parade was a diplomat, a representative from the Mexican consulate in Atlanta. He performed the act meant to remind Dalton's residents of their history: giving "the yell of independence" (*el grito de la independencia*), the reenactment of the moment when a priest took to the steps of his village church to declare Mexico free of Spain's rule. Later, the diplomat from Atlanta told his assembled, resettled countrymen, "We should never forget everything we've suffered to get to this country."

missed the parade, but read about it in the Spanish-language newspaper *El Tiempo*, one of three Spanish-language newspapers then circulating in Dalton. *El Tiempo*'s founder was Homero Luna, twenty-six years old on the day I met him, with crescent sideburns that pointed toward a clean-shaven chin, and dressed in a new, olive-green blazer because it isn't every day a writer from California comes to call. Besides, he was also headed later that afternoon to a meeting of the Rotary Club, having received an invitation from a local businessman who wanted to sound him out about his Mexican compatriots and the business prospects they represented. "We're being taken seriously," he said with a big smile. "And we like that. Because we're serious people."

Homero was feeling Homeric that day, and who could blame him, given the great hurdles he had overcome to become what he was at that moment: arguably Dalton's most important dispenser of culture, his weekly paper a window on life in north Georgia, as hefty and widely circulated as the English-language *Daily-Citizen News*, which had just launched a Spanish-language supplement to compete with him. His story was in many ways similar to those of nineteenth-century pioneers of frontier America, men who set off on a journey to an unknown place and made fortunes with such ease that they came to believe it had been their destiny all along. Homero had arrived in Dalton six years earlier, at the tender age of twenty, as just another peon, hired help at a chicken factory. Back home in the city of San Luis Potosí, he had edited his high-school newspaper and afterward tried to start a business, transporting produce to some of the smaller towns in his province, until drought wiped out the local vegetable crop and did him in. Then an old friend called from a place called Georgia with stories about the ridiculous amounts of money to be made there. On a lark, he dropped the business and bought a bus ticket to the border. By the time he'd made it across the Rio Grande and up through Texas and Louisiana to Georgia, his friend had left town and disappeared, the first sign that maybe things wouldn't be so easy after all. Still, he got a job almost immediately, but then someone stole his shoes from the ConAgra chicken plant's employee dressing room his very first day on the job. Without any money to buy replacements, he had walked around Dalton for two weeks with his boots on, stranded in a trailer with strangers, feeling thoroughly humiliated and wondering how he could have been so stupid as to have come two thousand miles to work at a job he would have never considered doing in Mexico. Going back wasn't an option, so as soon as he could he escaped the sickly smell and noise of "live processing" for a job in the personnel department. There he could at last show his true feathers: leather shoes with a spit shine, a new coiffure free of the obligatory hairnets worn by the lower class of workers. "It was like he stepped out of a fashion magazine," his former coworker Lynn Norris told me. She had set her eyes upon a species rarely seen in these parts: a big-city *mexicano* dandy.

Neither the chicken plant nor the carpet plant where he worked next would be the arena where he pursued his ambitions. He wanted to start a business and strike out on his own, but in what? He didn't want to sell tacos, or drive his own taxi, or cut lawns, which were the kinds of businesses *mexicanos* usually started in Dalton. The answer came to him as he puttered around Dalton on errands, from the grocery store to the bank to the butcher's, encountering first *mexicanos*, and then *salvadoreños* and *guatemaltecos* at every stop. "It was something that happened from one day to the next. All of a sudden, we woke up and saw these brown faces all over town. I think it scared the Anglos at first that we wouldn't leave. They would say, 'Oh, the Mexicans will go home for Christmas and probably never come back.' But no. We'd come back from Christmas with twenty relatives." The Piggly Wiggly and the bank and the butcher didn't have any advertising vehicles to reach this expanding Latino customer base, and the Latinos didn't have anything to read, so he would give them both a newspaper. He worked a night shift at the carpet plant and would come back home early in the morning and then work the afternoon on his newspaper, writing stories, selling ads, taking pictures, laying it all out. As the community grew, so did the newspaper, so he made it *El Tiempo*'s motto and put it on the masthead: *"Creciendo con la comunidad."* He had in his head a map of his future empire, with Dalton at the center; already, *El Tiempo*'s tentacles reached to Rome, Cedartown, and Chattanooga, Tennessee. One day, he might follow Sherman's old route and march southeast from Dalton to the biggest prize his imagination could take in, Atlanta, where some 100,000 Latinos lived.

El Tiempo succeeded because it gave its readers what they *wanted*—pictures of Latin American celebrities and stories about their weddings and scandals, and game reports from the Dalton soccer league. It also gave them what the publisher-editor thought they *needed*—interviews with Dalton's English-speaking city council members and stories about how American democracy worked and how *El Tiempo*'s readers might fit in and learn to live with democracy's institutions. And finally, it showed them the face of what they most *feared*—those forces that would have them expelled from their Georgia paradise and sent back home to Mexico in the back of a Border Patrol van.

The paper rode the tension between want, need, and fear in each week's issue, just as its Spanish-speaking readers lived it every day of their lives. Issue Number 106 revealed that the Colombian pop singer Shakira was preparing to record a mariachi record, something sure to bring pangs of pride to *El Tiempo*'s mostly Mexican readers. The sports pages gave a detailed account of two matches from the Dalton Soccer League, both played at the city's Taco Bell Field, complete with color pictures of heavyset, off-duty factory workers in spiffy uniforms kicking the ball around in poses vaguely reminiscent of the pros. But the front page displayed a fuzzy snapshot taken at Dalton's Flea Market, showing a white man with a sign that identified him as a member of the Council of Concerned Citizens of Georgia. He stood next to another sign that read: "Help Stop the Immigration Invasion." Homero Luna's response to the affront of this image was an editorial with the headline "In the Country of Liberties" (*En el país de las libertades*), which informed the paper's Mexican readers that the great men of American history were all on their side.

"Illustrious men like Benjamin Franklin, John Q. Adams, Thomas Jefferson, Abraham Lincoln, Martin Luther King Jr., among others, have established the rights of human beings as an expression of liberty in all its forms." Homero Luna had once played the Mexican revolutionary Emiliano Zapata in a high-school play, gluing a handlebar mustache to his baby face to become one of the founding fathers of Mexican peasant militancy. Now, as a newspaper editor in Georgia, he invoked the founding fathers of North American democracy in defense of a right not enshrined in either the Declaration of Independence or the Constitution: the right of Latin Americans to cross the United States frontier in the pursuit of happiness. For *El Tiempo*, the right was self-evident, the immigrants had earned it with their labor and the wealth they produced. Those who would try to keep Latinos out of the country were "trying to block the sun with a finger," he wrote, quoting a Mexican saying. "It is precisely the migration of thousands and thousands of men and women which has strengthened the greatness of this country. Our goal is not to invade. Rather, we believe, as a wise Cherokee saying goes: 'Whatever our culture is, our race, our language or religion, we are all one people.'"

In the thinking of *El Tiempo*, borders didn't or shouldn't exist. The advertisements that graced its pages offered proof that this philosophy was something more than a flight of fancy. *"¡Queremos hacer negocios contigo!"* (We want to do business with you!), a full-page ad for *"Tiendas* Piggly Wiggly" in Rome declared. "We are hiring bilingual people," the ad said in Spanish peppered with grammatical errors. "Come today and fill out your application. And we are stocking new products every day for our Hispanic community." Apparently, you could buy La Victoria salsa and pinto beans along with grits at the Piggly Wiggly now. Ed Kirby Chevrolet in Dalton bragged that it was "the number one dealer in growth in the Hispanic community," and potential car buyers were told they need not "suffer with the language" thanks to Dana, the new Spanish-speaking saleswoman.

Homero Luna and his staff envisioned their readers as more than passive consumers or hired labor for the city's factories. They were trying to gradually introduce Latino Dalton to the idea that they might want to take an interest in city politics, a completely English-speaking affair up to that point. "The highest authorities in the city are the Mayor and a team of five people called the *Mesa Directiva*," the newspaper explained in Issue 110, searching around for a good translation of "City Council." "The Mayor holds office for four years. . . . The main work of the Mayor and the *Junta Directiva* is to 'govern the city,' a job they do part-time, and you could even say it's volunteer work, since the Mayor receives a very small salary and the *Junta Directiva* receives only expense money. . . . Out of a population of twenty-five thousand residents in Dalton, there are twelve thousand registered voters, including Latino residents. Up to the moment, NO *hispano* leader has stepped forward to be a candidate, [and] unfortunately there has been no candidate who has stepped forward to make the basic problems of immigrants part of their campaign." One day, the article concluded, some leader might bring "the hope of the many" to Dalton city government.

Homero talked to me about this future day as we drove through the wintry streets of the town, off to a meeting with a handful of friends who formed a committee of Dalton's most ambitious and forward-thinking Latinos, La Alianza Comunitaria Latinoamericana, the Latin American Community Alliance. They were already talking about running a candidate for office one day, though the moment wasn't right then, because even though Latinos were already a majority in at least one of the city's council districts, hardly any of them were registered to vote. The man most likely to be elected to the council was the Alianza's president, Norberto Reyes, who also happened to be one of its most affluent Latino citizens. He owned a chain of restaurants called Los Reyes, The Kings, including one two-story affair on the outskirts of Dalton that functioned as a sort of restaurant–cum–convention center. Reyes would soon become a member of the board of trustees of the local state college and join the chamber of commerce. But a council candidacy still looked a long way off because of the low Latino voter registration.

In the meantime, *El Tiempo* would keep beating the drum of American democracy to its readers. In Issue 110 it took to the streets and asked, "If an *hispano* were elected to office, what would be the first thing you would ask for?"

"I would ask him to work to make racism fade away," said Raul Vejar, thirty-four years old and a native of the northern Mexican state of Durango. "I would ask him that, as a *hispano*, he would not change [his culture], that he would follow the same traditions. And also that he be strict because there are people who drive drunk and they should be punished with all the weight of the law."

Most of the other people interviewed by *El Tiempo*'s reporter that day said the same thing. They were concerned about their second-class status in Georgia, about their inability to get driver's licenses, especially, or insurance for the homes they were starting to buy. Georgia was sending them a double message: We want you, we need you to work, but you are not like us, not equal to us just yet. At the same time, they felt the need for someone to help to enforce community discipline.

"I think I would ask both sides [North American and Latino] to work closer together, and also to make less harsh the laws that discriminate against *hispanos*," said Fortunato Márquez, twenty-seven and a native of the Mexican state of Querétaro. "Sure, you have to be hard against those who deserve it, but the majority of us come to work and to contribute to the economy."

"I would ask that a place be established to help *hispanos* find jobs and housing, because there are people who arrive here with a lot of problems," said Angélica Rendón Rodríguez. "Also there should be workshops where people are trained according to the jobs that are available in Dalton."

Homero dreamed of the day when his fellow *mexicanos* would go to the city council and act like New Englanders and present their demands. "Eventually, it will happen, it's inevitable," Homero told me as we sat in Los Reyes Restaurant, where the walls and the ceilings were covered in kitschy and historically implausible murals of Aztec warriors in feather costumes walking past Spanish colonial churches. "One of us will put our name forward and run for office. Then they'll have to listen to us in the city." The lunchtime crowd filed in, a mostly white group of men in ties and women in prim go-to-work blouses, settling into booths, dipping chips into the fresh salsa. These were the people who, for the moment, still controlled the fate and future of Dalton, looking at the lists of burritos and enchiladas on the menu, asking the waitresses "Are the chile ray-yeh-nos really spicy, or just sorta spicy?"

On the other side of town, Flocelo Aguirre didn't have time to worry about city councils or the Rotary Clubs or American elections. If *El Tiempo* and Homero Luna were the cultural arbiters of a nascent Latino identity in north Georgia, Flocelo was its most successful mass mobilizer. He had helped found and nurture the largest social club in town, the Dalton International Soccer League. Also known as La Liga Mexicana de Fútbol, it had thirty-six teams with about one thousand registered players, coaches, referees, and linesmen; hundreds of unregistered team mothers; and "team queens," who competed each year in an annual beauty contest. Once a week the league met in a small storefront in the oldest and most rundown part of Dalton, next to the pawnshops and down the street from the train station, which apparently hadn't seen a passenger car roll in for quite some time.

Flocelo took me to the office, a claustrophobic space that brought to mind the inside of a moving van, filled with rows of folding chairs that were arranged before a chalkboard. "On the nights we meet, you can't find a seat here. We have people standing outside on the sidewalk," he said. In this small space the league carried out a small exercise in community democracy and in Latin American culture, organizing the central event in the nonworking lives of Dalton families, a few hours of recreation that broke the monotony of the chicken plant or the carpet factory. Here the league held elections for board of directors, settled the finances, and dealt with complaints about refereeing. Two years before my visit a couple of academics from UCLA and the University of Monterrey had stopped by to study the league, declaring it "the most important organizational experience of the immigrant community," part of the "social capital" they brought to their new homes.

Flocelo had cut his teeth in the Los Angeles *fútbol* scene, with its hundreds of leagues and the sophistication brought by expatriate Latin American professionals, which regularly produced young gems snapped up by teams from Mexico, El Salvador, and American Major League Soccer, all of whom had scouts scurrying about the metropolis. At the highest levels of the Southern California *fútbol* scene, there were young Latino men who were being pulled in opposite directions, their skills coveted by college athletic directors who dangled scholarships before their eyes, and club teams from Guadalajara, Buenos Aires, and Germany, who dangled the upfront money of big-league contracts. I had talked to young men torn between these two visions of the sport, which roughly mirrored the cultural divide in the metropolis. There was Aaron Lopez, a *mexicano* kid from Santa Barbara who had been aggressively recruited by professional teams in Mexico but at the suggestion of his American foster mother chose UCLA instead, where he majored in Spanish and scored the winning goal in the 2002 NCAA championship game; and Bensaheth Solis of Anaheim, whose *fútbol*-crazy Mexican father and uncles studiously ignored the phone calls and letters from North Carolina universities because he was being recruited by the team the men in the family had followed since they were kids kicking a ball around a horse corral in their *rancho*: Atlas of Guadalajara.

Next to Southern California, Latino soccer in Georgia was decidedly minor-league; at first, Flocelo had encountered an anarchy similar to that Dr. Frankie Beard had found in the schools. There were games that ended in brawls and fistfights with even the team mothers getting into it, allegations of match-fixing, and just a general sense that everyone was running around the field without a sense of order and direction. "We had problems with the *pandilleros,*" Flocelo said, using the word for gang members. Someone had pulled out a gun at one game and caused players, referees, and spectators to dive to the ground for cover, but thankfully no one had been shot. The gangster wannabes were in Georgia now, and not in Los Angeles or Chicago or the other cities from which their gang affiliations had been exported, carried in the brains and on the skin of young men who came to Dalton with their parents. People were less ruthless here, less sadistic. And anyway, drawing a firearm wasn't something completely out of the ordinary in this part of the country; just the week before I arrived in Dalton four white high-school students had been suspended for showing up at the school parking lot with a shotgun in the back of their pickup truck the day after getting into an altercation with a Mexican student. Still, the small brush with the exotic violence of faraway, Spanish-speaking cities had scared the town fathers and gotten the soccer league banned from Dalton parks and school grounds for a while, until Taco Bell and some other local companies stepped in and helped build the new fields.

"We managed to get rid of the *pandilleros,*" Flocelo told me in Spanish. "Then we took care of the referee situation. But money is always a problem." He paused, because talking about money is always a touchy subject, especially when that money is supposed to belong to that amorphous and contradictory thing called a "community." "At one point, I was handling what people around here consider to be a lot of money. I try to be open with people. There were some ugly insinuations, so I handed that job over to someone else." Flocelo recounts this with a big-city, ironic smile on his face. When he lived in Los Angeles, everything and everyone moved faster, at 78 rpm compared with the 33 rpm of Dalton. He was working with small-town people who were naturally suspicious of anything big, but eventually he had won them over to his vision of what the Dalton Soccer League could look like. These days it was thriving and growing. It had achieved in miniature the sophistication of Los Angeles, with teams whose names drew from the legendary clubs of Latin America—River Plate of Buenos Aires, Pumas of Mexico City. Flocelo did all this while working in the carpet factory five days a week; he had an understanding employer who let him off early on Saturdays when he had league business or a game to attend to. Being a factory worker, he regarded with skepticism the plans of Homero Luna and his friends, who looked to him suspiciously like bourgeois *mexicanos*. "We need real leaders in this city, not just people who are going to sit down and drink coffee with the *americanos*," he said. "Look, you drive through the city and if you have brown skin, the police can stop you and harass you and no one says anything about it. It isn't easy to be a *mexicano* in this city. We need leaders who will fight for us, who will stand up to these people."

Flocelo didn't need to see a Mexican face on the city council to feel his community was making progress. All on their own, he and his fellow immigrants had managed to organize the soccer league and the yearly Independence Day parade, which was attracting some two thousand people, a huge crowd for a town of Dalton's size. They had filled the tiny Catholic church downtown every Sunday until the parish leaders had finally raised the money to build a new one. A few years earlier, Flocelo had been with the parish priest to see scrubland north of town where the new church would rise, thanks in part to a $1 million donation from a local carpet magnate. "He took me out there and I cut up my legs on all the branches and brambles out there." Now the new St. Joseph's church rose like a kind of Catholic resort on a forested hillside facing a lake. It had been designed by Thomas Gordon Smith, a University of Notre Dame architect and proponent of classicism in American design, who gave Dalton a church in the post-Renaissance tradition, inspired by the San Gregorio Magno church in Rome, complete with Latin-inscribed walls of Indiana limestone. In the context of small-town Dalton, it was a building monumental in scale: you could have fit five of the small Ashland chapels inside this cathedral-sized building. Outside, standing in a freshly landscaped nopal cactus garden, there was a six-foot-tall concrete sculpture of the Virgin of Guadalupe.

The Latino community was like the sprawling ground of St. Joseph's: new and growing in its self-confidence and the sense of its identity. In Dalton, I saw something I had seen in no other Southern town I had visited: a large Mexican flag waving from the window of a passing car on a weekday afternoon, an act of cultural defiance that had become so common in Los Angeles no one noticed it anymore. Here I was, deep inside a "red state," one of those places where Samuel Huntington's Anglo-Saxon Protestant values were undoubtedly strongest, and yet even here cultural assimilation was being rejected by large numbers of Latino people. Dalton had become a small-town version of Los Angeles, a place where you could feel comfortable in your *mexicano* skin; for that reason Flocelo had no immediate plans to return to his *pueblo* in Mexico, or to California, where all five of his children were born. One of his adult sons was buying the home next door to his on Georgia Avenue, and one of his sons had just started kindergarten at Roan.

Let Homero and his friends worry about city planners and election districts and voter registration. For the moment, Flocelo would concern himself with a pet project: the Dalton Soccer League All-Star Team, which he hoped to match against teams from Atlanta and other nearby cities. "We've got some good players here, and other people should see them." Maybe one day a soccer prodigy would emerge in Dalton and go on to bigger and better things. When you took your soccer as seriously as Flocelo did, you aspired to cultivate a talent that would leave your mark on the game. Therein lay a dream that was, for the moment, much more attainable and real to the *mexicanos* of Dalton than control of the city council, or even a single seat on that body: that one day they might turn on their satellite televisions to Univision's weekly broadcast of Mexican League games and see a son of Dalton running across the green rectangle of Azteca Stadium—the Field of Dreams of Mexican sport—sending a ball skimming across the grass to the cry of *"¡Go-o-o-o-o-o-o-o-ol!"*

Chapter Six

OUR SECRET LATIN HEARTLANDS
Los secretos machote

Rupert, Idaho · Frankenmuth, Michigan · Grand Island, Nebraska · Liberal, Kansas

Being a good Mormon, Benjamin Reed traveled far in service of his faith. From the rolling grasslands and foothills of southern Idaho, where towns are laid out in a compass-point numbering system that mimics the streets of Salt Lake City, his "mission call" took him to northern Argentina. He was nineteen years old. With the Argentines, he sipped *mate* and ate fire-grilled beef with *chimichurri* sauce, and learned the peculiar verb conjugations of the *vos* pronoun that are sprinkled throughout the Spanish of the River Plate region. He learned to say "I love you" in the Indian language Guarani, and fell head over heels for an Argentine woman and married her.

When the time came to return home and he set foot again in Idaho, he came to a startling conclusion about himself: he had a Latin soul. He liked to talk loud and embrace people. He was a *machote* who could also weep when something hurt inside. "I'd look in the mirror and see a white face, but my heart was brown." He quenched his thirst for Spanish over the Internet, tuning in to the deejays who dominate the radio dial in Los Angeles, men like Pepe

Garza of Que Buena, who had become famous playing the *narcocorridos* of Los Tigres del Norte and other groups, helping to set off the explosion of that cross-border musical genre. Listening to the deejays' quick-witted double entendres and off-color humor, he picked up Mexican intonations and vocabulary, and could mimic the accent when he met the immigrants who came to work in the beet fields and the potato harvest. When he got a job on an Idaho radio station and tried to imitate Garza's over-the-top style for his English-language listeners, his boss told him that he was "coming on too strong." Even worse, he was letting a Mexican accent slip into his English, which made him sound like some kind of weird Mormon gangster.

One day he heard that a station in nearby Rupert was going to switch to a Spanish "regional Mexican" format. Country music station KBBK 970 AM would become KFTA, *"la fantástica,"* and Benjamin Reed would transform himself into *Ben-ha-meen Roberto Reed.*

The studios of KFTA sit in the middle of a beet field, a corrugated metal box with several satellite dishes clustered nearby like giant white mushrooms that have been pulled out of the ground and pointed toward the heavens. Inside that box, in a control room whose equipment resembled the inside of the alien craft in *Plan 9 from Outer Space,* I watched Ben Reed become El Chupacabras, the goatsucker of Mexican and Caribbean legend. At 2 P.M., precisely, with the sound of braying goats and accordions on tape announcing the beginning of his daily show, the phone began to ring with people calling in requests. They all seemed to be on a first-name basis with Ben-ha-meen. "Ester Calderón! It's been so long," he said into the telephone. *"¿Cómo te complazco?"* He scribbled down a song title and then talked to a man working at a company called Butte Fence who asked for a song by the group Mandingo. After taking half a dozen calls, he went on the air live, grabbed a microphone the size of a soda can, and wrapped his palms on a series of big control knobs to make his voice echo, bullet-style: *"Chu-chu-chu-pacabras."* He shaped his baritone voice into a Wolfman Jack–style radio persona, a Spanish version of the "boss radio" of American AM radio circa *American Graffiti.* He spoke in Spanish with hardly a trace of an accent and his listeners might have imagined him to be the epitome of *mexicano* manhood, with a droopy mustache and a ten-gallon Stetson and leather boots. But no, Benjamin Reed was a balding thirty-year-old man in a button-down, short-sleeve shirt, and a noticeable paunch over the waist of his polyester slacks. He looked like a copier repairman who had wandered into the station, grabbed the open microphone, and suddenly begun to channel his inner Mexican.

"¿Cuál es la que suena?" he asked a young woman he had put on the air. (Rough translation: "What station rocks?")

"¡La Fantástica y el Chupacabras!" the girl shouted back.

Outside, an antenna mast rose several hundred feet into the air, sending Ben Reed's modulated Spanish voice and his faintly lecherous Wolfman act over a farming town of railroad tracks and silos and a water tower shaped like an old coffeepot. His voice reached, too, across the Magic Valley (or *el valle mágico,* as he called it in on the air), a place where the Snake River cuts a fissure through rolling green hills, where men born in adobe villages tend to horses and watch potatoes roll down conveyor belts and sleep off hangovers next to their girlfriends and then call Ben Reed to ask for a song by Los Temerarios.

"Once, I got a call from a couple and I put them on the air," he said. "They seemed to be engaged in the act of love." A Mormon couple wasn't likely to do that. But the Mexicans of Rupert were an unpredictable breed; their emotions might burst from their skins at any moment, they might reach for the phone and call a stranger and ask for that song that would give their intimate moment a flavor of romance. "This is my dream job. Sure, I'm in a small market in a beet field. But there's so much freedom. I can make a fool out of myself." He switched back to Spanish, a habit of his, it seemed, with bilingual people like me who could understand those things that were said more naturally in a romance language. *"Es un alivio,"* it's a relief, the lifting of a burden. *El Anglo,* he said, is a closed person *(una persona cerrada).* Whereas *el latino* is a walking embrace, he is more *cálido,* a word that means hot when it refers to the weather and warm when attached to a person. He switched back to English again, to address the issue of his own place in this scheme: "I was born an Anglo but I identify myself as a Latino culturally."

A Honduran musician friend of mine in college at UC Santa Cruz had a name for Americans like Ben Reed: he was a *"latinófilo,"* a Latinophile. My friend used it to describe the people who were drawn to him when he picked up his guitar and started singing romantic Cuban songs, the people from Massachusetts and Minnesota who came to California and after a semester or two found themselves swept up in all things Latin American, carrying stacks of Pablo Neruda poetry around campus and taking salsa classes in which they learned to sway their hips in circles. The Latino population of southern Idaho had reached a number great enough to nurture Ben Reed's journey into *mexicanidad,* a Mexican way of being that redefined his self-image, his aspirations, and even, as I would learn later, his politics.

In Los Angeles, *latinidad* had reached a critical mass that reversed the momentum of cultural assimilation. It swept up people who looked in the mirror and saw brown skin and the face of a Tarahumara Indian but who spoke less Spanish than Ben Reed did when he left Idaho on his mission call, people like my future wife, who signed up for a language program at UC Santa Cruz designed for Latino students trying to reverse-assimilate. We had signed up for Spanish for Spanish Speakers to get in touch with our brown souls, and I tutored her on the seemingly baroque intricacies of Spanish irregular verbs such as *poder* (to be able to) and *tener* (to have), and where to place accents in words like *cálido* and *penúltimo*, rules of grammar I had mastered myself only a few months earlier. We studied so that we could talk and write letters to our grandparents, only to discover, years later, that our college lessons would also be useful for asking directions in Rupert, Idaho, and for understanding what pulled at the heart of people like Ben Reed.

Ben Reed's linguistic skills allowed him to "pass." For the hour he was on the radio he was a *paisano*, and every one of his regular listeners on the radio would have been proud to have him over to their home for some goat-tripe tacos. Ben Reed became Latino. He was not the first white American who I had seen do this. When I went away to college, to refamiliarize myself with Spanish and rework the language muscles that had atrophied during my high-school years, my best friend was a guy from the Southern California surf town of Manhattan Beach, a Greek-American kid named Gus Gregory. He had lived in La Ceiba, Honduras, for a year as an exchange-student teenager and could rattle off Central American slang and idioms like a native. Gus could have passed, in certain Latin American countries, as a member of the fairer-skinned European tribes that settled the region. Latino identity is, after all, a malleable, open set of qualities, molded from indigenous, European, and African cultures; you can be Latino and have sandy-blond hair, or blue-black skin, or the last name Rosenthal or Fujimori. But what really allowed Gus to pass was his outgoing and garrulous spirit, and his mastery of the small formalities of Latin culture.

One night in California, Gus went to a nightclub and met a very nice, slightly younger Peruvian-American woman named Dolores Fernández and charmed her the way a Latin lover would; with humor, flattery, and a good dance step. They headed off together for the mountains of Peru, to live in a rural village and work in a development project. After a few months, they got married in the church in Huancayo, a town of whitewashed stone buildings. A local newspaper had found out he was a gringo and snapped their picture, Dolores wearing the same purple print skirt she had been wearing in the nightclub where they met. Soon after, a little Gus was on the way.

With the United States becoming a more Latino country, it is a truism that more people without any Latin American heritage will, like Ben Reed or Gus Gregory, find their lives linked to the Spanish-speaking south. In California, Florida, and Texas, where the rates of intermarriage between Latinos and non-Latinos are highest, it isn't rare to learn, in the midst of a political campaign, that such-and-such candidate has a Latino relative of one kind or another. Faced with a tough and ultimately doomed bid for a third term, Gil Garcetti, the district attorney of Los Angeles County, recounted again and again the story of a great-grandfather who was caught up in the Mexican Revolution. The two president Bushes, George W. and George H. W., have three Mexican-American relatives, the sons and daughter of Florida governor Jeb Bush and Columba Garnica Gallo of Guanajuato, Mexico, now the first lady of Florida. It was George Bush the elder who once infamously referred to his eldest grandson, George Prescott Bush, as "the little brown one."

Many years ago a writer friend of mine from Portland, Oregon, married a Nicaraguan woman, which turned out to be an exciting, unpredictable, and ultimately complicated thing to do, involving as it did linking his bloodline to that of a large and poor Managua family with a history of tragic dysfunction. In Spanish Los Angeles, Jesse Katz was known as Chuy, the diminutive of Jesús, and we shared an office at the *Los Angeles Times,* in a cramped little space where we compared notes on how the country was changing around us, and how the secret world of Latin passions and the unpredictability of our families was infecting the city we lived in.

One day at lunchtime, Jesse walked into our office with his Texas-born friend Abel Salas, a publicist in the Tejano music scene. Both were carrying Styrofoam plates with black-bean quesadillas they had procured from the cafeteria. This set off a long discussion on the black bean, and how it was that the coal-colored legume might make an appearance at the company eatery, next to the plates of Jell-O, the tuna melts, and the beef casseroles. "When I was growing up, I thought I was the only person in L.A. who ate black beans," I observed. Black beans are what Guatemalans eat and they weren't very common in 1970s Los Angeles; the brown pintos of Mexican cuisine completely dominated the bean landscape back then. My mother scoured the markets of Hollywood for black beans, and when she found them she boiled them all day, then put them into a blender and fried them into what's known in Guatemala as *frijoles volteados,* which roughly translates as "turned-over beans." Three or four nights a week she would place this black slurry on a plate before me; I worried someone would knock at the door and see me with what would look—to them—like a disgusting plate of slop. On the weekends she served them at breakfast alongside scrambled eggs. I loved black beans, even though no one else I knew ate them. For all I knew, my family and I were culinary freaks.

These days everyone eats black beans. They are a hip and healthy accessory to a cosmopolitan urban life, as familiar to the

Southern California palate as wonton soup or pastrami sandwiches. You pay outrageous prices for black-bean concoctions at restaurants on the Westside, where chefs have been brought in from Miami and other tropical locales to splash them alongside shrimp and trout and other dishes my mother would have never imagined. I explained all this to Jesse. "I don't have to hide my *frijoles volteados* anymore," I joked. "Black beans have crossed over."

The black beans around us, I decided, hinted at deeper transformations afoot in the culture: they suggested our link to bean-eating traditions stretching back across the millennia and to the hands that teased them from the soil. Where, I wondered out loud, did the beans come from? Were they raised by peasants and shipped northward on the backs of peons? Was there a man dressed in the clean white shirt and straw hat of the famous Colombian coffee-picker Juan Valdez (the one in the television commercials) patiently dropping beans into a basket, daydreaming about the Americans who would eat them? In short, I felt the black beans of Jesse and Abel's quesadilla calling out to me; find our home, they said, and you will learn something about yourself, you will find the small black bean at the core of your soul.

A week or so later I was driving across the vast pancake of ash-gray loam that is the thumb of Michigan. It had taken me fifteen minutes on the Web to find out that the cradle of the American black bean, the place where the black beans in Jesse and Abel's quesadillas had probably been born, was the moist and cool peninsula around Saginaw and Port Huron. This in itself was quite unexpected: who would have thought that the seemingly tropical black bean was born in the colder latitudes of mid-America? More surprising was the black-bean explosion then going on in the heartland: the year before, black beans had displaced white beans as Michigan's top legume for the first time, with some 135,000 acres of black beans harvested. It was part of a Latin mini-revolution in American agriculture fueled by the spread of the burrito, the taco, salsa, and other dishes that was causing farmers from North Dakota to New Mexico to switch crops.

My search for the black bean would be the first step of a journey deeper into the North American continent in which I would discover the many subtle and small ways—and sometimes sore-thumb big and obvious ways—in which the heartland communities of the United States were being connected to that great mass of Latinoness of the coasts, of Los Angeles, New York, and Miami.

I arrived in Frankenmuth, Michigan, where bean broker Lyle Ackerman greeted me at his office overlooking the meandering, greenish-brown mirror of the Cass River and the only grain silo in town. "Black beans is major in Michigan," Lyle announced. Black beans did well in Michigan's thumb because its climate was similar to the highlands of Guatemala, where peasants had been growing the plant as their main source of protein since before the Spaniards arrived. Both were cool places where the summer temperature hovered around an optimal 75 degrees; protracted heat is lethal for the black bean.

Once upon a time, the navy beans in "pork and beans" were the Michigan farmer's bread and butter. But domestic consumption of black beans has increased tenfold since the mid-1980s, and Americans now eat more than 100 million pounds of black beans each year. The expanding bean market means Michigan growers have new competitors in places like Quebec and Manitoba, where many farmers are switching away from peas and lentils. Michigan farmers knew very well that the abundance of their fog-covered land was helping feed people in sunny, southern places, and they had tried to adapt of few of these distant culinary tastes for themselves. "We've got a restaurant near us that serves a black-bean something pizza," said Bob Green of the Michigan Bean Commission, based in the town of St. Joseph. "And how many places have black-bean soup? It's really grown. Is it a yuppie thing? Is it a Mexican thing? Is it a Cuban thing? Yes, it's all of the above. Whatever it is, it's something we're really excited about."

The export market was growing too, despite Lyle's complaints to me about the machinations of Mexico City bean brokers, who were conspiring, he said, to keep Michigan beans out of Mexico despite the free-market guarantees of NAFTA. Otherwise a politically con-servative bunch, Michigan farmers were also outraged at the con-tinuing U.S. embargo against Communist Cuba, where not a single Michigan black bean was served among the millions eaten there every day. Fidel Castro, it turned out, had friends in Saginaw and Frankenmuth.

Behind his desk, Lyle Ackerman had his buyers' products stacked on a shelf, canned black beans with bilingual labels and cooking instructions from companies called Goya, Garcia's black beans, and La Criolla. He chatted up the superiority of Michigan blacks to their Mexican and Brazil competitors as we drove outside town to a bean-processing plant the size of a Navy battleship, where streams of legumes flowed into conveyor belts for cleaning and packing into half-ton sacks bound for Los Angeles, Mexico City, and other points south. I was mesmerized by a machine in which a stream of beans was fired at seventy-five miles per hour past an electric eye that could find the split or the odd red bean among tens of thousands of others, the offending bean zapped with a burst of air that sorted it into a separate pile. The split beans were shipped to Guatemala, Lyle said, where they were made into "a puree product that is very popular there."

"Yes, *frijoles volteados!*" I responded immediately and perhaps too forcefully, causing Lyle's eyes to startle with confusion. I was probably the first person he'd ever met who actually ate "the puree product." Later, we drove through the fields around Frankenmuth, where I learned that black-bean plants look like any other bean plant while they're still growing, except for the distinctive purple color in the veins of their leaves, and then the purple flowers that bloom in spring; kidney beans have lavender flowers, and pintos bloom white. My black-bean pilgrimage took me next to the Michigan Bean Commission's test farm, where Greg Varner, a research agronomist, walked me through patches of pinto, black, and red beans and showed me the storage shed where he had collected varieties of blacks from across the hemisphere, dried pods from Brazil and Guatemala stacked on shelves. "I grew up on a bean farm," Varner told me. "My dad and my mother basically served us white beans our whole life. Now in my pantry I'll have some refried beans and some black beans."

Lutheran German immigrants founded Frankenmuth in 1845, and in the twentieth century the town had molded itself into a "Bavarian village" tourist trap. Lyle insisted on giving me a tour of the town's top attraction, Bronner's Christmas Wonderland, "the world's largest Christmas store," a warehouse-sized assault of plastic reindeer (for rooftop decoration), plaster nativity scenes, and "relaxing Santa" glass ornaments. I had a pair of custom stockings made for my two sons by a plump and very pleasant woman in a faux-Bavarian peasant dress who patiently strung together a string of tiny white tiles that spelled D-A-N-T-E and D-I-E-G-O. I am very far from Los Angeles, I thought. The only thing vaguely *mexicano* in the place was the display of "hot pepper" Christmas lights.

In the surrounding towns and fields, the international fraternity of the bean had led some of the farmers to become friends with

Spanish-speaking counterparts from as far away as Patagonia, as I discovered when I drove across the thumb to the town of Sebewaing and the farm of Dick Gremel. A few months earlier, Gremel had visited Argentina and its rugged interior of humid weather and *chacras*, small farms with pitch-black soil where muscle did most of the work. "Over there, when a guy wants to cultivate his field, he just hires four hundred Indians and they do it by hand." Gremel and his three sons did the same work with a single John Deere tractor that stood two stories tall. A year earlier, a group of Argentine farmers had visited Gremel's 3,200-acre spread, treading around his bean plants, gawking at his tractor, chattering in Spanish about his new and expensive combine. "We're not in a little world anymore," he told me. "It's amazing how the world shrunk." In his barn, Gremel had a computer that updated him routinely on news of droughts in Mexico, the impact of El Niño conditions on Brazilian farmers, and free-trade negotiations with Chile.

The same computers could be found in farmers' toolsheds in Nebraska, where I traveled next, on the trail of that other half of the basic diet of Mexican and Central American peasants, and its main source of carbohydrates—the corn tortilla. I had come to visit O'Malley Grain in Fairmont, a little metropolis of grain silos parked along the railroad that links Omaha to Denver. Based in Illinois, the company had just built this new facility in Nebraska to be closer to the fast-growing market for high-grade "food corn"—their specialty—for tortillas in California and Texas. The facility was a spotless zinc-and-concrete monument to the discerning taste buds of Latino consumers, Mexicans and Central Americans who'd grown up eating tortillas and could tell the difference between a real, full-bodied tortilla and its anemic, mass-produced imitators. O'Malley sold "white corn" to high-end tortilla makers, pale-yellow jewels that would be cooked in big vats to make tortilla dough, called *masa* in Spanish. Most factory-produced corn tortillas are made with corn flour, which is essentially corn that has been dehydrated and ground. O'Malley sold whole corn kernels to producers who boiled them directly into *masa*. "People who know tortillas say it's like the difference between drinking fresh milk and powdered milk," O'Malley vice president James L. Thomas told me.

"Anyone can make a corn flour tortilla," Lalo Espinosa, O'Malley's bilingual salesman piped in. "But to make a fresh tortilla, you have to be an expert."

Like their colleagues in Michigan, the people at O'Malley Grain were discovering how big and how Latin their world was becoming. Dale Byrkit, the plant manager in Nebraska, went to California routinely on the Midwest Airlines flight from Omaha to Los Angeles, which had become their very own tortilla shuttle. "I was in East L.A., on the Hispanic side of town," Byrkit told me, a geographic explanation that was probably necessary to the overwhelming majority of Nebraskans he talked to, their image of Los Angeles as a land of convertibles and suntanned starlets having been formed by decades of detective dramas and Academy Award shows. "There's a new tortilla place opening up every month out there. I drove for miles and miles, to Riverside and other places. All I had seen before was Disneyland." He watched Nebraska corn transformed into *masa* rolling off conveyor belts like little pancakes in the hundreds of mom-and-pop *tortillerías* that dot Southern California, operations that might have a single tortilla machine the size of a Volkswagen going in a room behind the front counter, using a half-dozen fifty-pound bags of O'Malley corn each day. They made the kind of tortilla you would send your daughter or son to buy at the corner grocery, so that you could eat the tortillas when they were still warm, the same way my grandmother in Guatemala City sent me down the hill from her house to fill up a basket from an Indian woman who made them by hand on a griddle (a *comal*) placed over a barrel of fire. So that its corn more closely resembled the kind used by Guatemalan *tortilleras*, O'Malley treated its corn with "gentle handling," trying to avoid split kernels, and working with "the farmer and the way he sets his combine" so that the kernels weren't tossed around and beaten. In essence, they tried to produce, within the mechanized agriculture of Nebraska, the care of the handpicked harvest of Latin America. Their bags proclaimed O'Malley corn *"el número uno para masa."*

Dale walked me over to the O'Malley loading dock, to watch a farmer unload a thousand bushels of corn, the grains falling with the sound of rushing water into an underground pit. I was admiring this golden Niagara when one of O'Malley's customers showed up. Vitalino González, the founder and owner of Sofía's Mexican Foods in the Los Angeles suburb of El Monte, had come to tour the O'Malley facility too. A dark-skinned man with a droopy mustache and a low-key air, he stood a foot shorter than all the tall lanky Nebraskans around him, men with wide belts and plaid shirts who were stooping over as they talked to him in the deferential tone Americans reserve for "the valued client."

"Mr. González, so good to have you here."

"Mr. González, you get in okay to Omaha?"

"Mr. González, we're going to take Mr. Tobar here to see the fields of one of our farmers. Would you like to join him?"

"I don't need to see corn," Mr. González said with a faintly contemptuous frown. He had once grown corn in his native Puebla, that was how he got his start in the food business, long before becoming the California tortilla baron he was today, a man who shipped product across the state, from Santa Maria to Brawley. "I know what corn looks like."

I had never seen American corn up close before, so I bade Mr. González farewell and went walking down the highway with Lyle to a field of man-high cornstalks where the corn cobs were still little green embryos. The only time I'd seen corn up close before was during my vacation trips to Guatemala, shortish stalks of *maíz* that clung to hillsides. Corn is at the heart of Mayan cosmology: in the Popol Vuh, the Mayan sacred book, God makes the first man from corn. Driving through western Guatemala, toward Tiger's Corner, where my grandmother was born, I saw the sons and daughters of that first corn man tending plants with hoes the length of their forearms, the stalks rising haphazardly and unevenly across their small plots of land. This Nebraska corn was, by contrast, of a sci-fi variety: we met a farmer who ran his tractor with a GPS-mapping system attached, downloading the data into a computer that plotted the yield and soil humidity of each corner of his field on color-coded maps. It was the best American technology put to service in the quest for a better, heartier tortilla.

Suitably impressed, I headed back to California with some Nebraska corn kernels and Michigan blacks to plant in my garden. I was driving in my rental car across a picturesque landscape of rolling prairies and distant farmhouses, bound for the Omaha airport on Interstate 80, when I turned on the radio and pressed the scan button.

"Is your alfalfa crop like a yo-yo? Up one year and down the next?"

The scanner sampled an easy-listening station and some "Cornhusker football talk radio," and then this: *"Ya está por comenzar el encuentro de esta tarde entre El Salvador de Grand Island y el equipo Xelajú . . ."* It was Spanish-language KMMJ, broadcasting live from a park in Grand Island, Nebraska, some sixty miles away, their remote van stationed at the edge of a soccer field. I stopped the scanner, pulled my rental car to the side of the highway, and started scribbling notes. *"Gracias por sintonizarnos esta tarde . . ."* Fields of flaxen grasses sprouted a few feet from the black asphalt pebbles on the road's shoulder, rising gently upward to a horizon upon which a clapboard house and cluster of trees sat perched. The scenery shouted out "heartland," its dry ruggedness suggested in solid, physical terms what I knew to be true in the abstract: that I was near the very center of the United States, far from those coastlines and border towns where *hispanohablantes,* Spanish-speakers, had first planted their flags. My Rand McNally road atlas verified that I was a two-day drive from the Mexican border, three days, at least, from California. *"Les habla Jacinto Corona, con ustedes para este gran partido . . ."* There was something vaguely thrilling about being in the middle of the United States and hearing the upbeat, rat-a-tat-tat Spanish of a *mexicano* deejay. It was like finding a can of *frijoles volteados* in the thumb of Michigan, something I could call my own in a place that seemed very far away from home.

Jacinto Corona, it turned out, had become a deejay by accident. Like Homero Luna in Dalton, Georgia, he'd come to Nebraska to work poultry—turkeys, in his case. A native of the hamlet of El Trapiche del Abra in the Mexican state of Jalisco, he arrived in Grand Island in the middle of a white-out November blizzard with his wife and young daughters. It took two weeks for the girls to ask their father, "Papá, can we go home now?," but he stayed, and for years he lived in a fog of unknowing about Nebraska life, confused by the way the people could seem friendly and welcoming one moment but then distant and moody the next. The

weather threw him for a loop too, especially that violent meteorological phenomenon called the tornado, which was unknown in
Jalisco, and the winters when a snowstorm might materialize from
clear blue sky in the time it took to work half a shift at the turkey
plant. No one who was Mexican—and with each passing year there
were more of his *paisanos* floating around town—seemed to know
when it was going to snow. The first one always took them by surprise, it caught them coatless and shivering as they left the mall,
whereas the native Nebraskans were snug and warm with parkas
and gloves. Was it some sort of unexplainable Midwestern intu-
ition? Could Nebraskans take a breath of air on a clear day and taste
the coming snow? No, that wasn't it, he soon realized; the *mexicanos*
were unprepared because there was no weather report in Spanish in
Grand Island, no Spanish-language news at all, whereas once his
English got good enough to listen to the radio, he realized all they
ever seemed to talk about was the weather. This was a farm town,
and farmers here were like farmers everywhere: they lived and died
with meteorology.

"It's a horrible thing not to know what the weather is going to
be, not to have any news," Corona told me inside his office at
KMMJ. "It's like living in a jail." He didn't know until weeks later if
the Chivas of Guadalajara had beaten Club America in the biannual
clásico of the Mexican soccer league, he didn't know what was going
on with the Zapatistas in Chiapas, or if the conspiracy behind the assassination of presidential candidate Luis Donaldo Colosio had been
solved. If it was snowing outside, he didn't have any idea when it
would end. "We didn't leave the house. We had seen snow before in
the movies but had no idea what it was really like." There was a way
you were supposed to drive in the snow, for example, but he and the
other *paisanos* had to learn that on their own.

The years without radio were symptomatic for Jacinto of a

larger problem. "The community didn't have any leadership. We didn't have any representation at any level." If you wanted a lawyer who spoke Spanish, you'd have to go to Denver to find one. "It was a very sad time, a moment of darkness" for Latinos in Nebraska. "Then we started to organize ourselves." As in Dalton, Georgia, straightening out the mess of fighting and drunkenness in the soccer league was an early priority. Jacinto became active in a church group, which formed a committee to talk to the owners of the radio station. One winter, they stood shivering outside the stores Latinos frequented and collected signatures, more than a thousand in all, making an inch-thick stack of petitions asking KMMJ's owners for airtime in Spanish. It was the kind of spontaneous, collective organizing effort I'd seen in other places where immigrants live. In Los Angeles, while writing about housing conditions in the "landing pad" neighborhoods of the city center, I'd run across buildings where a score of tenants had organized rent strikes in response to crumbling walls and backed-up plumbing. An American tenant, it seemed to me, would be more likely to call upon his instinct as a consumer to call city inspectors ("I'm paying five hundred bucks for this?") or simply move out, rather than reach out to the people across the hallway and ask, "Wanna get organized? Wanna do this together?" Seeking a group solution was the natural thing for Jacinto and the Latinos of Grand Island, who came from cultures with a stronger sense of collective identity. The idea of community was the antidote to their sense of powerlessness, that adrift feeling that had haunted my trailermates and me in Alabama. Their petition helped speed up a step KMMJ's owners would have probably taken on their own initiative eventually: the station was broadcasting polkas, after all, the music of choice of an elderly and fading demographic, the first immigrant wave of Nebraska's nineteenth-century birth. Mexicans, Guatemalans, and Salvadorans were the future.

At first, KMMJ agreed to give Jacinto and the Latino group three hours of broadcast time each weekend. Since it didn't make sense for KMMJ to hire a Spanish-speaking deejay to work such a small window on the station's schedule, Jacinto and his friend Oscar Erives—then an employee at an auto-parts store—would have to give it a go on their own. Turning on the microphone that first day at KMMJ may have been, in retrospect, the opening of a new chapter in Nebraska's very brief Latino history, but it was not one that began auspiciously. "We were so nervous, we were shaking," Jacinto remembered. For three months they put on what were little better than "practice programs," Oscar told me.

"We'd get the song titles mixed up," Jacinto added. "We'd look at each other with the microphone and say anything that came to mind." They did everything but stutter on the air. "But it was important for the community, so we kept going. We're guys who will try anything. A little defeat or failure can't stop us."

Eventually, the station went Spanish full-time, which led a rugged core of KMMJ listeners to call in to voice their anger at the loss of their beloved polka. How was it that one of Nebraska's oldest stations—the first, in fact, to broadcast full-time in the 1920s—could have suddenly, and without apparent warning, gone Mexican? "We had twenty, twenty-five callers complain," Lyle Nelson, the station manager, told me when I visited. "And maybe five hundred Spanish people saying it was good." The accordion-heavy polkas were relegated to Sunday mornings, switching spots with Jacinto and Oscar, who got serious about this deejay business. Their first on-air interview was with the ubiquitous Los Tigres del Norte, whose Midwestern tour had taken them to nearby Kearney. "You know, we just started out doing this," Jacinto told the group, trying not to look too starry-eyed. Los Tigres presented them with a box of CDs to give away to their listeners, a collection of oompah-pah songs laced through with accordions, melodies a polka band from Chicago might produce if they were exiled to Tijuana or Nuevo Laredo to live amongst the coyotes and the green chiles.

> *They came from San Ysidro, after leaving Tijuana*
> *They had their tires filled with weed*
> *They were Emilio Varela and Camelia la Tejana*

More bands showed up on what has become a regular Midwestern circuit for *norteño* bands. Mandingo came by too, as did La Sonora Dinamita, who played in Lexington, home to the massive IBP beef-processing plant. "KMMJ is still a country station," Oscar said. "It's just a different kind of country. My dad used to listen to the old KMMJ. He liked polkas. I'd tell him, Dad, shut off that music. I never thought that I'd be working in that station."

As the only Spanish speakers in town with access to the airwaves, Jacinto and Oscar became unofficial community leaders and spokesmen. Jacinto joined the Grand Island Chamber of Commerce and after a while became a member of its board of directors. Spanish-language radio spread throughout the state, with stations popping up in Omaha and Columbus. "All the state of Nebraska is getting these Spanish signals," Oscar said. "You could be on a hill, standing between a bunch of cows, and hear it. You can go to a ranch and hear the workers listening to it."

By the time I stopped by the studios of KMMJ one December, Oscar and Jacinto seemed at ease behind the microphone. I sat and watched them work in a predictably cramped studio where they cohabited with stacks of *ranchera* CDs and a thick book called *The Severe Weather Manual* on the table before them. "This is KMMJ Radio, covering all the corners of Nebraska, from Omaha to North Platte." Oscar plugged in a tape for a commercial. "On the eighteenth of

December, everyone come to Kearney, Nebraska, for the most spectacular rodeo! The best riders [*jinetes*] in the world!" I started scribbling in my notebook. "This 'Cowboy Cumbia' goes to *la familia* Sánchez here in Grand Island, and to the Cabral family in Shilton, Nebraska. . . . It's getting a bit ugly on the roads. All of you who don't have experience with the snow, don't worry. Go five miles per hour if you want to. . . . We want to give a greeting to a visitor we have in our studios today, a Mr. Héctor Tobar from the *Los Angeles Times*. Now, since Héctor just got here from California and doesn't know much about snow, we would like to recommend to him also that he be very careful driving out there today, just like all of you should be very careful. . . . Tomorrow you can put your nose to the grindstone because the forecast is for a sunny day. That's what the meteorological station in Omaha tells us. . . . And you better hurry because there's only a week left before Christmas. . . . It's gone very well for all of us here in Nebraska, hasn't it? Why deny it? The pay is good. Santa Claus is going to have to get a big trailer. And if my kids are listening, this doesn't mean you can ask for more presents. . . . *La migración* has a checkpoint between here and there. That seems strange to me. We're going to call the immigration office tomorrow and find out what it's about. I'm not sure if it's legal. . . . Actually, I'm sure it is legal. It's their country after all."

The Immigration and Naturalization Service had recently opened up an office in Grand Island, and the local agent in charge, Tom DeRouchey, had been in the station not too much earlier to talk to Jacinto and Oscar on the air about what *la migra* was up to. It goes without saying that the presence of a half-dozen officers from an agency whose express mission is to rid the country of immigrants without papers was a cause of some concern to the immigrant listeners of KMMJ. Would *la migra* sweep through town and clear them out? *Los paisanos* turned their ears to their radios like farmers following the progress of a plague of locusts across the plains, wondering whether their fields would be ravaged next, whether everything they had worked to build would be wiped out from one moment to the next.

I decided I should talk to DeRouchey too. After finishing up at KMMJ, I drove fifteen miles per hour across icy streets to Grand Island's brick-and-mortar downtown to meet with him at an old-fashioned soda fountain and café called Coffee and Cream. DeRouchey's previous assignments had taken him to the Canadian border in Vermont and to Temulca, near the Mexican border. "I told people I was coming to Nebraska and they said, 'Nebraska? What's in Nebraska?' It's a different kind of place than what we're used to. The nearest Border Patrol office is in North Dakota." People who worked in immigration were surprised to find themselves here, and surprised to find how busy they were. "You probably couldn't be farther away from a national border," an INS official in Omaha would tell me later. "We're in the heartland of America. Most people wouldn't think we would have an illegal immigration problem."

The "problem" was immigrant smuggling, human beings without permission to be in the United States being shipped across the United States in the backs of vans, cars, and trucks, on weeklong journeys from desert border crossings to destinations in Chicago, Atlanta, and Dalton, Georgia. Thanks to the crackdown I'd seen in place at San Ysidro and Tijuana (which had been repeated at other popular urban crossing points), the smugglers were taking a massive detour that wound through Nebraska and Iowa. The weekly printout of detentions in the Omaha office offered a hint of just how popular the Great Plains route had become: eighteen people detained one Wednesday outside the central Nebraska community of Aurora;

forty-four people the following Sunday in Kimball, near the border with Wyoming; sixty people over three days the following week in Iowa. The melodramatic theater of the border, with its *chiles verdes* chasing brown-skinned people through mostly barren, desert-like flora, was being staged here in the middle of corn and alfalfa fields and below the leafless cottonwood trees of winter. An overloaded van might struggle to maintain control on a windy stretch of Interstate 80, drawing the attention of a Nebraska state trooper, men in Smokey the Bear campaign hats and midnight-blue patrol cars who would pull the van over, open the back, and see a score of startled Mesoamerican eyes staring back at them. Disoriented by a landscape seemingly devoid of landmarks, hardly anybody tried to run away. "They wouldn't know where to go if they did run," Lieutenant Dave Anderson of the Nebraska State Patrol told me. "They'd be lost in a strange land."

Every once in a while, groups of immigrants would fill the holding cells, and then the classroom and the garage at Lieutenant Anderson's headquarters, a brick cube on the edge of Grand Island. "We'll put out mats for them in the garage. It's heated in there." In other corners of Nebraska, far from the nearest INS office in Omaha, a state trooper might decide holding a dozen or more hungry and distraught people was more trouble than it was worth and simply let them go. They might conclude, as Lieutenant Anderson did, they were more like victims of a crime than perpetrators. "You're talking sixteen or more people scrunched into a small van, standing up for hours, conditions that are not fit for humans, really," Anderson said. "You can understand why they're leaving. They're trying to make a better life. It's the smugglers who are taking advantage of them."

This was why Tom DeRouchey had been brought to Grand Island: to take the old Sears store on Third Street and make it an INS detention-and-interrogation center, so that the immigrants held in this part of Nebraska wouldn't be set free by kindhearted troopers. It was part of a nationwide effort to put the INS into rural communities far from the nation's borders, places like Fayetteville, Arkansas; London, Kentucky; North Platte, Nebraska; and Brush, Colorado. After my interview with DeRouchey was over, I walked a half block down Third Street to the shuttered Sears. I cupped my hands against the glass of an empty display window and saw bare carpets with the shadow marks of absent clothes racks and cash registers. How many pairs of Johnny Miller slacks had been sold here, how many Craftsman tools? The Sears had moved out to the Conestoga Mall, following the shoppers, who had been lured away from downtown as they had been in countless other heartland towns, leaving the center to age into a faded relic of Americana, where frayed telephone wires dangled from splintered telephone poles across narrow alleyways, and the stores smelled of mothballs. In Grand Island, one of the aging buildings of the city's prosperous past would become the theater of a human tragedy from the present. Immigrant men and women apprehended on the Nebraska highways would spend hours in the old Sears weeping over their broken dreams and faraway homes, inside cells built where mothers once picked out jeans for their sons, and fathers bought barbecues and power tools.

This was a different Great Plains from the one I had read about in the book of the same name by Ian Frazier, which celebrated a land of myth and opportunity still inhabited by the ghosts of nineteenth- and twentieth-century booms, by Crazy Horse and Mennonite immigrants, Lawrence Welk's accordion and abandoned farmhouses, nuclear silos and Bonnie and Clyde. There wasn't a single reference to *mexicano* immigrants in that book, which is understandable, as it was written just before the immigration explosion of the early 1990s. Latinos were only extras in the story then, maybe a guy sweeping floors at the back of the meatpacking plant, or a family in the old barrio in Kansas City. In little more than a decade, Latinos had added a few chapters to Great Plains lore, like the *mexicano* bandits of Nebraska, who in September 2002 took over a bank in Norfolk and killed five people in forty seconds, the bloodiest bank robbery in the state's history. Unlike Jesse James, who committed similar crimes in neighboring Iowa, no one romanticized the vicious crimes of Gabriel Rodríguez and his three accomplices, who saw in the small-town bank an easy mark without security guards or bullet-proof glass. In the meatpacking plants, meanwhile, Spanish-speaking laborers were introducing the Latin American–style class struggle that had already become a feature of life in Los Angeles and San Francisco. The writer David Bacon, who'd I'd last run into at the *LA Weekly*, where I edited his story about Central American farmworkers in California, was writing for *American Prospect* about "the Kill-Floor Rebellion" at an Omaha meatpacking plant. One of the activists was a survivor of the burned villages and death squads of Guatemala's civil war who called upon his experience in the revolutionary movement to help put together a successful campaign to unionize the plant. The turning point was a Catholic mass in Latino south Omaha, where a priest, in the best tradition of Latin American "Liberation Theology," told the workers in his congregation the time had come to choose sides in the struggle against poverty and inequality.

In Nebraska, Iowa, and Kansas, the beef plants were the powerful engines of a new economy that depended on low-paid immigrant labor. A generation earlier, as David Bacon explained, the beef plants had been monopolies, with a relatively well-paid and ethnically diverse workforce. Cheap immigrant labor changed everything; the beef plants adopted the industrial model of the *maquiladoras*, assembly plants along the Mexican side of the border, and their profits soared. In the Midwest, the beef plants and the wages they paid (several times what an unskilled worker might earn in Mexico) were the axis around which family life revolved for hundreds of thousands of people. In Liberal, Kansas, my next stop on the Great Plains, people talked about the beef plants the same way people talked about auto factories in Detroit and other American cities.

"There are towns that are composed of all these beef factories," José Gutiérrez told me in Liberal. His family had come to Kansas from Durango, Mexico, via Albuquerque a decade earlier. Nearly every male in his family had worked in the meat plants at one time or another, most in Liberal, others in Garden City and Dodge City. "Life is hard labor. I worked at National Beef. You get paid for everything you do. I worked in the knife section, making cuts on their cheeks. Every single head of the cow they killed went through me. I made three cuts on each side of the cheek. A cow has big teeth. We broke it up and sent it down the line. It's about nine dollars an hour. Kids that don't finish school end up there. And my dad's still working there. He picks up the meat that falls on the floor. He was in the knife section but they transferred him for his age and now he's only picking up the meat, cleaning and washing it and putting it back. He's fifty-eight years old."

José had gone to Seward County Community College and escaped the monotony of cow heads by getting a job at an auto-parts store, and then at the radio station when it switched from oldies to regional Mexican. When I met him, he was selling ads at the station, managing the part-time deejays and news staff—pretty much running KYUU as his own Little Ranchera Station on the Prairie, the second stop of my grand tour of the Latin airwaves of the inner North American continent.

The beef plants were KYUU's most consistent advertisers, what with one plant always trying to lure its workers away from the other.

"Are they treating you with dignity and respect on the job?" one ad asked in Spanish. "If not, join the IBP team. With IBP, you can make nine dollars and up to thirteen fifty-five if you qualify. This Wednesday is your opportunity to change your job to IBP!" This was quickly followed by another ad, for José's alma mater, National Beef, paying nine dollars an hour in the *departamento de matanza,* which can be translated, literally, as "the killing department."

You could walk around Liberal and see a small town, but for Latinos it was an industrial village, a sort of Flint, Michigan, or Akron, Ohio, where life was dominated by the round-the-clock rhythms of the massive plant on the edge of town and its 3,200 employees. You could get in a car and in a matter of minutes stand on the open sand dunes and sagebrush of the Cimarron National Grassland, imagining caravans of wagons crossing the prairie, but inside Liberal's city limits life took on a mean, urban texture: sometimes it seemed there were a dozen alienated youths produced for every million or so of the steers their mothers and fathers slaughtered at National Beef. Listening to the news report on KYUU, I could close my eyes and imagine myself in Los Angeles on those weekends when I had to do the Vietnamesque "roundup" of the "body count" for the newspaper, the summary of the Friday- and Saturday-night gunplay and carnage. "A young man was arrested and is charged with attempted murder after an argument at a party on Sunday," Indira Amparán said in a sweet Spanish voice on the KYUU afternoon news, happy Muzak playing incongruously in the background. Indira sold jewelry in her other job, and she read the news about this carnage in the same tone she'd tell you those earrings were simply delightful. KYUU, like KMMJ in Grand Island, was staffed with rookies mostly, who were learning their trade on the air. "In another incident, another youth of fifteen is under arrest for having assaulted a police officer on Sunday after an argument. It seems that the police officers found out about a meeting of gang members on the 200 block of Princeton Avenue, where they made contact with ten gang members. And that's when they found marijuana and other drugs. The police took three young people to the police department to ask them questions and that's when one of them attacked the officers. The youth of fifteen is also in the Juvenile Detention Center (*el centro de jóvenes*) in Garden City."

Indira spoke softly, without a trace of menace in her voice, unlike the alarmist stories you read in the national press about young men like those in her news report, tattooed warriors who were spreading the culture of alienated urban Latino youth to places such as nearby Dodge City, Kansas, and the Shenandoah Valley in Virginia. The gangs followed the beef and chicken workers across the United States. They were the "bad brother" Pedro tagging along after the hardworking "good brother" José, supposedly to work in the big food plants but discovering there were more lucrative, untapped possibilities in methamphetamine and other substances with high dollar-per-gram exchange rates. All of this gave more work to the gang professionals of Southern California, war-weary detectives who found themselves sending faxes to Kansas and Nebraska that explained what these organizations called 18th Street and Mara Salvatrucha were, and how they had started in smoggy and overcrowded Los Angeles neighborhoods, and the various shades of meaning behind their exotic tattoos and how to decode that elaborate system of hand and finger gestures that kids were suddenly flashing on the streets of Liberal and Garden City.

A Spanish-speaking parent who worked at a factory in Liberal and was at a loss as to what to do about his wayward son could switch the dial to FM and listen to KZQD, the personal crusade of Mario Loredo, an evangelical pastor who ran a string of churches in Kansas and the Oklahoma panhandle. My visit to the KZQD studios was also my introduction to that niche musical genre known as "Christian *cumbias*," an evangelical message sung to a hip-swaying, Caribbean rhythm. "Let it move, let it move, let it move," went one song (*que se mueva, que se mueva, que se mueva*). "Let it move the spirit of God!" But the songs were only filler in between Laredo's three-hour sermons, a spiritual anchor tossed to all the lost souls he saw around him, and the only commercials on the station were for other sermons. "At the Centro Cristiano of Tyrone, Oklahoma, come to listen to the word of God with *el hermano* [brother] Jesús Castañón. Also, Pastor Mario Loredo will be there to pray for the sick and the needy. Come and don't miss this great blessing."

KZQD's blessings were part of a potpourri of Latino culture that was making this corner of Southwest Kansas more like the southwestern United States. In the 2000 census, people marking the box labeled "Hispanic or Latino" made up 43 percent of the population in Liberal, and are probably the majority there as you read these pages. The city fathers put up a Spanish website so that immigrant residents could find *la biblioteca conmemorativa de Liberal* (the Liberal Memorial Library) and other city services. José Gutiérrez of KYUU invited me to the old train depot, now refurbished as a cultural center, for the graduation of a "leadership" program for young Latinos, sponsored by the Chicago-based National Hispanic Leadership Conference, designed to hone future pillars of Liberal. José was just twenty-three years old and perhaps already qualified as a pillar. Every day he linked the Latinos of Liberal to the Latinos of California and the rest of the United States via a satellite feed from San Jose, California, of nationally syndicated Z Spanish radio, with its anchor morning show El Chulo de la Mañana (the Handsome Morning Guy), which was also broadcast in De Queen, Arkansas, Minneapolis, and Dodge

City, just up the road from Liberal. José also gave his listeners regular local news, *tornado alertas* when the weather turned ominous, and jalapeño-eating contests at the local supermarket. Sometimes he broadcast from the store of Guadalupe Contreras, one of the station's most loyal advertisers. "We started to grow when the radio station started," Contreras told me. "They are the only ones who pay attention to the *raza,* the humble people. And the people love them back for it."

Contreras was a barber, and I interviewed him as he gave me a haircut. He was also a haberdasher. If you wanted a new Stetson, he had a wall of ten-gallon hats to choose from, along with rows of leather boots, and stacks of cassette tapes of Los Tigres del Norte and Mandingo. He was a beautician too, if you needed one, and he could give a man that ponytail-pompadour look that was popular in central and northern Mexico. He had a full line of ladies' clothing, assorted jewelry, jerseys of Mexican soccer teams. He offered an entire mall of Mexicanness in a room not much bigger than your average liquor store; as I sat in the barber chair, which he'd placed on a small rise in the center of the room, I could spin around and see a place much like Liberal itself, a mini-world of *latinidad* stuffed into a small package, a town where eleven thousand people huddled together against the winds that blew in from the Cimarron grasslands.

I followed the *cumbia* and *ranchera* signals of Spanish-language radio across the middle of the United States, from Grand Island and Liberal to Rupert, Idaho, where I met Ben Reed at the station in the beet field. By then it was spring, and Rupert was gearing up for its second annual Cinco de Mayo parade, which was going to wind past the park in the center of town with its gazebo and miniature windmill, and past the barbershop of Dagoberto Martínez, with its dual Mexican and American flags. For Latinos in Rupert, this Cinco de Mayo was going to be a transcendent event, their coming-out party, the first mark on the public life of the city. Cinco de Mayo has been a feature of Latino life in California and Texas for a generation; in a certain sense, it's more important to Mexicans in the United States than in Mexico, where it commemorates an obscure battle of that country's war against the French Empire. In California, teachers in the public school took up Cinco de Mayo as a way to celebrate Mexican identity because Mexican Independence Day, September 16, falls too early in the school year. Its appearance in Rupert and other farm towns and cities from the Midwest (Duluth, Minnesota) to the Great Plains (Garden City, Kansas) and the Pacific Northwest (Pasco, Washington) was, like radio stations in Nebraska and bean farms in Manitoba, another landmark in the march of Latino culture across the North American continent.

Ben Reed interviewed the six contestants for Cinco de Mayo queen on Rupert's English-language station, the other half of his job at the KFTA studios. "I just want to be a role model for the young people," one of the contestants said in English. "I just want to say to all the Hispanics out there, *que sí se puede,* yes you can do it." It was the slogan of the United Farm Workers of César Chávez in the 1970s and had become a catchall rallying cry for every Mexican-American since. César Chávez and the UFW are the only Mexican-Americans canonized into the American public school curriculum, and maybe *sí se puede* is the only Spanish in most American high-school history textbooks. In the case of Belén López, a seventeen-year-old who was one of the contestants on the radio that day, it would have been an entirely appropriate thing to say, since her parents were farmworkers. They discouraged her from running for queen because they thought the dress would cost too much money, but she'd gotten around that problem when her aunt agreed to make the dress for her, as she told me later when I met her at Minico High School. Her dress was a flared crimson outfit with blue stones and ersatz diamonds on top, a small act of rebellion against family members who had insisted on white, and in the end every woman in the family had helped sew it. She had convinced them all that *sí se puede.*

Mexican-American farmworkers had been coming to Idaho since the 1940s, but they had been a small group of people in the city, perhaps only slightly less isolated than my friend Gregorio and I were in the trailer park in Alabama. Paul Andrade had come to Rupert to work in the Ore-Ida potato plant in 1955 and stayed; for decades a Cinco de Mayo parade in Rupert would have been an impossibility, he said. "There wasn't a lot of Mexican people you could gather around before. There was maybe the Montoyas, and us and a few others." At the end of the twentieth century, Latino farmworkers from Mexico and south Texas had started planting roots in Rupert, becoming a large enough group of people to be called a "community," and Paul could celebrate his Mexican identity in public with several hundred other people. He was going to drive his low-rider 1962 Chevy Impala in the parade, and if the mood was right he'd set off the hydraulics and have the car bounce along the street a bit. The low rider is a barrio icon, of course, originating in Southern California in the 1950s, a symbiosis created at the moment when the pachuco zoot suit was fading from view and a car culture was being born. They were and still are illegal in many communities, and surely this was part of their original appeal: they became a kind of dressed-up illegality, a gesture of creative defiance, a metallic zoot suit that over the years has evolved to take many forms, the latest being the low-rider bicycle, which was born in Mexican towns among young people who could never dream of having enough money to buy a car. In this context, Andrade was a traditionalist, sticking with a Chevy and eschewing the low-rider pickups and the other newfangled low-rider creations. He worked on his low-rider every weekend, fussing over details like the big dice that hung from the rearview mirror—"to me, they stand for nostalgia." On the day I saw it, its black paint and chrome wheels gleamed with the reflection of the clouds of the Big Sky country.

"It's a work of art," I said.

"That's what I built it for," Andrade answered. "To show people what you can do."

Like Andrade, teacher Oralia Palomo was a Chicana, which was what U.S.-born persons of Mexican descent started calling themselves in the late 1960s. She was born in the Rio Grande Valley of Texas, and her father had been a famous accordion player in San Antonio; he taught her that "nothing was impossible," an idea she passed on to her students as Cinco de Mayo pageant coordinator at Minico High. "To be a queen takes a lot of commitment," she said. "You do it because you love it." Besides the dress, the girls had to come up with an act for the talent competition and, most important, a "platform" for their reign as queen, how they would bring the spirit of Cinco de Mayo to Wal-Mart when they made an official visit there, or to the kindergartners who would crane up their necks to look up at the queen in her crown.

In the major cities of the Southwestern United States, Cinco de Mayo had become a highly commercialized event, but here in Rupert, where it was brand-new, there were no beer-company sponsors or T-shirt giveaways from soft-drink companies. Instead it was a celebration of the Latin and of the possible, of "what you can do." Most people in the Latino community were farmworkers, after all, which is as close to a caste existence as there is in the United States. When you are a farmworker, you live out of your truck like the Joads of *The Grapes of Wrath*, or travel from one trailer to the next. You are a prisoner of circumstance, a slave to the cycles of the harvest and agricultural economies. In Rupert the wandering was coming to an end. People wanted to celebrate their emancipation by making dresses and singing "Cielito Lindo" with the mariachis and cruising down Oneida Street in their low riders. Probably in future decades Cinco de Mayo in Idaho would be divested of this original significance. It would be as trivialized an event as it was in Los Angeles or San Antonio, as meaningless as chocolate bunnies on Easter, but for now people talked about it with a genuine earnestness.

"You do something so that you can shine in front of the people, you show what you know how to do," said Antonio Carrillo, a twenty-seven-year-old with piercing eyes the color of green chile salsa who was arguably the most talented person in the parade. Antonio was a champion of Mexican *charro* rodeos who earned his living as a horse whisperer and trainer at an Anglo man's farm on the edge of town. *Charros* like Carrillo took the skills of the Mexican countryside and transformed them into a costumed ballet of man, rope, and animal called *charrería*. He showed me a video of his performance for the Fourth of July parade as we sat on the floor in his small trailer, which was down the road from his boss's house and the corrals of the half-dozen or so horses he looked after. We watched a platoon of soldiers marching with a Confederate flag, the float sponsored by the Idaho Republicans, and then Antonio, walking with his son in matching brown *charro* outfits with embroidered sombreros, spinning the "rope flower" (*flor de soga*), doing a quick hop in and out of its big hoop. Then he popped in another video of a *charrería* (horsemanship) exhibition in Mexico. Young boys made spinning rope circles and tackled calves. Men roped a horse's hind legs at a full gallop, pulling the animal to the ground with an elegant violence that would surely have made the SPCA wince. There weren't very many good *charros* in Idaho, as there were in Zacatecas or California, Antonio said. There were other *charros* in Twin Falls and in other parts of the United States, as far away as Kentucky. In his hometown of Jerez, Zacatecas, Antonio performed during Carnaval. "They do things a bit differently there. In my town, the queen has to be accompanied by *charros* and mariachis." Rupert hadn't reached that level yet. Maybe one day it would.

n Rupert's town square, where the parade would go past, the scene was of a Norman Rockwell painting where half the characters—the barber, the soda jerk, the smiling teenage couple in *After the Prom*—had been replaced with Mexican faces. Dagoberto Martínez was the barber and a man who appreciated Rupert's Rockwellesque qualities, how on the weekends the young couples circled around the town square arm in arm with a parent keeping a steely eye nearby. "Come out here Sunday afternoon and the place fills up with young people." They make eyes at each other, and it would be just like Mexico, he observed, except for the American policemen standing nearby to make sure there wasn't any trouble.

Dagoberto hoped that one day Cinco de Mayo would be as big a deal as Fourth of July, which saw hundreds of out-of-towners descend on Rupert for a slice of small-town Americana you couldn't see in Boise. Mayor Audrey Neiwerth hoped Cinco de Mayo would take off too. She was counting on burgeoning Latino business to help push forward the town's efforts to revitalize downtown.

Neiwerth was from the south side of the railroad tracks, the scrappier part of town, which these days was where most of the Latinos lived. I'd come upon this division in other rural towns I'd visited in the Rockies and the Great Plains, and also big metropolises like Salt Lake City, some three hours from here by car, where the Latinos lived to the west of the tracks and the rail yard, alongside the working-class white families of the city who are Mormon Sharks to the Mormon Jets on the east side. Over the years Neiwerth had gotten to know some of her Mexican neighbors in south Rupert well because she did their taxes. When she ran for office, she got to know more by knocking on their doors. She was in her sixties then, retired from the school district, and her neighbors might have mistaken her, with her thick glasses and her classic beauty-shop do, for the Avon lady but for the campaign pamphlets she carried with her. "I had a flyer in Spanish if they didn't speak English. That seemed to impress them. No one had done that before." There were people registered to vote who had never stepped into a polling place. Mayor Neiwerth quickly learned that in a town like Rupert, being on a first-name basis with all your constituents, even those who didn't vote, was a philosophy that would keep her in office. "A Hispanic guy called me last night," she told me. He was concerned about Rupert's planned annexation of property on the edge of town. "I explained to him that he wasn't going to lose his chickens and his calves. They'll all be grandfathered in. And he was happy."

Neiwerth regarded the city's Latinization as an economic inevitability. "Everyone here knows that our potatoes wouldn't get harvested, our beet fields wouldn't be thinned, if it weren't for the Hispanic laborers." Well, not exactly everyone. When I stopped by the Minidoka County Historical Society Museum to check out the turn-of-the-century soda counter, and the wagon wheels and log cabins of Rupert's pioneer past, I made the mistake of asking the docent, a sixty-four-year-old Irvin Hardy, if he was going to the Cinco de Mayo parade. He responded with a rant about the local Mexicans and their gangs, and wondered why English wasn't the official language of the United States. "The trouble we've had is that most of them are wetbacks. When the Border Patrol would come through, they'd hide. Then they get their green cards and come out of the woodwork. If we go down there, they don't do anything for us. If they come up here, they think we're supposed to kiss their butts."

Ben Reed had heard people talk like this and it hurt him. He was one of the few people in this town of 5,000 able to slip back and forth across its cultural and linguistic divide, and the tension had caused him to reexamine his own worldview, which up to the time he became El Chupacabras had been Republican libertarian. I had heard a hint of the old Ben when I turned on the radio while driving around Rupert and caught him hosting an English-language talk show on KFTA's sister station, which occupied another studio in that building in the beet field. He was trying to goad his listeners into calling in with a soliloquy about Attorney General Janet Reno and the simmering war in Miami over Elián González, the Cuban castaway who had become a cause célèbre for American conservatives because the Clinton administration was trying to reunite him with his father, a loyal Communist.

"Janet Reno wants to send this boy, this six-year-old boy, back to the loving arms of Fidel Castro," he said. Ben Reed the conservative talk-show host spoke English in the same bass voice of El Chupacabras, but English Ben couldn't make the phone ring, and across the airwaves you could feel the doubt in his mind growing. *Is anyone listening? Am I all alone in this beet field?* "No one is calling. I guess they're part of the sixty percent of the population that doesn't care what Dictator Reno is doing." The silence on the radio was thick and uncomfortable. Poor Ben: I almost wanted to call the station and offer some bogus opinion.

Next he tried to get his listeners going with a controversy that might hit a little closer to home here in the Mormon heartland: the lawsuit brought by a gay man against the Boy Scouts, a case then winding its way toward the Supreme Court. "What about this so-called 'Boy Scout'? Doesn't the sacred union between a man and a woman mean anything anymore?"

Again, silence.

Two years later, I called Ben up to see how he was doing, what was new in Rupert, how the station was doing. "I'm not doing English-language talk anymore," he said, sounding immensely relieved. "I've become probably a more moderate liberal. I've seen too much abuse, too many problems. I've started to take an advocacy stance to a certain degree." He does talk radio in Spanish now, and no longer is he forced to stare at a blank bank of phone lights, what with his listeners anxious to call in and turn his show into a litany of complaints about the authorities. "When the INS is in town, we do an alert," he said in a defiant, subversive tone. "Sometimes the INS chains people together. We don't even do that with convicted murderers." He was still doing battle with the Justice Department, only now from the left. "Since nine-eleven it's more popular among the politicians to say to hell with the immigrants." His position as a visible advocate for his Latino audience, he told me, had earned him some "disgusting" phone calls from local Klan members. Ben Reed had become what Norman Mailer called in the 1950s a "white Negro," a man who cast his loyalties with the oppressed minority because he saw in them something pure and uncorrupted, an antidote to the hypocrisy he had come to see in the culture in which he was born and bred.

Like Ben Reed, my friend Gus Gregory crossed over into *latinidad*. In Peru, he was known as Tino, a diminutive of his Greek name, Constantine. A few months after his marriage, while driving on a road in the Andes, he was ambushed and killed for reasons that are still not entirely clear some sixteen years later.

We buried him in California, in a cemetery high on a hill in San Pedro. His widow, Dolores, was five months pregnant, and we friends took solace in the baby on the way, but Gus Gregory's son was born with a hole in his heart and died just a few days later.

Gus was born in Torrance, California, but was married and shed his blood in the mountainous heartland of Peru. His son, conceived in South America, died in the United States. Gus probably spoke his last words in Spanish, a language that had come to express a part of himself that did not exist in any other tongue. In Spanish, he could tell a man he loved him, which was what he told me not long before he died.

"I love you too, dude," I answered him in English. It was true. He was the brother I never had.

In Idaho, when Ben Reed got sick with a very serious stomach problem, he too found strength and comfort in the Spanish language. His Mexican friends—many who knew him only as a voice on the radio—came to the hospital to look after him. They were his new brothers and sisters, linked not by blood but by a way of talking and feeling that Ben Reed did not know in the Idaho of his youth. More than likely, some of the *mexicanos* were surprised to learn that *el chupacabras*, the "goatsucker" and Wolfman Jack of Spanish-speaking Rupert, was the somewhat pale and pudgy man in the hospital bed. But when he opened his mouth to thank them for coming, and to tell them they had filled his *corazón* with happiness, they heard that familiar voice from the radio, muted but still unmistakably *machote*. It was the voice of the man who made them laugh while they were working in the green, undulating fields of El Valle Mágico.

Part Three

MANIFEST DESTINIES

Chapter Seven

UNCONQUERED
La reconquista

Cordova, New Mexico · San Fernando, California · San Antonio, Texas

I walked along the top of a ridge, across a field of talcum desert soil overlooking the Sangre de Cristo Mountains, following a drunk man who was guiding me through a forest of shellacked pine crucifixes and plastic wreaths with nylon flowers. He was small and wiry, and already nice and toasted at ten o'clock in the morning, although he had proven adept at guiding me around town and then to the cemetery. We had driven from the center of Cordova, New Mexico, a town of seven hundred people, where I had found him standing with three other men near the adobe Church of San Antonio. The church and its locked, weather-beaten wooden door faced a plaza where a low-lying tan fog of dust drifted down streets that in two or three hundred years of human habitation had never known asphalt, where you half expected to find a horse-drawn wagon or some other ancient form of locomotion just around the corner, or even the Spanish conquistadors in bronze helmets who trooped through here in search of the mythical Seven Cities of Cibola. From his perch on a bench before a local dispenser of spirits,

William Trujillo had answered my call for directions by rising to his feet and jumping into my rental car, which quickly filled with the aroma of his drinker's breath. He guided me some two or three blocks to the home of the late Allen Sandoval, a friend of his who had overdosed on heroin a few months earlier, and then a mile or so outside town to the cemetery where Sandoval is buried, under a mound of dirt with a plaster angel on top.

"It's over here someplace, I think," William told me, suddenly looking disoriented as we stood in the center of an undisciplined grid of graves. "Yeah, yeah, over there in the front."

Allen and two of his friends had died of heroin overdoses in Cordova some months earlier. One hundred more had died in surrounding Rio Arriba County, a death rate more than triple the national average. I decided I could hang a story on the incongruity: an urban cancer sweeping through a landscape of ocher- and rust-colored vistas, where fireplaces sprayed the perfume of juniper trees into the desert air. Certain kinds of tourists came to northern New Mexico because they felt it was an oasis of natural and spiritual purity. They filled up bed-and-breakfasts in Taos, drove up the prices in Santa Fe jewelry stores that sold Hopi earrings and Navajo pottery, and bought reproductions of Georgia O'Keeffe paintings of skulls and desert flora. I had come to New Mexico many times myself as a tourist, soaking up the atmosphere of the old *santuarios* and plazas and sensing that I was treading on land marked by Spanish and Mexican history.

When my future wife and I were dating, we drove to Tierra Amarilla near the Colorado border to see the place where in 1967 a man named Reies Tijerina led an uprising against the Anglo legal system that robbed Hispanic farmers of old communal lands, taking over the county courthouse with a group of armed men. The event is commemorated with a plaque, which brought a smile to my lips when I saw it: there aren't many places in the United States where you can say "this is where the peasants rose up." For the most part, New Mexico's Hispanic history (people here don't use the word "Latino") has been a series of disasters and disgraces: from the subjugation of the indigenous pueblo Indian culture, to the invasion and conquest of the Mexican province of Nuevo Mexico by General Stephen Kearny and the U.S. army in 1846. Reies Tijerina's motto was *¡Tierra o Muerte!*—the old Zapatista cry of Land or Death. But neither he nor any other New Mexico farmer ever did win the battle to have the old Spanish and Mexican land grants recognized by U.S. courts. When I called the top public health official in Rio Arriba County, Lauren Reichelt, to ask her why so many people were overdosing in her domain, her answer was a pithy summation of that history: "Cultural dislocation and cultural oppression. People are in pain." For her, the story of the heroin-shortened lives was all about the sorrow of dispossession.

My journey to New Mexico to write about Allen Sandoval and his friends took me first to Albuquerque, where the lists of people and things that survived them could be found in file cabinets of the state medical examiner. Then I traveled to Cordova, where the texture of subjugations and resentments past lived on in the unpaved streets, with their sinuous scars cut by rain and snow, and in the ruins of a pair of burned-out adobe stores, their collapsed roofs and mud bricks singed black, as if they'd been hit by a pair of cannon blasts a century or two earlier and never been repaired. Like heroin addicts elsewhere, Allen Sandoval and his friends were the weakest men in this place, town punching bags. More than once Allen's mother had to walk the three blocks from her house to pick up her bloodied son from the ground in front of the old church, guiding him back home to clean him up, patch his wounds, and weep over him because he was thirty years old but still as helpless as a little boy.

The church that looms over the plaza was built in 1832, sixteen years before the town officially became part of the United States after what's known in American history books as "the Mexican War." As in other conquered places, the locals in Cordova and the rest of New Mexico lost the right to be educated in their own language and in general became second-class citizens. It was a common outcome of nineteenth-century wars of conquest: in the colonized Ireland described by Thomas Keneally in *The Great Shame*, the English Penal Code kept the Irish from being attorneys or teachers, part of a series of practices that conspired to make the rural Irish "poor, powerless and stupid." In American New Mexico, a new social construction was born that would dominate the next 150 years of Latino history in all the territories that had once been part of the Republic of Mexico: the barrio.

Barrios are insular places, born of de facto and de jure segregation. They have produced proud community leaders, a sense of identity and defiance vis-à-vis the outside world, and also a variety of self-destructive behaviors, from gang banging to paint sniffing. Before heroin arrived in northern New Mexico in the late 1990s, Allen and his friends' self-destruction would have taken a decade or decades to complete, because alcohol would have been their weapon of choice. Allen's father had been an alcoholic who died in a car accident when his son was twelve. The heroin in New Mexico was called "black tar," one of many variants then sweeping through rural America, preying on the sorrowful, taking their victims not in years but after just a few flutters of their eyelids.

Brian Romero killed himself with an accidental overdose of alcohol and heroin one night in late May. A day later his body was lying on a table in Albuquerque, where an especially assiduous medical examiner took note of the markings on his body, a gallery of symbols of *la vida loca*, the crazy life. "A 12 by 4 inch tattoo of a woman and a dragon on the right anterior upper arm, antecubital fossa, forearm, and wrist; a 2½ by ½-inch tattoo of a cross and a flower on the right posterolateral upper arm; a 5 by 4 inch tattoo of a dog with a baseball bat . . . a 2½ by 2½ inch tattoo of a cross and the name 'Tracey' on the left anterior forearm; a 1½ inch by 1 inch tattoo of a bird's head on the left posterior wrist." Writing about Ireland, Thomas Keneally pointed out that even after the worst injustices of the code had been repealed, the rural Irish continued to "practice the habits the Penal Code had created, the habits of powerlessness, masked feelings, apparent subjection, slyness, and dreams of vengeance." Brian Romero carried his powerlessness in the milligrams of morphine that ran through his veins, and his slyness on his skin, in the form of that dragon and the bat-swinging dog. When the coroner finished with him, he was shipped back to Cordova, to be buried in the cemetery overlooking the town and the juniper and piñon forests that surrounded it.

Allen Sandoval was one of the people at Brian's funeral. He wept during the memorial service at the mortuary, then took off his sunglasses and approached Brian's coffin. His mother watched him linger over Brian's body, touching his fingers to Brian's cheeks, hands, and chest. "I didn't know they were friends like that," she would tell me later. Brian was laid to rest in one of those traditional New Mexican burials where all the attendees grab shovels and pitch in to fill the grave, the sound of the blades cutting into the dirt filling the afternoon air in that tiny patch of a cemetery overlooking the town where they'd both spent days and nights drinking.

"I don't want to die like that," Allen told his mother afterward. Allen was a muscular man with a caterpillar mustache whom you could have mistaken for a barrio tough guy, but for his eyes, which were pools of loneliness and hurt. In his last days he seemed to be gripped by an overwhelming fear of death. He carved his initials in the tree in front of his mother's home, an act of parting, though his mother didn't realize it then. "I'm going to my friend's to see if he has some vodka." These were the last words his mother heard him speak, even though many weeks later, after Allen had been mourned and buried, she would be sitting in her small living room and hear him calling, "Mom!"

On the morning of June 3, Allen's sister found him collapsed on his back on the ground outside her house, his arms folded across his stomach. A day later it was Allen's turn to lie on the medical examiner's table in Albuquerque. The examiner made note of various "scattered minor trauma," the scars of those wounds his mother had cleaned and bandaged while he was alive. The objects on his person when he died were duly noted: "A white metal necklace; a black cord bracelet with a white metal pendant; a yellow metal religious medal; a religious card in a plastic cover with a white metal religious medal; an empty bottle of Visine eyedrops; and thirteen cents in change."

It was a cold winter morning when I visited the cemetery in Cordova. William Trujillo finally located Allen's grave, and then showed me the resting places of several other *carnales* who had died of drug or drink. "Everything was smooth here until heroin and cocaine showed up," William told me. "They bring it here to town and shoot up just to be high. Older people, younger people. You see them one day and the next . . ." There were sixteen votive candles on Allen's grave. I stood there for a few moments, watching the wind tug at the satin flowers, examining the dates on the crucifix, while William looked away, staring at the asphalt curve and the double yellow lines of the nearby state highway, where no cars drove past. Allen was buried next to Genaro Trujillo, who had died of an overdose on April 10. I had a copy of his autopsy too, and knew he had parted this world with the words "low rider *y mi vida loca*" tattooed on his upper right arm, a fifty-four-year-old man whose liver had shown signs of "chronic alcohol abuse."

William said he had known Genaro, Allen, and Brian and the three other men who had died of overdoses in the previous year. He had shot up heroin himself a few times. "It makes you happy for a little while." When we reached a little bare spot of dirt in the middle of the cemetery he said, "This is where I'm going to be buried."

I had been talking to William in the cemetery about the dead for perhaps half an hour when he suddenly looked up at me with his bleary, bloodshot eyes and grew silent. I was wearing a long black wool overcoat my wife had bought me, and I had dug my hands deep into the coat's oversized pockets. I could see snow on the Sangre de Cristos, and the December air was cutting a sharp chill into my bare scalp, so I pulled the coat's big black hood over my head too. William's eyes were locked on mine in a weird stare, as if he'd just woken up from his alcoholic haze and realized something incredibly frightening. "Maybe you're a god," he blurted out. No one before or since has looked at me with such terror or surprise. He inched away from me and screamed, "You're one of the angels!"

"No, I'm not," I said with a mean-spirited guffaw. I later recognized this as the laugh of my Guatemalan grandmothers, neither of whom had any time for fools or any sense of pretense. Of course I felt superior to William the alcoholic at that moment, though I would later wonder if I had any right to be. At any rate, my laughter broke the spell of me, the menacing aura of a hooded stranger in black who had come to talk about the dead. William seemed immensely relieved to find out I was not an angel come to whisk him away from the land of the living.

A few minutes later a funeral party showed up to bury an old woman, a resident of Cordova who had died, mercifully, of natural causes. William, by now a bit sobered up, walked toward them and shook hands with several people. After the priest had spoken and led the mourners in prayer, William joined the men in the final ritual, picking up a shovel, tossing dirt on the casket.

Buried underneath the concrete geometry of Los Angeles there is a town like Cordova, New Mexico, an eighteenth- and nineteenth-century village of adobe, tumbleweed, and wood. This other Los Angeles was swept away by the violence and muscle of American commerce and jurisprudence, which in turn arrived in Southern California courtesy of Stephen Kearny and his troops, after their march across the Sonora and Mojave deserts from New Mexico. The United States had reached the Pacific; the Manifest Destiny prophesied by its most hawkish leaders had been fulfilled.

During the years I worked in downtown Los Angeles, I spent many lunch hours wandering the Civic Center in search of traces of this settlement of the Mexican Republic and the Spanish Empire. In 1769 an expedition of priests and explorers had given the settlement its name—lohs-AHN-heh-lehs in the original Castillian pronunciation, before it became loss-ANN-juh-liss. Prior to its conquest by the United States Army, Los Angeles was an outpost of Spanish-speaking ruffians and farmers, its family life centered on a small dirt plaza with a chapel built between 1816 and 1822. The chapel, the only public building of Mexican Los Angeles that survives today, still functions as a barrio church, hosting mass baptisms of the babies of Latino immigrants on the weekends. About a hundred yards away stands the city's oldest remaining adobe building, built by the Avila family in 1818 and rescued from destruction in 1930 by the preservationist Christine Sterling, who is also responsible for saving the street around it, now the tourist attraction called Olvera Street. Just about everything else has been wiped out in the frenzy of urban renewal and skyscraper building that swept through Los Angeles in the twentieth century. I carried old maps and 150-year-old sketches of a village with fields and orchards stretching across open valleys and could sometimes place myself near the location where the artist stood, looking up to see the pastoral idyll of one epoch replaced with the squat, smoggy urbanscape of the next. All that walking and study yielded one insight: just as San Francisco had risen from a strategic bay, and New York City at the spot where the Hudson opened a path into a continent, early Los Angeles owed its location to a key element of physical geography: it was built on high ground at the junction of two rivers. For the first 150 years of its history, until its center was rendered irrelevant and invisible by the habits of automobile commuters, Los Angeles remained anchored to that piece of real estate, climbing up the hills around the spot where the Arroyo Seco flows into the Los Angeles River, just like San Francisco and its bay.

On a small peak above the river junction, the United States of America built its first military garrison in Southern California in 1847. Visiting that peak today you find the Fort Moore Pioneer Memorial, perhaps the largest monument in California to the American conquest of Mexico's northern frontier. I liked to walk the four blocks or so from my office and read the plaques and look at the bas-relief sculptures of covered wagons and American soldiers and tributes to "the troops who helped to win the Southwest." Like the tourists who visit the beaches at Normandy, or the meadows of Gettysburg, I thought I might glean some truth about the wide sweep of history by merely standing there, by imagining what the air tasted like on those final days of the reign of the Californios who built *ran-chos* and planted vineyards, drawing water from the nearby river, which was now channeled into a massive concrete storm drain.

Every time I visited, I had the place completely to myself. In a metropolis famous for its historical amnesia, the Fort Moore Memorial was an especially lonely monument. But it was not always that way. In the *Los Angeles Times* archives I found newspaper clippings of its dedication on July 4, 1958. The assembled dignitaries watched 7,000 gallons of water a minute pour over the monument's four-story-high artificial waterfall. The Stars and Stripes was raised and the monument's bas-relief sculptures were unveiled, tributes to the New York dragoons of the U.S. Army and the Mormon battalion of Council Bluffs, Iowa, who crossed deserts and mountain ranges to extend "the frontiers of our country to include the promise of this land."

Mexicans and Mexican-Americans were a minority group in 1958, which was more or less the apex of Los Angeles's history as a "white" or "Anglo" majority city. As the workers poured the cement for the Fort Moore Monument, and laid the tiles of its fountains, the idea of a barrio—the Spanish equivalent of "ghetto," a word with which it shares many connotations—was well established in the city's Latino consciousness. My mother- and father-in-law grew up nearby in the Mexican-American barrios and were young adults when the monument was dedicated; they'd walk over from the old Alpine Street barrio and picnic next to the wet breeze of its waterfall. Today, fifteen minutes walking or less in any direction from the Fort Moore Memorial still takes you into some of the city's oldest ethnic neighborhoods: Chinatown, to the north; Little Tokyo to the east; the Central American neighborhoods to the west of downtown; and to the south, the Mexican shopping district that occupies the old storefronts and theaters of Broadway.

The city's first barrio was Sonoratown, at the base of Fort Moore. A thirty-minute walk from the fort to the southwest, over the hill now home to the new, Gehry-designed Disney Concert Hall, and past the towers of the city's Financial District, brings you to a shallow valley perhaps half a mile wide, known today to city planners as Temple Beaudry, and to the people who lived there as Diamond Street. During my walks through the center of the city, I was drawn to the place by the scene of devastation it presented: a vast open space of vacant, rubble-strewn lots, roughly equal in size to the space left in Manhattan by the destruction of the World Trade Center. There was something haunting in the way the place was returning to a kind of natural state, to the knee-high grass swaying in the wind. About two or three homes still stood on a gently sloping land where perhaps dozens had stood before. Mostly, there was the odd, sickly palm tree, the remains of concrete driveways and stairs. The ground upon which the Diamond Street barrio rested had become valuable in the real estate boom of the 1980s, and developers had bought up all the parcels, evicting the residents and tearing down their homes, clearing the land for skyscrapers, which, it turned out, were never built.

Once cadres of young men had tattooed DIAMOND STREET into their skin and fought street battles with the police and with other young men who had different names tattooed into their skins. I tracked down some of the old residents, including a burly former member of the Diamond Street gang called Vicente Rodríguez who told me nostalgia-tinged stories of fights with the police. One year, his aunt Betty Plasencia organized the Diamond Street gang members into a football team that played a group of Los Angeles police officers. She became the barrio's leader-mother figure and lobbied the school district to put an elementary school there, and today the campus posthumously carries her name. When she died, four hundred schoolchildren gathered outside her home to mourn her. Some years later, when word came that the Plasencia home would soon be demolished, the remaining young men of Diamond Street set fire to it instead, a pyre that set an angry column of smoke spiraling high into the smoggy air.

Vicente said the little valley of Diamond Street would always be his *tierra*. When he lived there he awoke each morning to a sun rising over the tenements and old Victorians on Bunker Hill, where Raymond Chandler had set many of his mysteries, and then in the shadow of the Harbor Freeway when that chunk of noir L.A. was itself wiped out. Vicente's youth in the 1970s coincided with the beginning of Diamond Street's end. He remembered an encounter with strangers on the afternoon of the Academy Awards, an incident which, in retrospect, announced the coming end of his barrio. A limousine headed to the Oscar ceremonies broke down in front of his home, less than a mile from the Dorothy Chandler Pavilion and its awaiting red carpet. "These people came out, all dressed up and fancy, and they looked at us like we were going to hurt them or something." Years later, their stares still hurt him, because they spoke to the breadth of the city's social barriers, and to his barrio's status as a place feared and misunderstood by outsiders. In the end, wealthy outsiders like the people in that limousine had imagined the Diamond Street barrio out of existence.

The Diamond Street barrio is gone forever. But so, too, is the world that gave Los Angeles its memorial to conquest at Fort Moore. Every Fourth of July, a small band of local Mormons dress up as pioneers to reenact with a "musket salute" the 1847 raising of the flag by the U.S. Army. Perhaps they are the last people in California to really care about what the monument declares in its plaque and bas-relief sculptures: "Water and power have made our arid land flourish. . . . May we keep faith with the pioneers who brought us these gifts." I stumbled upon them one Fourth on Olvera Street, while enjoying a holiday lunch with my family at one of my favorite Mexican restaurants in the city, La Golondrina Café. The restaurant resides in the city's oldest brick building and I like to bring out-of-town visitors there to show them that Los Angeles does indeed have places tinged with history. The "pioneers" were wearing bonnets and straw hats and ill-fitting costumes that made them look like workers evicted from a Wild West theme park.

Every other day of the year, the Fort Moore Memorial is a forgotten relic. Los Angeles is a Latino city now, and it's hard to gather a crowd to celebrate the defeat of the Mexican army. The waterfall and the fountains at the base of the monument were turned off during the drought of 1977, when we Angelenos were asked to put bricks in the backs of our toilets and to stop watering our lawns. The drought ended but the memorial's waterfall and fountains have remained dry. A generation later, the tiles are falling from the waterfall's parched face, one by one adding up to a pond of broken tiles dissolving into the dust and soot that fills the old fountains. The floodlights that once illuminated the waterfall are broken. There is a flagpole, the same one from which the Stars and Stripes was raised at the dedication in 1958, but I never saw a flag flying there. There are signs promising punishments for loiterers, and on some visits I found blankets and bottles left by homeless men and lumps of soiled clothing. One night in 1986, a serial killer deposited one of his victims at the memorial, a dark and abandoned place where there was little danger of stumbling into witnesses.

Today it could be argued that all the barrios in Los Angeles are either dead or dying. Because the whole city is a barrio, swept up by Latinization, there can be no barrio as such, no segregated, insular place to which people with Spanish surnames are relegated. In the 2000 census of the City of Los Angeles, there were more people in the Hispanic/Latino category (47 percent) than any other. The 1.7 million Latinos in the city were dispersed in large numbers throughout all but its wealthiest neighborhoods. A similar transformation had taken place in most of the other cities and towns wrested from Mexico in nineteenth-century wars, including San Antonio, Texas (56 percent Hispanic/Latino), Tucson, Arizona (36 percent), and San Jose, California (37 percent). In certain nativist circles of the Southwest, this re-Latinization is part of an elaborate conspiracy to rejoin the old Southwest to Mexico, what they call, using a Spanish word, *la reconquista*, "the reconquest." All of the metropolises located within the boundaries of the territory ceded by Mexico to the United States in the Treaty of Guadalupe Hidalgo have substantial Latino populations, even those that were not yet cities or even settlements during the Mexican period—including Salt Lake City (19 percent), Phoenix (34 percent), and Dallas (35 percent).

Most of the major cities of the Southwest have substantial numbers of elected Latino representatives. Every year, the number of city council members, city managers, county supervisors, city clerks, and other government functionaries attending the convention of the National Association of Latino Elected and Appointed Officials grows. At the 2000 convention in Denver, while perusing the buffet spread at the Coors Field baseball park lounge, I met a tall and somewhat awkward young woman in black pants, an oversized sports coat, and oval-shaped glasses whose name tag identified her as CINDY

MONTAÑEZ, SAN FERNANDO CITY COUNCIL MEMBER. Had it not been for the name tag, I might have mistaken her for one of the many college interns and low-level staffers floating about the convention. She said she was trying to get a Latino café/cultural center to open up near the civic center of San Fernando, a Los Angeles suburb located within the valley of the same name. She was imagining a place modeled on the trendy Espresso Mi Cultura, a café on Hollywood Boulevard—two blocks from my alma mater, Grant Elementary School—which regularly hosted Central American and Mexican poets reading bilingual verses.

"You know, I went to this place, and it was jam-packed with Latinos listening to poetry and drinking cappuccinos," she said. "So I thought, Why not put one in San Fernando? There's a lot of young Latinos in my city who need a place like that. Why should we have to drive all the way to Hollywood to find one?"

"Sounds like a great idea," I said, trying to suppress the natural pessimism with which I greet just about anything said by an elected official, even a young hipster like Cindy. I told her I had covered the San Fernando City Council a decade earlier, when it was made up mostly of old white men from the Rotary Club set and hardly anything of interest happened there. "I could have used an espresso to get me through those meetings without falling asleep." I had written a brief history of San Fernando at about the same time, talking to old-timers about the town's segregated past, when the railroad tracks divided the city into a white north side and a Mexican south side. I had even gone to the Los Angeles County Registrar Recorder's office to look up the old restrictive covenants that had once kept this segregation in place, and found one written by manual typewriter, prohibiting the sale of a home "to persons of Mexican, Chinese, Japanese and Ethiopian descent."

"The city's changed a lot," Cindy said, stating the obvious. "And so has the city council." Her very presence at the convention was evidence of that. Montañez didn't have the pedigree of most city council members I'd met over the years, most of whom were longtime homeowners and chamber-of-commerce types who approached city governance with the penny-pinching outlook of small businessmen surveying the world from behind their front counters and cash registers. The most noteworthy item on her résumé when she ran for office was joining a fourteen-day hunger strike as an undergraduate at UCLA to force the university to create a Chicano Studies center. She talked with the intensity of someone devoted to a holy cause, and with the earnestness of a small-town official, which was what she had become at the age of twenty-four, defeating a three-term councilman named Doude Wysbeek, one of the council members who had been responsible for my bouts of somnolence. She was unemployed and still working on her degree when she ran for office, making most of her flyers and campaign materials herself. Her campaign kickoff was an all-you-can-eat *barbacoa* fund-raiser.

Cindy Montañez was ambitious for herself and for her city, which was probably why she talked to me forty minutes after finding out I was a reporter for her hometown newspaper. As she looked into my brown eyes, no doubt, my irises became printing presses spinning with headlines: MONTAÑEZ MOVES SAN FERNANDO FORWARD. Such stories would soon be written, though by other people and not me. In the coming years, Cindy would bring big plans to a city that hadn't dreamt big in a long time. Her fellow council members would eventually appoint her mayor and her café would get built, along with a yoga studio, a Mexican restaurant, and a barbershop at an urban renewal project called Library Plaza. Then at the age of twenty-eight, she would head off to Sacramento after winning election to the State Assembly. Some months later, the City of San Fernando would break ground for one of the projects approved during her term as mayor: the 23,000-square-foot César Chávez Memorial.

At the center of the monument stands a statue of the late farmworker leader and Chicano icon holding a dove. The bronze César Chávez looks out at a line of bronze farmworkers, the one closest to him hunched over and toiling in a field with the infamous, backbreaking "short hoe." In front of this farmworker, another one squats up, and the one before him rises higher still, each one standing a bit straighter than the next until they have become a line of bronze marchers carrying bronze flags and picket signs. Behind César is a fountain in the shape of the stylized eagle on the UFW flag, an enduring symbol of Latino pride that itself is an echo of the eagle on the Mexican flag. The memorial fountain to California's Mexican-American identity in San Fernando is much smaller in size than the memorial waterfall to American conquest in downtown Los Angeles, just six feet tall, against the forty feet of Fort Moore. Unlike that other fountain, however, the César Chávez Memorial has water. Running down the wings of the eagle, the water flows into a pool, where it is prudently recycled, an idea that hadn't occurred to anyone back in 1958.

One half-block north from the Fort Moore Memorial runs a street known since 1995 as César Chávez Avenue, or, on some traffic signs, as Avenida César Chávez. The former Brooklyn Avenue, a major thoroughfare linking several Eastside barrios, was renamed thanks to Gloria Molina, a barrio activist who had become first a Los Angeles city councilwoman, and then a Los Angeles county supervisor, the first Latino to serve on that body since the days of the *californios*. Renaming streets, schools, and libraries in honor of Chávez became a municipal fad throughout the old lands of the Treaty of Guadalupe Hidalgo at the cusp of the twenty-first century, just as naming public places and institutions for George Washington, Abraham Lincoln, or John F. Kennedy had been in earlier American epochs. If Washington was "the father of his country," Chávez is the father of an identity. Thus there are Chávez Elementary schools in San Francisco, Davis, Corona, and Coachella in California, and also in far-flung cities like Madison, Wisconsin, and Hyattsville, Maryland, and also in Pharr, Texas, where I had once jumped on the bus to Alabama. There is a César Chávez Street in Austin, Texas, and César Chávez Parkway in San Diego. Elsewhere, the efforts to honor César Chávez had mixed results. In San Antonio, a group of Chicano activists wanted to rename San Antonio International Airport in Chávez's honor but met with the resistance of city leaders, who delicately pointed out that Chávez had fought nearly all of his battles in California and had never been associated with Texas.

At the turn of the century, San Antonio was the most Latino major city in the United States, which was why it made sense to some people to name the airport for the country's leading Mexican-American icon. San Antonio had already become the kind of place where you could turn on the radio and hear not just a dozen Spanish-language stations but also odd phrasings of the bilingual deejays who constantly swung back and forth on some stations between Spanish and English, even while doing the traffic reports: "There's an accident on Nogalitos, *mucho cuidado por allí*." I wanted to take in the sounds and imagery of what will one day be the first American metropolis to pass wholly into Mexicanness, so I went there too, to eat enchiladas and anything else spicy from the self-proclaimed "birthplace of the fajita," to see the new public library and other buildings designed by Mexican architects, and to meet with the writers, artists, and thinkers who had created in that city a Latino salon of artistic expression and activism.

San Antonio is just a couple of hours' drive up Interstate 35 from the Mexican border at Nuevo Laredo. Its old commericial center rises around the downtown "riverwalk," where the turtle-shell green waters of the San Antonio River are channeled into a tame little canal resembling the one that meanders through the Pirates of the Caribbean ride at Disneyland; you can go there and partake of good Mexican cuisine and tequila shots at a riverside table and watch the tourists glide by on gondolas. Beyond the city center there are the old wood-frame houses and brick storefronts of twentieth-century San Antonio, where I visited two of the leading lights of the city's vibrant *arte* scene, the painters Rolando Briseño and Ángel Rodríguez-Díaz, who had arrived in south Texas by way of New York City, where they had both been trained as oil painters and then lived for several years, until they'd been driven away by the coldness of the city, the increasing abstract and emotionless art scene, and the high rents. Rodríguez-Díaz painted the human form, which a lot of people in New York considered passé, and he infused his work with subtle political themes. His paintings cried out for a Latino audience. "Out of all the places in the United States, this is where I feel most comfortable," Ángel told me. Rolando wanted to live where he had been born and raised, closer to the food that had become a central theme of his work. "There's more Mexican-Americans in Los Angeles, but they don't have the power we have here." In San Antonio, they found an old grocery store in the city's Beacon Hill district and converted it into a studio and home, which was filled with their paintings and sculptures on the day I visited, their explorations and experimentations with a mélange of artifacts from Mexican and Puerto Rican culture.

There was Briseño's sculpture of the University of Texas tower in Austin—the same one where Charles Whitman went on a shooting spree in 1966—built entirely from tortilla chips with a chile on top. (Later, he would build mini World Trade Center towers from tortilla chips too.) The tortilla tower faced an easel with his five-foot-tall *Birth of the Tuna*, a painting of a dish covered with an arrangement of flowering nopal cacti, a Mexican delicacy and one of my wife's favorite dishes. Ángel guided me across the studio to his self-portrait, *Chupacabras*. This was another Chupacabras entirely from the one Ben Reed became in Rupert, Idaho: I saw the same soft-spoken, goateed artist who was standing before me rendered as a half-naked man climbing to the top of a cliff, blood dripping from his mouth while black helicopters circled in the background. "This is an allegory about Puerto Rico," Ángel told me. "It's about how these remnants of the local culture survive against the pressures of modernization and assimilation."

The writer Sandra Cisneros stared at me from one of Ángel's unfinished portraits, leaning back in a chair while an image of the Virgin of Guadalupe began to take shape over her shoulder. A native of Chicago, Cisneros was one in a long line of Latino intellectuals to have moved to San Antonio, where she had found the voice in her story collection *Woman Hollering Creek*, tales about being Mexican-American in a border-land where legends and dreams are translated back and forth between languages—thus the title story, taken from a traffic-sign renaming of what locals call La Llorona Creek, after a mythical weeping woman who steals naughty children. Another of Ángel's portraits of Cisneros was in the Smithsonian American Art Museum. *The Protagonist of an Endless Story* depicted Cisneros against a sky the color of burning embers, wearing a strapless black dress that wrapped around her lean frame like a piece of embroidered armor.

In real life Sandra Cisneros had recently gone to battle against the city over the color she had painted her house in the historic King William district. "Periwinkle purple," it turned out, was a violation of municipal code 35-7200, which stipulates that homes should be painted only those colors found in the neighborhood during its German-American heyday. The city ordered her to tone it down—suggesting various bland earth tones—but of course she refused. "Color is a language, and either you are bilingual or not," Cisneros told my colleague Jesse Katz, who had traveled to San Antonio a couple of years earlier to write about the controversy. "Either you understand the color, or the color needs translation. . . . Colors that I consider Mexican and beautiful, they consider Mexican and garish. . . . This is really a story about the absence of color, about the absence of Mexican people when you talk about history in this part of the world." She turned the City Hall hearing on her purple house into a skit on history and culture, arriving in a ruby dress and with a coterie of supporters dressed in purple. "This is not Mexico, but it's not the U.S. either," she wrote in a statement she submitted to the city. "It's a netherworld of neither and both, a spiral, a helix, one contained inside the belly of the other."

The battle of the purple house—which ended up staying purple—was only one of several over Latinoness and public space in San Antonio. At about the same time, Rolando, Ángel, and their intellec-tual and activist friends in San Antonio's Grupo de Cien (the Group of One Hundred) stopped a plan to place a statue of Davy Crockett and other defenders of the Alamo at the site of that famous battle of the Texas War of Independence. Rolando had grown up Mexican-American in San Antonio, which meant having the Alamo story-myth crammed down his throat, those images of evil Mexican soldiers in tin hats pouring over the walls to murder the brave Texan defenders in floppy pioneer felt hats. Since Briseño was then on the city's Historic and Design Review Commission, his objection carried some weight, and more weight still when El Grupo de Cien showed up at a public meeting of the commission to call the statue proposal "insensitive" and "culturally inappropriate."

"We're very militant here," Rolando told me. "There's still a Southern politeness in this city. You're not supposed to make waves." Anglos still controlled the economy of the city, including funding for the arts. He felt he had been blacklisted from the arts community for taking his stand against Davy Crockett. "I come from a colonized country," Ángel piped in. "I recognize one when I see it." There was no more segregated barrio in San Antonio. You could be brown-skinned and live on the northside now, as Rolando and Ángel did, but the city was still divided. "They let the purple house go because by the time they got around to seeing it, the color had faded," Rolando said. "One day they'll wake up and say, 'Yes, this is a Mexican-American city; yes, it's a border town.' When that day comes, then San Antonio will reach its true identity."

In the early 1990s, the city fathers took one especially brave step to embrace a Latin-American identity in the city's public space. They hired a Mexican architect, Ricardo Legorreta, to design the city's new library. Legorreta gave them a modernist cube, then painted it a blindingly bright red that readers of the *San Antonio Express-News* described, variously, as "truly repulsive red," "bleeding heart liberal red," and "enchilada red." To assorted Anglo commentators and residents, the look of the library, Sandra Cisneros's house, and other buildings that followed was a bit unsettling: it seemed "the Mexicans" were intent on splashing paint all over the city, colors previously confined to the city's segregated barrio. "Spanish culture is beautiful, but sometimes you can go overboard," one council member would say. "These people came to San Antonio to escape the Mexican influence."

I drove by the public library to see what was so shocking and subversive about it. Perhaps the hue had faded in the sun by the time I saw it, a half decade after its inauguration. The color, more of a brick now, I did not find especially shocking, as much as the quantity of it, the idea that a wall eight stories tall could be painted any color besides white or tan. Inside the library the walls were lemon and plum. These were the hues people painted their houses in poor barrios from Watts in Los Angeles to La Boca in Buenos Aires: it was a relatively inexpensive way to declare your domicile's individuality. That bright palette has infected the tastes of middle-class Latinos like my wife and my sister-in-law, who make it a ritual to cover the interior white walls of every house they inhabit with mango, peach, or adobe brown paint. Once I asked my wife to decipher the deeper philosophical meanings underneath these colors and why so many people we knew embraced them. "To me, it's about taking a risk, doing something brave and not being afraid to say who you are," she said. "Once you start painting, you're committed. You've got this bright color and you have to live with it." As with tattooing the Virgin of Guadalupe on your forearm, or a picture of your favorite low rider and the words *la vida loca* on your chest, Latinos went for bright hues as a statement of boldness. Legorreta had taken a similar risk, and now all of San Antonio—American, Mexican, Chicano, and so on—had to live with his daring every time they drove through downtown.

Rodríguez-Díaz fought another, much smaller and quieter color battle after winning the commission to put up a mural at a new municipal building. Inside the under-construction Business Service Center—a one-stop shop to apply for things like building permits—he was to create a 54-foot mural called *Birth of a City* and also work with the architects to create "design elements" like the color of the tiles of the floor in the lobby, which he planned to make aqua, in honor of the nearby San Antonio River, even though it has probably never been that hue. For the walls of the main lobby Ángel planned green and yellow, along with some broad splashes of indigo. Word of the plans reached a "financier" of the building. Secondhand, Ángel was told the financier was concerned Ángel would turn the Business Service Center "into another library," à la Legorreta. The financier worried that the businessmen who would file through the building would flee before the rainbow-colored walls, though he was eventually persuaded Ángel would refrain from excess, that he would not transform the Business Service Center into a kitsch garden of pink and green pastels, like some gaudy Mexican *sarape*.

When the building was finished, Rodríguez-Díaz took a look around. Beyond his indigo-and-aqua lobby—in the offices where the clerks, secretaries, and bureaucrats would set up shop, and which he had had no hand in decorating—he found a snowstorm of white: white walls and white cubicles, white chairs and white desks. "I saw all that white and then I understood. They were absolutely terrified of color." For Ángel, the new building was an apt metaphor for modern San Antonio. The public space was splashed with his chartreuse and turquoise Latin shadings, but the inner workings of the building, the conference rooms and executive offices where decisions would be made and plans approved, remained completely white. Colorless.

Chapter Eight

THE OLD MEN AND THE BOY
Los balseros

Miami, Florida

The old men of Little Havana have sun-blotched arms, and teeth stained the color of tobacco and espresso, because in Miami they have been unable to escape either the climate or the habits of their youth. Cuba is just over there, on the other side of the wet breeze that ruffles the leaves of the tamarind trees. The ocean waves that lap on the sands of Biscayne Bay are the same ones that lap at the rocks on the Malecón, the seaside promenade where their thinner, younger selves walked arm in arm with sweethearts. Today they have grandchildren, businesses, multiple mortgages, and electric wires running to their aortas, but in their minds they are still those same, spry young men who zipped about La Habana at the helm of V8 chariots from one conspiratorial meeting to the next, looking over their shoulders to see if they could spot the dictator's spy in the crowd. Today they drive from Coral Gables culs-de-sac to storefronts on Calle Ocho, in fuel-efficient Hondas with air bags and maybe a car seat for the granddaughter in the back, to new rounds of conspiratorial meetings in restaurants and cafés, not bothering to look over their shoulders because there are no spies at the next table, only suburban mothers who have come to try a bit of exotic Cuban fare, tempting their toddlers with spoonfuls of white rice and black beans. Talk to one of the old men alone and they might confess to you that they are tired, that Fidel Castro the Communist dictator will outlive all the exiles, who are slowly filling up the best plots at Miami's exclusive Woodland Park Cemetery. But their public face and voice is unyielding: They will return to the old country one day, the dictator will be sent fleeing, it is an inevitability.

The central irony of their lives is this: once they rose up in rebellion against a tyrant, a former sergeant named Fulgencio Batista who became one of the Caribbean's most venal banana republic dictators. The sergeant-president fell, quicker than they might have imagined, on a New Year's Eve of fireworks and champagne toasts and celebratory bursts of gunfire. Then a new dictator emerged, a fellow revolutionary and a man of their own generation, poised to rule during the span of their entire lifetimes. They rebelled against the rebel. Eventually they would become senior-citizen counterrevolutionaries. When I met and spoke with them, in offices and homes furnished with plaques and awards and black-and-white photographs in which they are standing inside Cuba, they filled their conversations with the names of battles that they had fought and mountain ranges they had marched through as young men: Escambray, La Sierra Maestra, Bahía de Cochinos.

One group of old men operated a radio station to transmit their voices to the small and isolated (some would say mythical) band of followers inside Cuba itself, including the speeches-cum-sermons of Dr. Diego Medina, "vice secretary general" of the guerrilla group Alpha 66. Perhaps his listeners on the island imagined Medina inside an expansive studio, at the base of a large radio tower looming over the Caribbean. In fact, he broadcasted from a cramped, three-foot-wide storage area lined with egg cartons, a sort of hut at the back of a Little Havana storefront. He was a doctor who never became rich, his friends said, because he spent too much time at the radio station and in Alpha 66 meetings. Alpha 66 had actually "invaded" Communist Cuba in the 1960s, a series of botched landings that ended with all its troops either killed or captured. In Miami Dr. Medina had spent a good deal of time arguing with the American FCC, which was responsible for the humiliation that temporarily took Radio Alpha 66 off the air once; U.S. marshals descended on the studio with weapons and sealed the doors because neither Dr. Medina nor anyone else at the station had bothered to get a license.

The closet studio lined with egg cartons was also the scene of his final "battle," at his post before the microphone. Every evening at six or seven, after a day of seeing patients, he came to the studio to record his show. On this last day he began to falter and after a few minutes turned to his longtime collaborator Andrés Nazario Sargén and said, "Look, I need you to close the show for me. I don't feel well." He made it to his car, turning down Sargén's offer of a ride home. He labored to keep his car from drifting onto the shoulder, but made it home, where he died a short while later, thirty-eight years of struggle ending with a last bowl of soup on the table before him and with Fidel Castro still lording it over Cuba.

They buried Dr. Medina in Woodland Park Cemetery, next to Jorge Mas Canosa, who was supposed to be the first president of a "free Cuba," but who instead died of cancer at the relatively young age of fifty-eight, after three decades of leading the struggle against Castro with a Washington lobbying campaign par excellence. All the old, dead anti-Castro fighters are buried at Woodland Park. When I went to see Mas Canosa and Medina's graves there, I found freshly mowed green lawns circling a two-story mausoleum, marble obelisks, a monument to the dead Cuban soldiers of the Bay of Pigs invasion, and graveside flower arrangements of Cuban flags made of white and red carnations, with the flag's stripes made from white carnations dyed blue. It was a lush, affluent place to lie for eternity, another world from that last, rustic cemetery I'd visited in Cordova, New Mexico. Up in the mausoleum I found the resting places of exiled ministers and presidents, men like Carlos Prío Socarrás, president of the Republic of Cuba from 1948 to 1952, who died in Miami in 1977. Standing in that cemetery was like being in the backstage closet of the defunct theater of twentieth-century Latin American history, a place where all the costumes and props of farcical coups and bloody tragedies had been tossed away and forgotten. Jorge Mas Canosa's burial here was supposed to be a temporary arrangement, his followers said, "until he can be reburied in a free Cuba." At that moment, the only grave marker was a picture of the living leader in a heroic pose against a backdrop of windswept palm trees. His gaze drifted off to the right, as if he were making a conscious effort not to look at the marble building the size of a van rising directly in front of him about one hundred feet away, which contained the crypt of one of the cemetery's more infamous residents.

ANASTASIO SOMOZA DEBAYLE

PRESIDENTE DE NICARAGUA

5 DE DICIEMBRE 1925

11 DE SEPTIEMBRE 1980

AMO A SU PUEBLO

The dictator of Nicaragua, deposed by the Sandinista revolution in 1979, assassinated by rebels in Paraguay a year later, "loved his people." Nevertheless, at least one of his former subjects had come to take revenge against him in death, shattering one of the windows to his mausoleum, leaving a splash of glass shards that the groundskeepers hadn't noticed or cleaned up yet. Whoever had come to vandalize Somoza's resting place had done so relatively recently, coming here with a rock to avenge wrongs committed a generation earlier. He or she had hung on to that anger for some twenty years, much as the Cuban exiles did who went to bed each night for forty years with visions of their nemesis, a bearded torturer who would not die, no matter how much they willed it.

M ax Lesnik was my entrée into the world of the Miami exiles. He greeted me from behind his desk inside an office located next to a beauty parlor in a Little Havana mini-mall, a man with a big smile and a few wavy gray hairs dancing about his bald pate. "So I'm doing a story about the exile community," I said, "about the generation of 1960 and 1961 and how people are getting older. . . ." Before I could finish the question he launched into a torrent of words and history and names, all in rapid-fire, mushy Cuban Spanish, a dialect that requires the listener to ingest a Cuban espresso or two before it can be fully understood. More words and names and arguments came from the half-dozen or so old men who happened to be sitting in his office that morning, men like Manuel Martínez Barriegos, who had been director of tourism for the province of La Habana until "Castro betrayed our revolutionary principles and I stood against him, because what we wanted was a real revolution, a nationalist one, not a Communist revolution."

Most of the men there were fiercely anti-Castro, and to none did I mention my youthful admiration for Che Guevara, who was the "Supreme Prosecutor" of revolutionary Cuba and oversaw the execution of fifty-five counterrevolutionaries. Max's friends would have considered me a leftist radical, which was what they branded Max himself, since he had committed the almost unpardonable sin of sitting down and meeting with *el barbudo* (the bearded one) a few years back. Just as bad, Max routinely traveled to Cuba, seeing how his old Havana haunts had aged and how Cuba was being shaped by new generations of Castro-era babies educated in Communist-run schools. Max did not maintain the chastity of the other exiles, for whom strict adherence to the boycott on travel to Communist Cuba and all business dealings there was an article of faith. "In political matters, we're enemies," Barriegos said. "But on a personal level, we tolerate each other." Now that their exile was coming to an end—how many more years could they live waiting for Castro to die, really?—they were starting to forgive old enmities. Or maybe they remained friends because, with so many lingering resentments in their lives, they didn't have room for new ones. They gathered around in Max's office for an informal *tertulia,* or meeting of the minds, which I had unknowingly barged in on, though no one seemed to mind. They served me a little cup of Cuban espresso and blew cigar smoke across the room and talked in the high-volume half-shouts both Cubans and old men are known for.

"We get people from the right, the center, the left, those who defend Castro's government, those who criticize him, people in favor of every position," Max explained.

"I am more Cuban than you are!" someone said on the other side of the room, a statement outrageous enough to cause everyone else to turn silent for a second, breaking Max's train of thought.

"A dictator for forty years!" Barriegos piped in, apropos of nothing. "A dictatorship, no elections, *ni un carajo!* There are no laws. A country with no laws!"

Two decades earlier the Miami offices of Max's magazine *Réplica* had been bombed by men who shared the opinions of some of the friends in this room. Back then, the city was full of CIA agents and wanna-be counterrevolutionary guerrillas who trained in the Everglades on the weekends. The presence of a left-of-center exile like

Max among them was too much to bear, so they tried to terrorize him with bombs. Of course that only made Max more stubborn. In the long run those bombings and other acts of violent intimidation turned out to be little more than a colorful sideshow to the bigger story of the rise of Cuban Miami. Cubanos became the most affluent and influential group in the multinational Latin American diaspora in the United States. Rather than armed revolutionaries or bomb throwers, most became fervent aficionados of that quintessential American pastime called making money. They came to Miami with engineering and medical degrees, with a merchant's nose for lucrative possibilities and untapped markets, and remade Miami into the capital of the Caribbean and South and Central American elites. "They came here and started working as gardeners and became millionaires," the exile novelist Celedonio González told me. "Now we have five thousand Cuban millionaires in south Florida alone." Cubans led a charge followed by wealthy Peruvians, Guatemalans, Brazilians, and Argentines, and then by tens and hundreds of thousands of the less-rich people of those and many other Latin American countries, who came to work in their restaurants and their gardens.

Once Little Havana had been an only child, but then her siblings Little Managua and Little Buenos Aires were born and Little Colombia too. Spanish-speaking Miami became a family of brash, self-confident, and extroverted expatriates. In Los Angeles, Spanish is the language of working people, appropriate for transactions at neighborhood *tiendas*, or for *cotorreo*, bantering with family and friends; but *mexicanos* and *centroamericanos* leave their mother tongues at home when they go to the parts of the city where real money is made and spent. In Miami, by contrast, Spanish is the language of the elite; if you look the slightest bit Latino the maître d' at a South Beach restaurant will probably address you with a *buenas tardes*, *caballero*, as will the clerk at the gift shop at a five-star hotel, or the woman behind the counter at a Miami International newsstand, who rattled off the price of my copies of the *New York Times* and the *Miami Herald* as *un dólar cincuenta*. In south Florida, Spanish is the language of commerce, culture, and thought. Latin American academics and bankers and diplomats routinely gather here for conferences, to sign treaties with the Americans and with each other. Fortunes made in São Paulo, Lima, and Asunción find their way to south Florida banks; when I moved to Buenos Aires, I sent my first rent check to a Chase branch in Miami, which was where my French-Argentine landlord squirreled away his money to avoid the prying eyes of the Argentine taxman. One morning, I took the elevator down from my hotel room on Biscayne Bay and found several hundred Peruvians in the lobby, part of a line snaking through the front door and out into the parking garage.

"What's all this about?" I asked the concierge.

"They're voting," he said.

"It's Election Day? On a Sunday?"

"In Peru it is, I guess," the concierge said. "They're all Peruvians. The consulate set up a ballot box in one of the conference rooms back there." In most Latin American countries, voting is mandatory, even when you live abroad. When Luiz Inácio Lula da Silva made history by becoming the first laborer ever elected president of Brazil, hundreds of Brazilians voted for him in Miami too, as did Argentines in their election, and citizens of many countries more.

Cubans laid the foundation for this mini–Latin American republic, the nineteenth-century "Liberator" Simón Bolívar's vision of a union of Spanish-speaking nations come true in the neon- and palm-lined boulevards of Miami-Dade County. It had all happened by accident, thanks to the humiliating disgrace inflicted upon a relatively small group of people on that island just across the water.

. . .

When your younger self is attached to a distant, long-unseen place, you can dream of going back and delude yourself that when you set foot there you will recapture a bit of your lost innocence. If you cannot return, you will never have the sensation of standing on the stage of your youthful glory and seeing how small that place really is, or how time has colored it, or rearranged the furniture of your reminiscences. You cannot see how the café you cherished has disappeared, or how the sidewalks of your old neighborhood have crumbled and been patched and repatched, how new people with unfamiliar faces have moved into homes where your friends once lived. The novelist Celedonio González lives with this kind of idealized memory of the country he left behind. Havana was a jewel in the turquoise sea, home to upright men who walked down orderly streets. He cannot imagine that the new generations arriving in Miami from the island really belong to that species of people known as *cubanos*. "Even the way they speak is different," he told me in his Miami condominium, inside a subdivision of orderly, identical homes. "It's another country. I look at them and I don't know who they are or where they came from. I will never go back to Cuba because Cuba doesn't exist anymore. When we die, there won't be any Cubans left." He'd written six novels in exile, all in Spanish and all about the Cuba and Cubans of his generation. He was a Miami incarnation of the novelist Isaac Bashevis Singer, who said he wrote novels in Yiddish, a dying language, because he believed in ghosts and resurrection and "millions of Yiddish-speaking corpses will rise from their graves one day and their first question will be 'Is there any new Yiddish book to read?'" The Cuba of Celedonio González was with each passing day a republic more of corpses than of living men. His acceptance of this made him one of the few anti-Castro exiles I spoke to who was willing to throw in the towel. "An exile that lasts forty years isn't an exile anymore, it's a failure. We're great at pretending. It's been twenty years since I went to a political meeting. They invite me, but I play deaf."

The battles Celedonio González was no longer willing to fight still raged most fiercely and defiantly in the imagination of Andrés Nazario Sargén, the leader of Alpha 66. He was seventy-eight years old when I met him in a Little Havana storefront on the Plaza de la Cubanidad (Cubanness Square), a patch of concrete where men played dominoes on the sidewalk and gazed suspiciously at any passerby under fifty. The guerrilla leader was a diminutive, dark-skinned man whose features suggested some East Indian heritage. Nazario Sargén had been in the mountains in the struggle against Batista: he gave me a Xerox copy of a picture of himself with Fidel Castro when they were both still guerrillas, and both *barbudos*, the tiny Nazario Sargén seemingly about to fall forward under the weight of his own theatrically long beard. We spoke in a bare room that had been arranged with chairs to double as both an office and a meeting hall, where the walls were lined with eighteen pictures of men circa 1970, arranged in rows like the page of a high-school yearbook; they were martyrs of the Alpha 66 invasion commemorated by a large painting of a map of Cuba that covered one wall, a large arrow indicating their landing spot on the island's north coast. "We are a legend inside Cuba," the guerrilla commander told me. "The Cuban people will respond to only one name, Alpha 66, and to one leader, whose name is Andrés Nazario Sargén." He still went into the Everglades to train with his troops, though truth be told he was more like a chaperone to a group of Eagle Scouts than the *comandante* he imagined himself to be. Alpha 66 would go down fighting, somehow, even as its founders were becoming members of the great Cuban Republic of the Afterlife.

All the old men were being united in death, running into one another at the masses praying for the health of Jorge Mas Canosa, and then at his funeral, and at the funeral of Dr. Medina. The novelist González and Nazario Sargén and the other exiles had gone to these events, running into old friends, including a certain radio personality, or *locutor*, who was one of the hard-liners of the exile community. On the radio this *locutor* continued to preach the total break with the regime and its economy that had been the First Commandment of Miami Cuba. Even sending money to your desperate family members in Cuba was a no-no. The *locutor* fought with his own brother and sister on the day he left Cuba and they did not utter a word to each other for the next two decades, so maybe it was easier for him to demand obedience of others. When the *locutor* left Cuba, his brother and sister called him a traitor to the revolution, and they remained on opposite sides of a great ideological and emotional divide until word finally got back to the *locutor* in the 1990s about the desperate straits his brother and sisters and nieces and nephews were in Cuba. He secretly sent them $500.

"Don't put that in your story, because, you know, I don't want people to know that I did this, because of all the things I said on the radio," he told me. "I was always an opponent of sending money. But what are you going to do if a relative of yours is going to have an operation and he needs some medicine and he doesn't have the money to buy it? You can pick who your friends are, but God sent you your family, and you can't leave them behind." *El locutor* blames Fidel Castro, of course, for the moral quandary that forces him to choose between his family and his principles, and he says he will never return to Cuba as long as Castro is in power. He is the sixth person to tell me this.

Salvador Lew is the seventh. Lew is a tall man of pure-white hair which is a kind of snow-covered peak to the black mountain of his finely tailored suit. Like most of the other men in the exile movement, he could recount his personal run-ins with Fidel Castro: he had been, briefly, an official in the revolutionary government, and on the day I met him he was still waiting, in theory, for Fidel to return his phone call from 1959 about a $200 million loan from the Americans. "It's been forty years and he still hasn't called me back." The fate of his stamp collection has been nagging at him for forty years too. He remembers the especially beautiful stamps from the Soviet Union, engraved with those red flags and hammers and sickles that looked exotic and unthreatening to him when he was an adolescent, and not the symbol of the evil empire that would one day lord it over his island home. "I started it when I was a kid and it would be worth a lot of money today, though money doesn't interest me. It's that I made it with my own hands from the time I was ten years old. I had the stamps Cuba produced from the time of the beginning of the Spanish colony to the period in which I was exiled."

When he ran away from Cuba, he left the stamp collection stored in his closet, fully expecting he would return there soon and retrieve it, after the political situation sorted itself out. "I thought that, at most, the regime would last two or three years. I was a victim of that stupid belief that you couldn't have Communism ninety miles from the United States. I left because I didn't believe in the system, because I could have been a member of that new ruling class. My business partner was the minister of education, Fidel was my friend. I have no reason to deny it. He was always polite to me. But I preferred liberty." After the mess with the Soviet missiles, it became clear Fidel would not fall so easily; it was the event that sealed the fate of the exiles, because President Kennedy secretly agreed not to invade Cuba again in exchange for the missiles' removal. Salvador asked a friend to retrieve his stamp collection and bring it to him in Miami. Unfortunately, that friend was himself declared persona non grata soon afterward and dumped off the stamp collection at the Spanish embassy, where it ended up inside a closet. During some unexplained diplomatic crisis, a Spanish official had emptied the contents of the closet and had them incinerated. Salvador Lew's stamps, his album of six hundred family photographs, and his collection of newspaper clippings detailing his glory days as a revolutionary student activist all disappeared in a column of smoke drifting over Havana.

Salvador Lew tells me this story in his Miami office on Blue Lagoon Street, while Ronald and Nancy Reagan stare back at us from pictures on the wall. Later, President George W. Bush will name him head of the U.S. government station Radio Martí. He oozes the kind of success people in Dalton, Georgia, and Memphis, Tennessee, will spend their lives striving for. But Fidel is a cloud over everything Lew has accomplished. Lew says he killed off any remaining chance for friendship with Fidel when the dictator's sister showed up in Miami and he became her publicist. Thanks to Fidel, he shed his Cuban citizenship too. Lew had been part of a group of thirteen Cubans and two Americans who founded the first commercial Cuban radio station in the United States, and in order to become a full partner in the radio station he had to become a U.S. citizen. Having spent most of his adult life fighting for the freedom and prosperity of one country, it felt like a betrayal to profess loyalty to another.

"I spent the day crying, weeping actual tears," Salvador tells me. "My wife at that time—because I've had several, three actually—told me 'Stop. Please don't cry anymore.' But I couldn't. I hurt a lot not being Cuban anymore." He paused for a second to consider the weight and relative truth of this statement. "But I haven't stopped being Cuban. I would like to be buried in my *pueblo*. I don't know why, because every *tierra* [the word means both "dirt" and "homeland"] is the same when you're underground."

Such was the state of mind of the founding members of Miami's Latin Republic: their dreams and nightmares were still in Cuba, and no amount of success in the United States could erase that central tragic fact of their lives. They imagined themselves saviors of the country across the water and were thus doomed to the fate of other liberal reformers of Latin American history: like Simón Bolívar, the Liberator himself, they lived their last years wandering about in lands that were not their own, trying to fight off the nagging sense that all their struggle may have been for naught.

Rather than surrender to such maudlin laments, Max Lesnik had gone back to the other side, figuratively speaking. Even if his body was still in Miami, his state of mind had returned to the island and the people who ruled it. "Now, with the wisdom of many years, I see that Fidel's path was the right one," he told me. The socialist state was the only way to preserve Cuba's dignity and sovereignty. Max applied a similar principle to his personal life too, never surrendering his Cuban citizenship. "I have never sworn an oath to the American flag. And the reason is the following: a lot of people swear loyalty to the American flag and later tell you, 'I just did it for convenience sake, to have a passport, to be able to travel, to have access to certain benefits.' My response to that is if having access to those benefits means swearing loyalty to a flag I'm not ready to defend, it seems to me an act of double disloyalty: first to my Cuban flag, because I am still Cuban, but also an act of disloyalty to the flag of the United States, where I have daughters and grandchildren. I can't take an oath for something I don't believe in."

But Max recognizes that now that he's reached the homestretch of his life these are purely philosophical questions, a debate between the old men in the smoke-filled *tertulia* of his office. "All of us who came here in the sixties are beyond any possibility of exercising power in a future Cuba. In other words, the world becomes young.

There are new generations in Cuba and also here in exile [*el destierro*]. The new generations here are more American than Cuban. Most of them were born here, others have gotten used to American life. They might have strong feelings for Cuba, but they can't pretend to be something they're not. They can't go back to Cuba to govern." He looks at me inquisitively, through the haze of cigar smoke around us. "You're of *mexicano* origin?"

"*Guatemalteco.*"

"Well, imagine Guatemalans who have been here twenty or thirty years in this country who go back with very good intentions and try to govern Guatemala."

"It wouldn't be possible," I admitted. Never once as a boy, or as an adult, did I imagine that I might become president of Guatemala. I'm sure most Cuban-American children didn't entertain thoughts about ruling Cuba either.

"It's not possible to govern Guatemala without Guatemalans from Guatemala!" Max said, his voice rising to a shout because it was so obvious, a truth that applied just as much to the aging Cubans of Miami, who nevertheless lived in denial of this fact every day of their lives. When Max's generation died out, any idea of Cuban Miami returning to La Habana to rule the island would also die. Miami was already more famous as the site of the Latin Grammys and singers like Gloria Estefan and her producer husband, Emilio Estefan, the power behind Shakira, Ricky Martin, and a whole line of crossover Latino music stars, and baseball players like José Canseco, who even had a Miami street named after him. Counterrevolutionary Miami would soon fade into memory, like the society that had built the Art Deco palaces in South Beach in the first half of the last century. That was the story I wrote for my newspaper, a community obituary to the generation that had launched the Bay of Pigs, the Alpha 66 invasions, and many more wars of liberation in the mind, battles that unfolded over espressos on Calle Ocho and nowhere else. Even though their hearts still pumped caffeine-tinged blood through their veins, they were dead politically.

A month or so after I left Miami, a five-year-old boy, his mother and her boyfriend, and ten other people in the Cuban port city of Cárdenas climbed into a boat only slightly bigger than your average American station wagon. They pushed into the tepid water that attracts flocks of European tourists to the nearby resort of Varadero, hoping to catch the northern current that would take them to a landing in Florida. Soon the most intransigent of the Miami exiles would have a new symbol for their fight against Castro. My obituary would have to be retracted.

E lián González was the Miracle Child. Plucked from the sea by fishermen on Thanksgiving Day after days adrift at sea clinging to an inner tube, he would later draw pictures of the dolphins he said had circled around him as he drifted into the Bermuda Triangle. His small boat of refugees had been swamped by an ocean wave and ten of the twelve adults aboard had drowned, including Elián's mother and another woman whose body floated for at least forty-eight hours attached to Elián's inner tube by a rope. The fishermen brought Elián to shore and a waiting ambulance. A news photographer snapped a picture of him being carried away on a stretcher, his brown eyes wide and distant in shock. The local child welfare and immigration authorities took a quick measure of the situation—they had a boy with a dead mother, divorced from the father, who lived in Cuba. They handed Elián over to his closest living relative in Miami, his great-uncle, Lázaro González. This seemingly routine and innocuous bureaucratic decision set in motion a chain of events that would affect the lives of people far beyond south

Florida and Little Havana. You could even say, without it being too much of an exaggeration, that presidents would be made and wars launched thanks to that decision.

The Lázaro González abode, at 2319 NW Second Street in Little Havana, was a tiny stucco bungalow with a postage-stamp crabgrass lawn and a three-story Deco-era apartment building two doors down. This was the sort of home a Max Lesnik or Salvador Lew would remember from their first days in Miami: a bit cramped for their growing families but with a homey intimacy they would wax nostalgic about when they moved to the suburbs. It reminded me of the East Hollywood of my childhood, a neighborhood where immigrant clutter baked in bright sunshine under aging palm trees. Both neighborhoods were decades past their heyday and havens for English-challenged families. North Little Havana, where Lázaro's home was, was where the new Cubans in Miami arrived, the Cubans who were not exactly *cubanos* in the eyes of the novelist González. Lázaro González arrived there in 1985, as part of a wave of poorer exiles raised in the socialist state and perhaps less prepared to cope in hypercapitalist south Florida. He was an unemployed mechanic when his grandnephew came to live with him.

The Cubans who were not Cubans were known as *balseros*, rafters, because that's how they came to South Florida. They worked in construction, took jobs at fast-food restaurants, or traveled to the interior of the United States in search of better prospects, because in Miami there were too many other Cubans like them looking for work. They eschewed membership in the organizations led by the generation of Salvador Lew and Nazario Sargén, whom they saw as part of a distant, better-off establishment. They told crossing stories like those told by Mexican immigrants, only their desert was made of salt water, and they crossed it not on foot but afloat on rafts made from old inner tubes, on rusty pickups with oil barrels tied on the side, parched under the sun, begging the wind to blow northward. So many *balseros* arrived in the mid-1990s, that it became known in the south Florida media as a "crisis," a shorthand way of saying, How are we going to house and feed all these people and keep them from dragging our city down? Eventually, as in California, the chaotic arrival of these foreign-born crowds led to a clamor for new rules and barriers. The rules of Cuban migration changed. No longer were the fleeing *cubanos* automatically granted political asylum: if they were caught out in the water by the Coast Guard—and every year thousands were—they were undocumented illegals like the Salvadorans or Guatemalans and received the same kind of treatment.

Juan Valdez had set off for Miami when the *balsero* crisis was at its peak, in 1994, some five years before Elián's mother set off on her boat ride. He fashioned his raft from aluminum and plastic foam; the first time he set out, the weather turned bad and the raft turned back. The second time the Cuban coast guard captured him. "They hold you in jail for a day in Cuba, then they let you go," a description that sounded reminiscent of the revolving door of the U.S.-Mexico border. On the third try he was detained by the United States Coast Guard and shipped off to a detention center in Guantánamo while the Clinton administration decided what to do with him. He was in a limbo. Legally, he was on Cuban soil—the United States has leased the property for the base since the Spanish-American War—but under the watchful eyes of American soldiers, not quite at the destination he had imagined for himself and not quite the place he had left either, like those men I'd met in La Casa del Migrante in Tijuana, wondering how to get around *los chiles verdes*. In 1994 and 1995, tens of thousands of Cubans who missed walking through the only recently closed door to south Florida wound up in Guantánamo instead, in a vast camp where man-high loops and tangles of barbed wire kept them inside.

In Guantánamo, Juan Valdez made some friends he would keep

for the rest of his life. One was Gerardo Mir, an older man who was a kind of camp sage, writing letters for detainees and once taking action to stop the planned murder of an abusive U.S. solider by a group of outraged *cubanos*. To pass the time, and so that he would never forget the tedium and injustice of his ill-fated journey northward, Valdez decided to get a tattoo. He had another detainee make it for him, in the improvised, jailhouse way these things are done when you find yourself under armed guard. They fashioned a tattoo gun and tattoo ink out of a melted toothbrush and soap, applying the mixture to the skin around his biceps with a thousand pricks. What emerged was a ring of barbed wire, a few flowers trapped between the strands, a surprisingly delicate drawing given the conditions it was made under.

When he finally arrived in Miami, after President Clinton decided that more than a year of languishing in Guantánamo was enough, Valdez found himself sitting in a relief agency in Miami, with his friend Gerardo Mir. The two men caught sight of a flyer on the agency's bulletin board that had a large dollar sign on it. Come make $5.65 an hour, the flyer announced, working the swing shift at Tyson Chicken, in the not-too-faraway town of Ashland, Alabama. At that moment, they had only their Cuban experience to draw from; in Cuba the idea of making $50 American for a day's work was fantastical. So they headed off to Alabama, because if there was one thing that Guantánamo taught them, it was that bad things happen if you wait too long to begin your journey.

Juan Valdez and Gerardo Mir were already safely ensconced in Alabama by the time Elián's mother decided to try her luck on the Strait of Florida. The new rules of Cuban migration left just enough hope for island-trapped *cubanos* to say *"No es imposible."* Of course, it was *imposible* for Elizabeth Brotons, Elián's mother; she disappeared into the deep blue sea and inadvertently set off the Great Battle of the Castaway Boy. Lázaro González, the uncle who would have taken her and her son in for a few days while they got settled in Miami, instead found his Little Havana bungalow transformed into a fortress and a rallying point. In Cuba, meanwhile, Fidel Castro's regime put Elián's picture on billboards next to Che's; they, too, took up the image of the castaway child as an icon of suffering and injustice, and hundreds of thousands of people rallied in Havana for him to be reunited with his father, Juan Miguel González, a waiter at a resort hotel who became the newest hero of the revolution. Juan Miguel sincerely and adamantly wanted his son to live with him in Cuba, a simple fact that made most of Cuban Miami apoplectic with rage. He would soon be photographed at the side of El Barbudo himself.

Elián was already legend and myth in Miami and Cuba by the time I arrived there and set eyes on him for the first time. In Miami, they said angels had circled over him as he floated on his inner tube, and cited the supposed lack of sunburns or scrape marks on his body at the moment of his rescue as proof of divine intervention. In Cuba, family members revealed that his mother had had seven miscarriages before Elián, her only child, was born. Others pointed out that in the belief system of Afro-Caribbean Santería, children open and close the doors of fate for others. Elián was destined to fulfill prophecies, though people in Cuba and in Miami were split on exactly what exactly those prophecies were.

E lián brought out both the paternalistic and the warrior-like instincts of the anti-Castro lobby. Jorge Mas Canosa's son and successor as head of the Cuban American National Foundation, Jorge Mas, helped to orchestrate a smart and effective media campaign centered on the boy's elfin face and his miracle story. The foundation took a copy of that picture of him on the stretcher and made it into a poster proclaiming "Another Child Victim of Fidel Castro." They ferried the boy around south Florida to various photo ops, including the obligatory visit to Disney World, where poor Elián said he didn't want to go on the water rides. His sixth birthday was covered on local TV. With money from the foundation, Lázaro had the biggest swing set possible built on his tiny lawn, a prop for the photos in which he appeared daily in the press. Immigration officials ordered that Elián be returned to Cuba; his Miami relatives refused to comply. The controversy and the spectacle spun to ever higher levels of absurdity and diplomatic gravity.

The radio in my rental car the morning I returned to Miami offered the first hint of the Elián insanity gripping its Spanish-speaking homes. "That boy will be tortured in Cuba!" cried out the voice of one AM *locutor:* Elián would be subjected to a Castrista brainwashing program to make him into a loyal Communist six-year-old. Another station was calling on courageous *cubanos* to step forward and become "human shields" if the U.S. Justice Department sent in agents to enforce the court order that he be reunited with his father. The streets around Lázaro's house were all barricaded by the police, so I parked a couple of blocks away on a narrow street without sidewalks, and within sight of a sixteen-wheel tractor trailer that rose higher than any of the roofs on the block, a first hint of the madness going on in front of Lázaro's house itself. I flashed my LAPD press pass at the cop manning the roadblock, but he just waved me through with a half-disgusted flip of his wrist. I followed a half-dozen electrical cables around a corner and into the small village of media tents that had sprung up in the street and sidewalk directly across from Lázaro's lawn. About 150 sets of eyes, lenses, and microphones were trained on that spot, concentrated most thickly around a telephone pole that marked the patch of sidewalk closest to Elián's new swing set. Here, the scrum of photographers and cameramen had surged upward in search of better vantage points. I counted seven ladders, each a perch for a man or woman with a telephoto lens. Behind the ladders, on the front lawns of two of Lázaro's neighbors, were a pair of portable platforms rising three stories into the air so that cameramen with tripods could give a pigeon-eye view of the house (the networks were paying several hundred dollars a day for the right to park the platforms in the homeowners' front lawns). When the boy Elián peeked out of a curtain a few minutes later, the media cluster erupted with a chorus of clicking shutters and the whir of small electric motors pulling film forward. Two houses to the right, several dozen demonstrators gathered behind a steel barricade broke into a chant: *¡Elián, amigo, el pueblo está contigo!* Elián gave them all a six-year-old's nonexpressive look, as if he didn't quite care or understand that "the people are with you." He closed the curtain. A moment later all the clicking and the chanting and the whirring stopped.

Elián was a bubble boy inside that bungalow, subjected to an around-the-world voyeurism each time he stuck his head out the curtain, or dared to slide and swing in his great-uncle's front yard. It struck me as a kind of child abuse to subject a six-year-old to this much attention and intrusion. I half wanted to call the Miami-Dade County child-protection people and issue some sort of complaint: against Elián's Miami relatives, against the media, against myself for standing there and being part of the circus.

There are certain times in the life of a journalist when the best thing is to run away from the spot where all the other journalists are. This was clearly one of those moments. So I headed for Max Lesnik's office and his daily *tertulia,* for the relative sanity of old men in a smoke-filled room arguing about bearded dictators and who was *más cubano*.

Elián's story was one of the earlier versions of a turn-of-the-millennium parable: the real-life saga of a child in danger broadcast round-the-clock on cable news networks. But it was also a Little Havana obsession exported around the world, a Spanish *telenovela* translated into English for consumption on *Larry King Live*. Yet most people didn't quite understand why Cuban Miami was so worked up about the kid, why they were surrounding his house in a vigil and promising Miami-Dade County would break into open rebellion should Janet Reno send her minions in to spirit him back to Cuba. I decided to explore their obsession from the inside, to write a story about how the Elián story looked to the eyes of a "typical Miami Cuban family." Max Lesnik was a networker; he knew everyone, so I figured he would know someone "typical."

"I know just the man," he said. "A typical Cuban workingman."

Marcos Correa and his family had, in fact, been profiled some sixteen years earlier by the *Miami Herald* as a "typical Cuban working family." He was a longtime friend of Max's, and also a bus driver on the No. 72 line of the Miami-Dade transit system.

I arrived at the Correa household, about a mile or so from Elián's house in Little Havana, and sat down to talk with him and his wife Elena about the castaway boy. Marcos and Elena had met in the 1960s in Havana when they were both students at the university for teachers there. She now worked at an elementary school in Little Havana: if Elián had been enrolled in public school, María Elena might have been his teacher. Marcos left Cuba in 1961 because he found its growing revolutionary and socialist conformity stultifying. We talked in a dining room where the walls were lined with dishes bearing the seals of Cuba's provinces. My questions about Elián quickly set off an argument, with man and wife shouting so loudly those dishes on the wall started to rattle.

"My husband thinks you have to respect the father's rights," María Elena said to me. "I believe that the boy should stay in the United States. I think that he deserves that in exchange for the fifty hours he spent in the water, and for the mother he lost. He should stay here until he turns twenty."

"The mafia that runs the radio and television stations here has everyone worked up," Marcos said. "We have eight radio stations here controlled by the mafia. My wife and daughter and son listen to them all day long."

"That word 'mafia' is offensive to me. . . ."

"The whole world knows Fidel is using Elián as a political pawn," Marcos said. "But the father is the father. He has his rights."

"There is no gray here!" María Elena shouted back. "It's black and white. You're with Fidel, or you're not!"

She turned to me and said, "He thinks Fidel is smart. He respects him."

"Please!" Marcos shouted back, looking a bit wounded.

To my surprise, much of the Correa family was split along roughly the same lines: the men coming down on the side of the Cuban father, while the women were with the "Miami relatives." Everyone seemed to see an element of his or her life in Elián's story, an allegory about exile and loss, rescue and division. Elián's family was split, as were most extended Cuban families, by politics and geography. He was lost at sea, then found shelter in Miami, but his fate was being argued over by adults, just as the fate of the larger Cuban family was in the hands of politicians in Havana and Washington. For a growing minority of people—including Marcos Correa, his son-in-law, and his youngest daughter—the battle over Elián would drive home their frustration with the tunnel vision of the Miami exile leadership, even though they would only express these frustrations in private. In the Miami Cuban nation, there was a pressure to conform, to fall into line, much as there was in the rest of the United States during the debate over the decision to invade Iraq two years later: no one wanted to be accused of cooperating with the enemy, be it Fidel Castro or Saddam Hussein.

Talking with Marcos Correa and his family and friends, I would also discover how small and provincial a place Little Havana was; everyone, it seemed, could claim some personal connection or another to the story. One of Elián's cousins attended María's school. "I know the priest that is ministering to Elián's family," said Marcos's next-door neighbor, José López. "He goes to that house every day and conducts a mass there. I can tell you, because this man has told me, there has never been any pressure put on Elián to say he wants to stay here." Mr. López was pro–Miami relatives. "I am an extremist in the defense of liberty," he said, which prompted a sarcastic retort for Marcos: "I am moderate. That's why I want Elián to go back with his father." The two men began arguing, speaking over each other while I looked at them with an amused smile and raised eyebrows, but when it was over they shook hands and Marcos agreed to lend José his garden hose.

Next I drove Marcos in my rental car over to his oldest daughter's house. Marilyn Correa was busy feeding a baby in a high chair when we walked in. She was a paralegal and firmly in the stay-in-Miami camp, although not everyone in her house was. "My husband is a selfish male. His opinion is that a father has as much right in Cuba as anywhere else. But I don't believe this man has any interest in his son."

Marcos quickly pointed out that Juan Miguel González had recently appeared on worldwide television, asking for the return of his son, and had wept openly. Marilyn was unconvinced. *"Papi,* if this man wanted his son, he would have come when Elián's mother died." Marilyn looked up from the high chair and a baby covered with food to give her father a piercing gaze. "He is being controlled. His tears are not for his son. His tears are because he can't do what he wants!" Marcos, who had smiled slyly while debating his wife and neighbor, suddenly turned quiet, serious, and deferential. He said nothing as his daughter ripped into Fidel. "The monster is into Santería. That's why he's working so hard to get Elián back. The *santeros* told him that Elián has special powers. If he can't get Elián back, he's finished in Cuba. That's what the *santeros* told him. Nobody has been able to kill him all these years, so he's got something going for him. And it isn't God."

The Correas' youngest son, Orlando, was too busy to meet with me in person. I had to interview him by telephone. Orlando Correa had actually met Elián, an encounter he described as a life-transforming experience. This had happened because he had been a schoolmate and lifelong friend with Marisleysis González, Lázaro's daughter and a young woman then famous in Miami for two things: for being Elián's "surrogate mother" and for the fainting spells that would hit her when anyone suggested that the boy would probably be sent back to Cuba. "Whenever I'm with Elián, I see him like one of my nephews and nieces. He wants to enjoy the paradise of this country." Orlando had taken time off from his job to become part of the Elián saga and spoke of the boy in a weirdly reverential tone, as if he still emitted the aura of the angels that had saved him from the open sea. "The attachments that Elián has deposited with his cousin and his family in Miami have filled that emptiness in his heart."

None of this was Orlando able to discuss with his father. "I try to avoid the tension. I don't take anything away from what my father went through in Cuba. But my father puts that blindfold on his eyes.

I respect everyone's point of view, but there's a lot of ignorance out there."

The home of Marcos's daughter Blanca and her husband José Cespedes was my last stop on the Correa family tour. They lived in a home with polished hardwood floors and seemed better off than the rest of the family. Their views were also more forward-looking, despite the fact that José's father had been a political prisoner. José now sided with Elián's Communist-leaning father. "As a father, I would want my son with me. You wouldn't want anyone else raising him. He's my son, my blood."

Blanca agreed. "When this started, as a mother, I felt passionate about the kid staying here." The growing circus around Elián changed her views. "It's a disgrace. It's a disgrace that these Cuban politicians are exploiting these people who don't have a life. The old folks who have no life, who are all on Social Security are the ones out there protesting. The people who are young and up-and-coming are not out there."

I had come upon some unexpected cracks in the the armor of Cuban-American unity. Later, long after Elián was back at home with his father in Cárdenas, these divisions would become wider. In the 2004 election season, the Bush administration announced there would be new restrictions on travel to Cuba, new limits on those who went back to see their relatives, new limits on how much money they could legally take back to those relatives. This played well with the old-line exile crowd but not among the *balsero* generation. They were tired of the old men asking them to be faithful to the anti-Castro religion. They wanted to be free to travel back and forth to the old country as often as the Mexicans with papers did, to figuratively drive across the Caribbean to their homes in Cárdenas, La Habana, and Santiago and bring as many presents as they could in the back of their figurative pickup trucks.

s Janet Reno's deadline for Elián to be returned to his father approached, the crowd of "old folks" and "people without a life" grew in front of Lázaro González's house. The presence of the boy, the doe-eyed child, changed everything. He was like a living religious icon, a Virgin of Guadalupe in the flesh, and to think of moving him from his shrine on NW Second Street was a kind of sacrilege. They stood in front of the stainless-steel barrier about twenty yards from the house and leaned over it to chant and wave and perhaps catch another glimpse of the persecuted boy. I met *cubanos* from New Jersey who had driven day and night to be there. There were also self-appointed block commanders who were recruiting men for the "human chain" that would circle the block to prevent Reno's agents from entering Lázaro's property through the back door. "We need one hundred men! Not girls, but men! *Hombres!*" For half an hour I watched the block commanders run frantically around the block, trying to form the human chain, but they might as well have been trying to build a chain of cats; the men and women (in the end, the commanders settled for women) linked their arms but started to wander off after ten minutes or so, probably because they, like me, sensed that there would be no raid that day. I made my way back to the press area in front of the house itself and climbed to the top of the ladder marked *Los Angeles Times*. You would have thought Lázaro's little house was hosting a wedding reception it was so crowded, with several dozen people milling about the swing set, in the front yard behind the chain-link fence, and on the front steps. "Hey, look, it's Andy Garcia!" someone shouted. There, on Lázaro's crabgrass, stood the actor who had played the bastard son of Sonny Corleone in the *Godfather Part III*. Later the singer Gloria Estefan arrived too, and Cristina Saralegui, the most popular talk-show host on Spanish-language television. Miami's Cuban-American Mayor Joe Carollo was there too, as was Miami-Dade County Mayor Alex Penelas, who up to that moment was considered a rising star in Democratic politics. There were also a group of nuns in habits and priests in frocks. Anybody who was anybody in Cuban Miami was there that day. But the agents everyone expected would come to crash the party never arrived.

They came several weeks later, in the dead of night, in uniforms the color and shape of Darth Vader's outfit in *Star Wars*. One agent snatched Elián from the closet, where he was hiding in the arms of Donato Dalrymple, the housecleaner-cum-fisherman who had rescued him. A few hours later Elián was on a plane to Washington, and eventually to Cuba, while *cubanos* in Little Havana staged a mini-riot. Mayor Carollo wanted to fire Police Chief William O'Brien for not telling him the feds were on the way to Lázaro's house, but the city charter wouldn't let him do that, so he fired City Manager Donald Warshaw instead, which caused the police chief to resign. This was too much to bear for non-Cuban Miami. People started throwing bananas on the steps of City Hall—in bunches of two or three, or by the crateful. To make the meaning of the fruit crystal clear they draped a banner over the building declaring THE BANANA REPUBLIC OF MIAMI and replaced the Stars and Stripes with a green banner decorated with more bananas.

Carollo's political aspirations were ruined: left to choose between the compromises of American politics and the demands of the constituents from the country where he had been born, he'd chosen the latter. Mayor Penelas all but dropped out of Democratic Party politics: in the presidential election later that year, he declined to campaign for his own party's nominee, Al Gore, who ended up losing Florida—and thus the national election—by a few hundred votes. Your faithful correspondent returned to Florida once again, this time to West Palm Beach and Tallahassee to witness the very Latin American–looking farce of an election where votes were not votes and crowds of shouting men surrounded and stormed county buildings to keep officials from counting the ballots. In the end, a panel of judges named George W. Bush the winner.

Chapter Nine

FATHERS, DAUGHTERS, CITIZENS, AND STRONGWOMEN

El hambre y el orgullo

Barstow, Los Angeles, Bell Gardens, Maywood, Watts, and South Gate, California

The girl from the desert sat next to her father in the front of the family pickup truck as he navigated past stray rocks along the street that connected their home to Highway 58 and the city and the world beyond. The County of San Bernardino called this Waterman Road, a mile-long stretch of dirt that followed the Santa Fe railroad tracks along the valley of the Barstow River. The pickup would bob up and down sea waves of pebbles and dry riverbed until, inevitably, it would suddenly lurch to a stop, as if a solid and invisible barrier had suddenly risen from the road. The girl would listen to her father mutter and open the door, stepping out from the shelter of the pickup's cab into the oven bake of the sun outside. She would look through the windows and follow his path to the back of the truck, where he had placed a shovel for use at precisely such moments: to scoop bits of Waterman Road under the tires, and then restart the engine and move the pickup backward and forward again, until the next obstacle, when he would retrieve the shovel and once again begin to dig, grunt, and curse. Back in the cab, behind the steering wheel, he would look across at his redheaded daughter, the middle daughter of five, "the smart one," and ruminate about the base injustice. He had been a veteran of World War II. Why, he asked, did a man who had served his country in uniform, who never failed to pay his taxes, have to subject his family to the daily humiliation of this street?

A day, an afternoon, a morning after one of his struggles with the road and the shovel—she doesn't remember which, exactly, because the moment came decades ago—she was sitting at the kitchen table. She was in junior high school then, perhaps thirteen years old, and the kitchen table was where she had done her homework for as long as she could remember, and where she would continue to do it, after high school and into community college, until the day came when she left this town in the desert for a university by the blue ocean a day's drive away. Her father came into the kitchen and found her there, pencil in hand, doing some math problem perhaps. "Write this down," he demanded. At thirteen she was the family scribe, and this wasn't the first time he had uttered the command, but this time his words were not a letter to a friend, or a matter of family business, but instead a kind of declaration made in the first-person plural, the "we" of the community of families that lived along Waterman Road. It was a petition, demanding that their street be paved with asphalt.

The girl from the desert and her family lived between railroad tracks, amid the vast switching yards of Barstow, a hub on the line that linked Los Angeles to Las Vegas, Kansas City, Chicago, and the rest of the United States. Living by the tracks, in the chorus of horns, the clack-clack of boxcars, the drifting hoboes (as they were known then) defined the girl's notion of who she was. Her mother would enlist her and her sisters to make bologna sandwiches from the family's home-baked bread to give to the drifters who came bounding off the freight cars, and fill old marmalade jars with cold water, which the drifters always accepted with grateful smiles, because they'd just spent hours crossing the Mojave. They were hungry people trying to get to Los Angeles in search of jobs, many of them *mexicanos* beaten, bloodied, and cut up by the desert landscape and by the Santa Fe Railroad police. These encounters with violence and poverty on her doorstep left a mark on her ideas about her place in the world as much as that dusty drive down Waterman Road. The letter was, in its own way, a proclamation of the community's dignity, of its right to be included in the United States by having the road that connected its neighborhood to the rest of the country be not just a line on a map but a real, physical, usable link.

When she had finished writing her father's words at the kitchen table, she walked with him up and down Waterman Road, knocking on doors, standing silently behind him as he talked about getting the road paved and the Board of Supervisors and then watching people take the petition—the words she had written—and signing their names under his. We'll show them we count, her father would say; the humiliation of Waterman Road would not stand. She felt a sense of ownership to the words, an incipient sense of her own worth and ability. "They were my words," she would say years later. When her father came back from the board meeting to announce they had won, and when the county graders and trucks arrived to flatten out old Waterman Road and cover it with a smooth black layer of asphalt, she felt something more, a sense of the union between herself and her neighbors, and of their collective strength.

So began the journey of the girl who would one day become the state senator for the Twenty-fourth District of California.

loria Romero's father gave her the spark of the civic ideal and taught her the rudimentary skills of "organization," the art by which you could unite people in spite of those aspects of human nature that tend to divide and isolate them. For the rest of her life, the impulse her father gave her on Waterman Road in the mid 1960s would take her to city halls and courtrooms and county boards of supervisors, often as the spokeswoman for groups of social outcasts. The story about the shovel and Waterman Road was her answer to the question I put to her at her office in the State Capitol in Sacramento: Do you remember the moment of your civic awakening?

It came from her father, she said. "How he got to it, honestly, I really don't know."

I asked the question because I wanted to understand the force that moved people to that first act against apathy, and how they came to believe that they could participate in their own governance. Faced with an unpaved road or any of the other multiple injustices and inequalities of life in American immigrant communities and barrios—unemployment, police misconduct—most people choose to do nothing. At best, they will seek redress with the solitary tenacity of the day laborer Fidel Chicas, who staked out the man who owed him $600 until he finally got paid. The absence of a collective local voice vis-à-vis the political and legal system is one of the conditions that defines those places that immigrants and migrants call home in America. In the trailer park that was my home in Clay County, Alabama, most of us were strangers to one another, a sum of individuals easily manipulated by the chicken barons who had brought us there. Among the uprooted and the transient, family is the flag, the future of sons and daughters the rallying cry. Like my roommates Frankie and Linda, you work, you save, you don't look for trouble, you dream of the day when you have enough money so that mother, father, and son can live and prosper as one.

In the United States, a country founded on the notion of individualism, the "Citizen One" who steps forward to create the Latino community voice is by definition cutting against the grain; he risks being taken for a kook by the people he is trying to convert, mistaken for the evangelical preacher on the street corner haranguing passersby. And in fact the accounts of their conversions are often tinged with the mystery of the divine, like those stories of angels appearing to the Virgin Mary, or María herself appearing to the Mexican Indian Juan Diego. Citizen One has a vision. She steps out of the kitchen and walks over to her neighbor's house and knocks on the door.

A Citizen One encountered an especially daunting wilderness of civic fatalism and apathy in immigrant Los Angeles in the mid-1990s. In a vast swath of the city stretching from Sunset Boulevard and the foothills of the Santa Monica Mountains in the north, to Century Boulevard and Watts in the south, a majority of the people were not and could not be citizens. They were foreign-born and not naturalized, and thus ineligible to vote. There was a great abyss between the formal institutions of American democracy and the language and culture of the populace. The "more perfect union" conceived by Jefferson and other founding fathers—where authority originated from the "people" and the instrument of their will, the ballot box—was a hollow shell. The simplest civic act, the annual or biannual ritual of punching the number of a candidate in the same way one might choose a television program with a button on a remote control, was the reserve of a relatively small sect of devotees.

The contradiction of this state of affairs was plain to see on a typical Election Day in the neighborhoods of central Los Angeles. Here the machinery of American local democracy had been perfected circa 1960 (when John F. Kennedy accepted the presidential nomination of the Democratic Party at the Los Angeles Memorial Coliseum), and it continued to sputter along like an old Chevrolet from that era, still running on leaded gasoline, its old whitewalls stained and cracked. On the day of a special election to fill a vacant seat in the state legislature, I visited Los Angeles County precinct number 9007542, which resides a half-mile from the Coliseum and a few hundred yards from the busiest freeway interchange in the United States. I arrived in a neighborhood of tenements and stubborn maple trees rising from holes in the concrete sidewalks, looking for the address listed by the county registrar of voters, which turned out to be the front steps of Norwood Elementary School. But I couldn't find the flag that would show me where the polling place would be. A school security guard pointed listlessly to a space inside the maze of beige-colored bungalows that made up the campus, and eventually I found a stubby staircase leading to an open door with a white sign attached: POLLING PLACE.

I walked in and introduced myself to the poll workers, the usual trio of amiable senior citizens, sitting alone in what turned out to be the school's library, a shoe box of a room with three empty voting booths; the poll workers were so pleased to see me ("At last, a voter!" their eyes said), you would have thought they were three castaways and I the captain sent to rescue them.

"I got lost," I said. "I couldn't find the flag."

"We didn't put one out," said Pat Diaz, whose name tag also identified her as the precinct captain. "We're keeping it in here." She gestured at a spot near the door. Instead of being allowed to shimmer in the midday sunshine and be the beacon guiding voters to this polling place, the nylon Stars and Stripes was tacked to an inside wall, forced to share the cramped room with a cluster of kindergarten chairs and a table with the Vietnamese and Cantonese translations of the *Official Voter's Guide* and *Donde Viven los Monstruos*, the Spanish-language version of *Where the Wild Things Are*. "The last two elections, we put it outside and someone stole it. This time we're trying to keep an eye on it."

"Why would anyone want to steal the flag?" I wondered out loud, but no one answered.

I sat in a chair at the table and waited for a voter to show up. After a few minutes, I started leafing through *Donde Viven los Monstruos*, wondering if a voter would walk through the door before one of the volunteers dozed off the way Maurice Sendak's monsters do halfway through the book. Finally, a single elderly man walked through the door, gruff and in a hurry, like someone paying a parking ticket, wanting to get it over with, shaking his head when I asked him for an interview.

Five months later, I went to the same precinct on the day of a statewide primary for governor, Congress, the state legislature, and a number of ballot initiatives. The flag was once again a no-show: this time Pat hadn't received one from the county. "It wasn't in our packet," she explained, sounding defensive, a simple bureaucratic mix-up. Outside, neighborhood life went on in Spanish. I picked up a copy of *La Opinión*, the Spanish-language daily, which carried a front-page story on the election but dedicated most of the rest of the page to stories of more pressing interest to its Spanish-speaking readers: "Immigration Service Clarifies Rules on Workplace Raids" and "Five Arrested for Smuggling Immigrants." Four blocks away on Estrella Avenue, one hundred or so immigrant tenants were engaged in a protracted daily struggle with their landlord in a building I had visited a few months earlier, five stories of rotting floors and roach runs that had been a centerpiece of my exposé on the breakdown of the city's housing inspection program. All were immigrants and none could vote: if they noticed it at all, Election Day would have appeared to be an obscure ritual celebrated by small handfuls of the elderly. A few miles away in Koreatown I visited a precinct in a senior center where voters had been scared off when the police raided a group of suspected street prostitutes and drug dealers a few feet from the front door. The panorama offered by the institutions of American democracy in those neighborhoods of central Los Angeles was roughly analogous to that of the struggling owner of a corner grocery store who waits in vain for someone to buy his bread before it goes stale, and who worries that the next person to walk in through the door might be a hoodlum come to rob him.

Those voters who did make it to the polls sometimes carried out their civic duty with a startling naïveté. Jorge Muñoz, a twenty-seven-year-old poll worker and veteran of ten elections, told me it wasn't uncommon for voters to present him with their sample ballots and ask, "*Señor*, who do I vote for?" Just outside the polling place across the street from MacArthur Park, the central plaza of *centroamericanos* in Los Angeles, I was corralled by one such confused voter, Salvador Díaz, a sixty-six-year-old man in a dusty suit who looked as if he had stepped out of a sepia-tone photograph of Mexico City circa 1920. He saw the reporter's notebook in my hand and mistook me for some sort of official. "I want to vote on this," he said in Spanish, showing me a pale-green voting guide with a smiling portrait of Gray Davis, then the democratic candidate for governor. He pointed to the "No on 227" that Davis recommended, a rejection of a ballot initiative to end bilingual education in public schools. "But the lady working here told me I couldn't vote on that." I explained to him that I was a writer but said I would help him. We walked into the polling station, the lounge inside the Grandview Apartments, where I repeated what he had told me, translating into English for the four poll workers for a few moments, until it became clear that at least three of them understood Spanish.

"*Señor*," the poll inspector said in calm, even Spanish. "No one can tell you how to vote."

The woman who had helped Díaz vote the first time and could sort this out was gone, off to translate at another polling place. The precinct captain gave a sigh of resignation: there was nothing more to be done. In the United States, you can't vote twice, he said. You have to get it right the first time.

A few moments later, as I escorted the defeated Mr. Díaz back out onto the street, the real source of his confusion became clear. "*Soy analfabeto*," he blurted out—an illiterate. "By pure luck I was able to make out Gray Davis's name." Everything else was a blur.

In many Latin American countries, the ballots are festooned with the pictures of the candidates or the flags of political parties, precisely to keep the illiterate from getting lost as they cast their votes; in California the only official aid the state gives the voter is a prolix pamphlet filled with fine-print legalisms describing the proposed ballot initiatives, a guide that would be helpful if you were writing a master's thesis but useless to Mr. Díaz, who shuffled away down the street without returning my *Buenas tardes*.

Moments later, I was standing in front of the Grandview Apartments, next to its dutifully placed Stars and Stripes, debating which polling place on my list to visit next when two women approached me and asked for help. "We're looking for this place," one of them said in Spanish, showing me a business card with an address.

"Oh, that's just two blocks from here," I said in Spanish. *"Allí no más."*

They headed off in the direction I pointed, to the Mexican consulate, where the eagle and serpent of Mexico's tricolor flag rose from a pole attached to an office building, waiting for the rare summer breeze that would unfurl it for a few seconds so that it might call out to its citizens: come here to conduct business with your government.

Even though he was sixty-six, Salvador Díaz was the "new man," a freshly minted voter and civic actor. Like a baby fresh out of the womb and still covered with amniotic fluid, he was disoriented and blinded by the light of so much democracy. The American ballot offered too many choices, it asked him to opine on too many topics of weighty import, on bond measures and Indian casinos and even what language should be spoken in the schools. It asked him to pick judges, senators, city council members, and also congressmen and assemblymen—and what was the difference between those last two, anyway? And how was he supposed to know if he couldn't even read? In Mexico, everything was simpler. Usually you didn't have much of a choice on the ballot: you put your X over the party with the green-white-and-red flag. If you lived in a small *pueblo*—as many new Californians did at one point in their lives— the government wasn't made up of anyone you could say you had voted for. No, they were merely *hombres prepotentes*, high-handed men who came to the village to tell you how things would be, which land was yours and which belonged to the next village, like the "delegate" who shows up in Juan Rulfo's story "Nos Han Dado la Tierra," or "They've Given Us the Land."

In Rulfo's story, written at about the time Salvador Díaz was a young man, a group of *campesinos* march across a rock-dry, treeless plain, a place so empty "your eyes start to roll loose because there's nothing for them to hold on to." It's the land the government has given them to farm, and the *delegado* has told them all they have to do is drop some seeds in the ground and wait for rain, but the *campesinos* have been to this place and know the land isn't good for anything, not even for "raising vultures." They explain this to the delegate, but he brushes them off, telling them to "put it in writing." There's no water, nothing will grow, the peasants insist. "But he didn't want to listen to us." The story ends without anyone questioning the *delegado*'s authority. Instead, the *campesinos* walk across the dry open plain until they can see a line of green where there is a river and there are trees, a place that can't be theirs, because the government's *delegado* said so.

Traditionally in American history, the dislocation and political confusion spawned by the arrival of large numbers of immigrants like Salvador Díaz into the nation's cities is the fallow ground tilled by the political boss. In New York City circa 1850, where the Irish made up most of the low-wage workforce, the minions of William Marcy ("Boss") Tweed bedecked Tammany Hall in green on St. Patrick's Day and employed "emigrant runners" who plied the docks naturalizing Irish immigrants. With their legs still sea-weary after transatlantic journeys, they were made instant American citizens (in those days, naturalization was the purview of local authorities) and got jobs and housing in exchange for the votes that kept Tweed and the "Forty Thieves" of the common council in power. In Martin Scorsese's movie *The Gangs of New York*, you can see Tweed's "emigrant runners" dramatized. "Deliver these good and fervent folks to the polls on a regular basis," one Tweed operative says as Irish families step off a ship, "and there'll be a handsome price for each vote that goes Tammany's way."

Some thirteen decades later, in Cuban Miami, campaign workers for the candidates Xavier Suárez and Humberto Hernández performed a similar roundup in Little Havana. To humble houses, duplexes and apartments not far from Elián González's erstwhile home, the modern-day emigrant runners arrived with blank absentee ballots. The *cubano* operatives' prey consisted mostly of elderly, Spanish-speaking natives of the old country, for whom they filled out and punched absentee ballots. "My vote was stolen," one septuagenarian *cubana* told the *Miami Herald*. "They know our eyesight is not good and we are not well. What kind of person would take advantage of the elderly?" It was all part of a larger vote factory that also had campaign workers fraudulently signing stacks of absentee ballots. The dead voted too, propelling Suárez to victory as mayor, and Hernández to a seat on the city commission. Hernández got his relatives appointed to city jobs, until a judge overturned the result and threw him and Suárez out of office.

Such corruption is well known in Latin America, where it is part of a colorful and unpredictable political culture. Probably many Miamians simply rolled their eyes when hearing about the *cubano* vote fraud, since their city is filled with exiled officials who've specialized in such sleight of hand in their native countries. Over in Little Buenos Aires, people would have been reminded of the province of Catamarca, where a powerful senator and owner of a soccer team sent the team's paid hooligans to set fire to the ballot boxes to prevent an opponent's victory. In Little Peru, they would have remembered the "signature factories" President Alberto Fujimori set up so that stacks of his reelection petitions could be signed by teams of his employees.

The traditions of nineteenth-century immigrant America and modern-day Latin America live on in California, where new civic actors are beginning to fill the vacuum left by the slow death of the Anglo-Protestant political institutions Samuel Huntington eulogizes in *Who Are We?* They are city council members, city clerks, self-styled founders of community agencies, pamphleteer activists, and minor-league political bosses. Like the brothers José and Pedro García, they are idealists and cynics who approach the opportunity that the United States represents from opposite sides of the ethical divide. For some, California offers the chance to realize democratic dreams deferred south of the border, to achieve a level of liberty and self-expression unimaginable in the old country. For others, it offers a chance to operate on the fringes of the law as they manipulate the reins of local government in a venal, overt pursuit of self-interest, which is what you can do with even just a sliver of public power in places as diverse as Ciudad Juárez, Mexico, and Asunción, Paraguay.

Talk to enough of these cynics and idealists in Southeast Los Angeles County and you will hear a common theme in the stories of their civic activism: humiliation. Having crossed over borders and deserts, the immigrants arrive in a new territory as pioneers and pilgrims; they have overcome early tribulations to proclaim their permanence in their adopted land; finally, they can even say they have prospered, until Citizen One wakes up one morning to the realization "We are not free." In the rejection of his subservient status, he stages the equivalent of a Boston Tea Party and writes or speaks his own Declaration of Independence, a call to arms that might begin like this: "We hold these truths to be self-evident, that we are the Anglos' equal, and that the Anglos are laughing at us, that they have denied our inalienable rights as human beings and taken us for fools." The newly elected city council member or city clerk will tell you that he was made to feel small, brown, insignificant, that he was reminded somehow, someplace, of his humble origins, his lack of education, and that he decided he had something to prove.

D riving south on Interstate 710, the freeway that links central Los Angeles to the ports at San Pedro and Long Beach, you pass through the balkanized patchwork of Southeast Los Angeles County, a kind of New Jersey to the white-and-teal Manhattan of the downtown skyline that juts up from the brown horizon to the north. These cities have names conceived by land speculators during the great property booms of the twentieth century—Maywood, South Gate, Huntington Park, Bell Gardens—and are now home to several hundreds of thousands of immigrants, including an aspiring *mexicano* middle class. Families led by truck drivers and carpenters have bought up most of the single-family homes that you find there, clusters of affordable stucco boxes huddled between industrial parks, rail lines, refinery tanks, and the giant towers of the trunk lines bringing imported electricity into the heart of the city. These cities have fallen off the map for English-speaking Los Angeles; for Westsiders on a day trip to Disneyland, they register as little more than the names of freeway exits about halfway to their destination. Traveling at 65 miles per hour, you need a certain amount of concentration, for example, to realize you've entered Bell Gardens: the small, green, rectangular Caltrans sign that announces BELL GARDENS CITY LIMIT, POP. 46,650, ELEV. 125 is dwarfed by billboards for La Buena radio station and the old Vegas-style tower of the Bicycle Casino, a low-budget lure for addicted gamblers.

The undisputed founder of Latino political power in Bell Gardens is María Socorro Chacón. She is, by extension, a pioneer in the wave of civic activism that swept through all the other Southeast cities, making them all Latino-run. You could call her a Citizen One. "The sleeping giant has awoken," she announced in 1992, unaware or unconcerned that the phrase was already a ten-year-old cliché about Latinos (the 1980s was supposed to have been the "Decade of the Hispanic"). Hers was a rebellion born, in part, of self-interest. She owned several apartment buildings in Bell Gardens, and the Anglo-dominated city council had put forward an initiative to reduce "density" in the city by replacing apartments with single-family homes. María Chacón argued that this was a form of ethnic cleansing, because if there were no apartments there would be no more *mexicanos* in the city. She became the manager of the recall campaign that brought a record number of Latinos to the polls to kick out the old council.

María Chacón was a large woman with the moderately overbearing air of a know-it-all Mexican aunt and hair the color of a smoggy Los Angeles sunset. She had a matriarchal charisma that manifested itself chiefly as a blunt obnoxiousness before the Anglo city leaders and bureaucrats. In a place and time where most Mexican immigrants didn't rock the Anglos' boat, María Chacón looked especially courageous. Once in power, Bell Gardens' new rulers conducted a top-to-bottom purge, from the city manager and police chief to the lowly code inspectors who had once dragged María Chacón the landlord to court on charges of abusing her tenants. Eventually the city of Bell Gardens would pay at least $2.5 million to settle lawsuits when these former employees claimed they had been dismissed unfairly. A stack of legal briefs and newspaper clippings described María Chacón as the power behind the throne—not a U.S. citizen, she couldn't run for council herself, but she had a hand in picking who did. She had her foes arrested on trumped-up charges and put her friends and relatives in city jobs for which they were woefully unprepared. None of this dented her popularity with the city's newly assertive Latino voters: once she became a U.S. citizen herself, she was elected to the council too, and eventually became mayor.

Carlos Daniel López, once the president of the Bell Gardens soccer league, offered me some insight on how María Chacón got her way. As mayor, she had the city pay for the leagues' uniforms, and in exchange she repeatedly asked López to assemble his players and their parents at protests at city council meetings and school district hearings. They had become that essential member of the cast of the Latin American political farce: the dial-a-crowd, the loyal chorus I had seen at political rallies from Guadalajara to Argentina, crowds of needy people so dependent and beholden to a political boss that they have no choice but to gather when and where they're told to shout things like "Our *jefe* is right! *Viva* our *jefe!*" Lopez told me, "We would go to these meetings and chant 'Chacón! Chacón!' We realized we were being used as puppets." When he refused to go to any more rallies, the new boss of Bell Gardens reminded him of her generosity. So López and his players arrived at the next council meeting and dumped the uniforms before the dais—a public humiliation for which he would pay a price. Soon afterward, the Bell Gardens police showed up at his home and arrested him for allegedly embezzling $700 in city funds. The charge was thrown out of court, but López filed a federal civil rights lawsuit alleging Chacón had ordered the investigation. "She is an arrogant and despotic woman."

The only time María Chacón used a Spanish word when I sat down to interview her was when I mentioned the former soccer-league president. "He is a *malagradecido*," she said, an ingrate. "It's been devastating and painful for me to see that people you think you know, people you supported, can turn their backs on you so quickly." We were sitting at a table in the empty city council chambers, where the seats on the dais each had a name plaque in Spanish and English: COUNCIL MEMBER/CONSEJAL, MAYOR/ALCALDE.

Three of the four council members had recently turned against Chacón. The city council was now split into pro-Chacón and anti-Chacón factions, and the bimonthly council meetings had become raucous affairs complete with bilingual catcalls and shoving matches. "I stand up against corruption, so I am in the way of a lot of people who do bad things." One of the recent meetings had ended violently, with her husband Jesse in an altercation with the chief of police, and Chacón's arrest three days later on charges of disturbing the peace.

Nothing like that had ever happened when Bell Gardens was controlled by the old Elks and Rotary Club sets. "We're going through the agony of the birth of the new Bell Gardens," María Chacón told me. Bell Gardens was a model of municipal dysfunction, a place where seemingly everyone had been tainted with accusations of petty malfeasance. Minutes before sitting down to talk with Chacón, I had been across the hallway from the council chambers at the window of the city clerk's office to request the minutes of a recent council meeting but was told I'd have to come back another day: the documents were in the hands of the district attorney's office, which was then launching the first of what would become a series of government corruption investigations in Southeast Los Angeles County. Eventually, officials from South Gate, Cudahy, and Commerce would all be dragged into criminal court, and also the defendant in *People of the State of California v. María Chacón.*

The body politic had been orphaned and then adopted by new, Spanish-surnamed parents. Since there were few voters in the city, and even fewer people with the peculiar American obsession for small-town government, the new leaders operated in a vacuum of accountability. Chacón told me betrayal and humiliation had led her to turn against her most recent slate of handpicked council members and the new mayor, David Torres, who had become the leader of the anti-Chacón movement. Torres was pigheaded, another ingrate, Chacón told me. She was about to file the papers for a recall campaign against her former protégé. (In all, the city would have half a dozen recall elections, most of them successful, making Bell Gardens the Bolivia of Southern California politics, with stacks of signed petitions replacing tanks and bayonets as the preferred instrument of the coup plotters.) "Torres is history," María Chacón told me. "He is a nothing. He is pffft." I raised my eyebrows in surprise. The boss woman of Bell Gardens had just made a raspberry.

There's another Rulfo story about rural Mexico that might shed some light on the happenings in Bell Gardens. It's called "El Día del Derrumbe," or "The Day of the Collapse." An earthquake hits the village of Tuxcacuesco, leaving its residents in very dire straits indeed. A few days later, the governor arrives. "All of you know that all the governor has to do is present himself, and as long as people can see him, everything is taken care of," the narrator of the story recounts. Despite the destruction around them, the people of Tuxcacuesco spend all their money arranging a big meal for the governor, and when he actually sits down to eat with them they are mesmerized. Later, they will go over every detail of his meal: how the governor ate all his *guajolote* (turkey), and how he picked up one tortilla after another to dip in the guacamole sauce. After he's eaten, *el gobernador* launches into a long-winded and nonsensical speech, until he's interrupted by the yells of a man at the far end of the table, and someone shouts, "Shut that drunk up!" The man at the far end of the table begins shooting into the air, a brawl breaks out, and very quickly it spreads through the village. The men unsheathe their machetes, women begin screaming, and not even the band launching into the National Anthem can calm things down.

María Chacón, at the height of her power, was a leader with an aura like that of *el gobernador*. Certain residents of Bell Gardens would have seen her as the person who could raise the village from the ruins, and they would have posed for snapshots with her, telling their friends about the time they met her and what she was wearing and how they felt somehow stronger in her presence. Until the moment when the metaphorical voice came from the end of the table and proclaimed that the empress had no clothes, and the people of the village started to unsheathe their machetes.

Bell Gardens City Hall is a low-slung building in the functional style that could be called Suburban Municipal, a collection of pastel blocks with rounded corners, and lights inside globes of glass and stainless steel—Deco flourishes meant to counteract the disposable, prefab feel of the place. When I arrived, to see the spectacle of an American city council meeting divided into competing *mexicano* factions, the lights were giving off a grayish glow that was gradually overtaking the orange twilight, coloring María Chacón and her supporters with an eerie pallor as they staged a premeeting rally on the building's front lawn. The Chaconistas were for the most part a crowd of women and their children. Chacón had filled their ranks by circulating a story that the city council, with Torres at the helm, was going to close a popular youth center. This was, it turned out, a blatant lie.

After spending a few minutes chanting, *"El pueblo, unido, jamás será vencido"* ("The people, united, will never be defeated") and listening to María Chacón warn of wayward young men roaming about the city if the youth center was closed, the Chaconistas filed into the council chambers. One carried a drawing of a game of hang-man, with the names of Chacón's three council foes hanging from the noose. That image stayed with me; in Latin America, the mean-ing of the word "lynch," *linchar,* can drift rather easily from the fig-urative to the literal. Once while on the way to Bolivia's coca region, I happened upon a town outside Cochabamba where an effigy of the mayor hung from the balcony of City Hall—"he stole all our money and if he comes back here we'll lynch him," someone told me. The mayor stayed prudently far away. Later I went to a town in Peru where the mayor had in fact been lynched, having been pulled from his home and run through the cobblestone streets and beaten to death, his corpse tossed over the ruins of the bridge he promised to fix but never did.

The Bell Gardens council meeting that night only hinted at such expressions of mob justice. It began with María Chacón insisting that the mayor proceed immediately to public comment on an item she had placed on the agenda: the alleged city project to close the youth center. The mayor refused, setting off a repartee that ended with Torres telling Chacón several times she was "out of order," while she compared him to two notorious Latin American autocrats, including the one whose abuses Mexican children learn about in el-ementary school. "So you're an absolute power here? A dictator? Are you Porfirio Díaz or Fidel Castro?"

They went on for a good forty minutes more, almost entirely in English, though it was clear that Spanish was the mother tongue of four of the five council members. Below the dais, a woman with a headset and a microphone was methodically translating it all into Spanish, her calm repetitions of *"Estás fuera de orden"* carried by wire to the twenty or so people in the audience who were also wearing headsets. It would have been much easier for everyone, it seemed to me, if the council members had stuck to Spanish, but no, they kept getting nasty and angry with each other in this language that was not their own. After a while the effect was what the Spanish director Pedro Almodóvar might achieve if he ever decides to make a crossover movie with dialogue taken entirely from Robert's Rules of Order. "Mr. Mayor, you are not my father!" Councilwoman Chacón spat across the dais. "You are the person running this meeting!"

When the public was allowed to speak, a small, avuncular man was the first to walk up to the microphone. "It seems to me like there's two groups here fighting among each other," he said in Spanish, without a hint of irony. I had the sense he had grown up on a farm or in a rural hamlet, a place where you repeated what was obvious as a way of taking your time and thinking about what you needed to say. "We came to this country because we were hungry. We came because those people governing us in Mexico were killing us with hunger." He tried to set a conciliatory tone, though no one who spoke later would follow his lead. "We would like to ask that you work together. It should not be about fighting. *Ojalá* you will govern us with honesty."

Next a heavyset woman with a scowl approached the microphone. "Thanks to Mrs. Chacón, you are all there," she said in English, pointing at the mayor and his two council allies. "And thanks to Mrs. Chacón, we'll be able to get you all out!"

A dozen or so people in the audience began chanting, "Re-call! Re-call!"

Sam Macias, a former city public works supervisor, came up to speak. He had sued and won a $200,000 settlement after being laid off for refusing to hire one of Chacón's supporters to a city job. "This is a shame. A real shame. Not a *chame*, councilwoman," he said, mimicking Chacón's accent and causing some nervous laughter in an audience where most people had accents. "When she gets angry she speaks like a sailor. She's not worthy of sitting in that seat!"

After an hour or so the mayor declared the public comment at an end. Now the anti-Chacón council members would have a chance to rebut the accusations that they were going to close the youth center. It was another example, they said, of the manipulations of the woman who had helped put them in office. Addressing the crowd in Spanish—in words that went untranslated for the monolingual English-speakers present—Councilman Joaquín Penilla recalled the moment of his break with Chacón. "She told me, '¿Sabes qué, chiquito? [You know what, little man?]: I put you in, I can take you out.'"

Mayor Torres, looking thoroughly exasperated, spoke last. "Those people are giving me the finger. . . . If these are the kind of people they want to bring into the chambers, they're going to bring the city down."

"Liar!"

"Mentiroso!"

"Tell the truth!"

A few moments later, with the catcalls growing in volume, Torres declared the meeting adjourned and rose quickly to his feet. His two council allies joined him as he headed for a side door with the chief of police and a pair of nervous officers as an escort; they just made it out the door before it was swamped by the Chaconistas. With their foes chased out of the building, María Chacón's sister led them in another chant: "Re-call! Re-call! Re-call!"

H alfway through the last Bell Gardens City Council meeting I attended, a young woman of about twenty shouted out "This is embarrassing!" City Hall was suffering from an acute deficit of decorum, which was entirely understandable given how little experience the Spanish-speaking and immigrant civil society of Bell Gardens had in American municipal government. The small machine María Chacón had created in Bell Gardens was an imitation of the Mexican system, a set of relationships of favoritism, nepotism, and patronage that are known in Spanish as *amiguismo*, "friend-ism."

In Mexico, the alternative to friend-ism is to step outside the system and transform your hopes into a mass movement that aspires to pull the corrupt empire apart. Arturo Ybarra, the future founder of Latino civil society in the barrios of Watts and South Los Angeles, took the movement route as a young student in Mexico City. He was one of the tens of thousands who marched down the city's broad avenues, past the white marble of the Palace of Fine Arts, and the gleaming new Torre Latinoamericana skyscraper, demanding democratic reform. Having embraced that tradition as a youth would help determine the activist persona he adopted as a middle-aged homeowner in Watts. In 1968, he had been a twenty-four-year-old student with ruddy skin and a bush of curly black hair threatening to morph into an afro. His country was run by a mean, corrupt little man, and Arturo and the students believed they were living an emperor-has-no-clothes moment. They peppered their marches with funny rhymes about the president, a tonic against the undercurrent of danger and menace building around them, against the bayonets and tanks beginning to appear on the streets.

Today, Los Angeles is home to thousands of people who have known the exhilaration and sense of dread that come with living the kind of history made by large crowds and armed troops, be it in a rally in San Salvador at the height of that country's brutally suppressed revolution, or an uprising in the villages of Guatemala. One of the great joys of being a bilingual journalist in California is that you can sit in someone's peaceful American living room and listen as they transport you to the epic stage of recent Latin American history. Once, I spent several weeks visiting former Salvadoran soldiers, including one small man whose vivid descriptions of mountain battles, complete with his finger tracings of army and guerrilla troop movements on the blanket of his bed in a tenement near downtown, helped inspire me to write a novel that would capture the drama of it all. Arturo Ybarra first told me the story of his Mexican past in the modest space of the Watts Century Latino Organization, not far from the Jordan Downs housing projects and its community garden of man-high corn planted by immigrant families.

Arturo the university student had been a pamphleteer, running off communiqués announcing new marches and protests, until the "forces of repression" caught up with him and he spent four days in a *calabozo* somewhere, a dungeon of the intelligence services. The agents made fun of his semi-afro and dumped his head into a barrel of water and held him there until he started to pass out and drown, at which point they pulled his dripping face and curls out and demanded to know, "Who are the members of the committee of struggle?" The torture left Arturo with a nervous tic and a pathological paranoia about cameras and police surveillance that lasted for months after they let him go. The army crushed the student movement and chased the multitudes from the streets with bullets, opening fire on a crowd gathered at Plaza of the Three Cultures on October 2, 1968, a night when the demons of Arturo's torture chamber were set loose to inflict their violence on the city.

Arturo left for California, where he had a sister who lived in rural Ventura County. She tried to distract him with some sightseeing trips, but he panicked whenever she pointed a camera at him, because in his mind those were pictures the CIA could get their hands on and pass on to the Mexican army. When he turned on the television he was confronted by the sights and sounds of California in

1969; young people marching, carrying American flags emblazoned with peace symbols and letting their hair grow down to their waist or in great globe-shaped afros that made Arturo's look tame by comparison. Before he could join them, their movement started to disappear too—of a slower, more natural death than the homicide in Mexico—and he started to worry about how he would earn a living. His first job was in a restaurant earning 90 cents an hour, but he soon found better work, got married, joined a union, and bought a house in one of the few places he could find one under $80,000 in California's booming 1970s housing market: Watts.

Arturo the activist was resurrected one day near 103rd Street in Watts, when he happened upon a sign announcing a meeting for the city's Community Redevelopment Agency, which in turn brought him to a room filled with black people and, near the back, a small cluster of Spanish-speaking families. At that instant he felt a twinge of his Mexican self from twenty years earlier. When the meeting ended, the old pamphleteer in him walked across the room and introduced himself to these other *mexicanos* and invited them over to his house. "We were a group so small that we would look at each other with kind of a hunger to communicate with someone who could relate to us," he told me in Spanish. In his living room, they founded the Watts Century Latino Organization.

For many years, no other group would speak for the half million or so Spanish-speakers living in that conglomeration of traditionally black neighborhoods collectively known as South Los Angeles. The area was represented by African-American politicians whose base of support was the "block clubs" that had been instrumental in electing the city's first black mayor, Tom Bradley, in 1973. In the early 1990s, my duties as a reporter took me often to its oppressively long and straight thoroughfares. I would walk past low-rent mini-malls, wandering into the appliance stores specializing in refurbished stovetops, gazing up at the shuttered façades of the Central Avenue nightclubs where the Harlem Renaissance had played out decades earlier. Once I jumped into the ice cream truck of a *mexicano* driver-salesman and helped him pass out Popsicles to Latino and black children who flagged us down, waving quarters and dollar bills. When he saw a group of black teenagers, he swerved in the other direction. "I'm afraid of these black kids. They'll stone your truck if they don't like you," he told me in Spanish. But when I asked him how many times he'd been held up, he offered, "To tell you the truth, it's my first day on the job." Venturing into new territory, my ice-cream vendor had only old fears and prejudices to guide him as he drove through the grid of bungalow homes between the commercial thoroughfares.

Arturo Ybarra and the Watts Century Latino Organization worked to fill this vacuum of community consciousness. His new allies were working people from rural corners of Zacatecas, Jalisco, and other places—construction workers, maids, the raw labor of Los Angeles. The new group came to be known as Wacelo, using the Latin American custom of making abbreviations into pronounceable words. It fought battles over water quality and against the county Housing Authority. Arturo sprinkled his Spanish speech with leftist political terms like *organizaciones de base* (rank-and-file groups) that I recognized from my days with the Mexico City Left. Other organizations came later, but Arturo Ybarra's was the first—he showed what could be done. Arturo Ybarra was the Citizen One of *el sur de Los Angeles,* and in the years that followed people who founded new groups, or who ran for elective office, would come to seek his advice. "Here it's easier to have a meeting with a Congressman or some other high elected official than it is to meet with some *chichincle* in Mexico," he said in Spanish. I wrinkled my brow at that last expression, so he explained, "A *chichincle* is a second- or third-level functionary who gives himself so many airs that they're inaccessible. But here, I think they're obliged to give me the meeting with the Congressman." Arturo Ybarra had met with congressmen and United States senators. The arc of his life was not an uncommon one for people of his generation: from the streets and the iconoclastic marches of raised fists and red banners to quiet meetings in the halls of power. But Arturo had begun his Long March Through the Institutions—as a generation of sixties activists called their transition into the mainstream—in one country and ended it in another. This was one of the secrets behind the Citizen One: the contagion they carried could often be traced back to another outbreak; in Arturo's case, it was one that seemed to have run its course and exhausted itself decades earlier in Mexico City. The *mexicano* faces of his neighbors in that Watts meeting hall resurrected the dormant activist in him, and made him a living link between two political traditions ever more entwined across the border of language and culture that once separated them.

The Latin American political ideas carried northward by Arturo Ybarra and others very quickly began to filter upward in the civic life of California, reaching the marble rotunda of the State Capitol in the person of a handful of Los Angeles–area representatives whose careers were linked to the city's immigrant-dominated trade union movement. I went there to meet one of these elected officials, walking underneath the dome and then past the corridors lined with displays of the flora, fauna, and minerals of California's counties that I had last seen in 1979, when I was the Boys State representative for the now defunct Sierra High School of South Whittier, California. State Senator Gloria Romero's office was on one of the upper floors, down the hall from the governor.

After her epiphany as a thirteen-year-old in Barstow, Gloria Romero's life had followed channels carved into the desert by the tides and currents of Latin American history. She was raised by devoutly Catholic parents whose roots were in New Mexico, and her girlhood was a swirl of narratives about victims, martyrs, and rebels. An elderly uncle told her the Romeros could trace their ancestors back to the land grants made by the Spanish crown about the same time the pilgrims were stepping on Plymouth Rock, and that those ancestors had been disinherited by the Treaty of Guadalupe Hidalgo, which annexed New Mexico to the United States. At church she met a priest, a Father Ponce, who united the most inquisitive young people in his parish in a study circle that gave them a new vision of Jesus as a radical, long-haired idealist who bore a resemblance to a "hippie," a word that circulated like contraband through Barstow in those days. He was the Jesus of the Sermon on the Mount, of "blessed are the peacemakers," the Jesus of the Colombian guerrillas led by the warrior priest Camilo Torres, the Jesus of what would one day be known as "Liberation Theology."

At Barstow High her history teacher asked her to write a paper on "an important figure in American history"—any person, be it Jefferson or Harriet Tubman or Herbert Hoover. She wandered over to the school library, looked through the stacks in the biography section, and came across *The Bolivian Diary of Che Guevara*. She tells me this story today, sitting in her Senate office in Sacramento, with a look of astonishment, disbelief. How did a work of Marxist subversion end up in the Barstow High School library? It's another one of those questions she can't answer. She looked at the cover, flipped through the pages, and decided, "I need to read this book." In her telling, this moment is linked to the funeral she attended sometime earlier for Clarence Griego, a nineteen-year-old son of Barstow who died in Quang Tin, South Vietnam, as a draftee and army private.

The Bolivian Diary of Che Guevara and its tale of a visionary who is martyred for his beliefs carried a power greater than any Bible story Gloria had read, because it was a story born of her times. In the book, Che and his disciples take to the mountain jungles to battle the forces of poverty and darkness. They cross rivers and climb mountains and suffer many trials in the name of a greater cause: the equality of human beings. There was another contraband word tossed around the text, albeit one not much in circulation in 1970s Barstow: "imperialism." This was the word, she felt, that had lingered, unspoken, over the funeral of Clarence Griego, who had been buried without anyone stepping forward to talk about why he died. Much of this young Gloria Romero put in the book report for her history teacher, Mr. Harris, who was not amused. One day after class he took her aside. "I'm very disappointed, Gloria," he said. "You shouldn't be reading these books. If you keep reading books like this, you're going to turn into a Communist."

Gloria Romero did in fact become a kind of guerrilla fighter, a strident gadfly haunting the meetings of the Los Angeles County Board of Supervisors and the Los Angeles Police Commission, speaking out against police abuse. In my duties covering local politics I often crossed paths with her. Once she wrote a letter to the *Times* denouncing me for the sexist crime I'd committed by writing a somewhat critical profile of Gloria Molina, California's most powerful Latina politician. Gloria Romero was one of those strident, unrelenting activists you often find rallying behind hopeless causes, a person much like the man who comes to life in Jon Lee Anderson's *Che Guevara*, the arrogant Argentine who never tired of talking to anyone who would listen about the injustices suffered by Latin America's poor. Che backpacked his way into fame and future martyrdom when his path crossed in Mexico City with a group of exiled Cuban revolutionaries. Gloria Romero became an elected representative thanks to the hundreds of exiled Salvadoran and Guatemalan radicals and displaced Mexican unionists who found themselves busing tables, putting up drywall, and engaged in other low-wage pursuits in 1990s California. Immigrant labor had become a dominant force in the Los Angeles County labor movement. When the hotel workers marched in front of the old Los Angeles Hilton, or the janitors blocked Wilshire Boulevard in a campaign called Justice for Janitors, Gloria Romero did her best to be there.

One day a union contact from the American Federation of Teachers suggested that she run for the Los Angeles Community College District Board of Trustees, one of the more invisible bodies in local government. The trustees oversee the regional network of what used to be called junior colleges, and each is chosen in an at-large ballot that involves all 4 million registered voters in Los Angeles County. "This is the Siberia of local politics. Nobody knows who their trustee is," she explained to me. Her only chance at winning was to win the endorsement of the teachers' union; as a matter of routine, she would then win the backing of the Los Angeles County Labor Federation, whose deep pockets would put her name on "slate mailers" addressed to millions of prospective voters. But in the end the teachers' union leadership decided to back another candidate, in part because they were concerned that a Latina wouldn't be able to win. Gloria appealed to the County Labor Federation's Committee on Political Education, but lost there too. Her last chance came with the federation's House of Delegates, which usually rubber-stamped the political committee's recommendation. "The House of Delegates are your rank-and-file delegates. And a lot of them knew me—janitors and garment workers and hotel workers and laborers especially. They had seen me on picket lines." So it wasn't a surprise when, at a key moment in the debate of the House of Delegates, one of the union members stood up and said, "Hey, Gloria is a *sister*. We should be endorsing her and not this other guy."

In effect, the janitors, the hotel maids, the garment workers, and the other immigrants of the new, Latinified Los Angeles County proletariat gave birth to Gloria Romero's political career. The ascendancy of an uncompromising daughter of Barstow would not have been possible without the boost the union rank-and-file gave her in that first election, and in all her elections since, from the Community College trustee, to the Los Angeles City Charter Reform Commission, to the California State Assembly and finally the State Senate.

When Gloria Romero was first elected to the state legislature and set up shop in the Capitol, one of her fellow legislators shared with her a rumor circulating around Sacramento. "I heard you were a guerrilla and fought with the Sandinistas in Nicaragua."

Gloria Romero laughed. "I've never been to Nicaragua," she said.

The State Assembly would later elect two speakers with ties to the L.A. union movement. The first, Antonio Villaraigosa, was a Mexican-American former activist with the teachers' union who later ran for mayor of Los Angeles. I followed him around the city on his campaign, listening to him struggle with his Spanish as he addressed a group of striking grocery workers on the picket line near the farmers' market. Villaraigosa, like most other Latino politicians, made a point too of speaking out on behalf of immigrant causes. The plight of the immigrant carries a moral weight in the Latino community that far exceeds the immigrant voter's potential to influence any election. Latino politicos will probably always speak out in the defense of the immigrant, just as, for example, Congressional black leaders embrace the causes of Africa more than a century after the abolition of slavery. After Villaraigosa, Fabián Núñez, another assemblyman from central Los Angeles, became the sixty-sixth speaker of the California Assembly. He had been the political director of the Los Angeles County Federation of Labor, was one of twelve children from a San Diego family of Mexican immigrants, and represented a district where three in four residents were Spanish-speakers. His own Spanish was impeccable, the best I've ever heard from an American politician. I listened to him on KMEX-TV's *noticiero* as he explained calmly that he didn't take very kindly to hearing that the new governor, Arnold Schwarzenegger, had referred to him and his Democratic colleagues as *mujercitas* (little women), the only Spanish-language translation anyone could think of for the governor's untranslatable, German-accented insult: "girlie men."

The election of the Latino-speakers hinted at a deeper change afoot in the city's public life. Voter registration, that basic thermometer of a community's civic health, had begun to rise again. The twenty-five-year decline in voting that had ended with the nearly abandoned precincts I saw in central Los Angeles just a few years earlier had slowly begun to reverse itself. You could see this most clearly in Southeast Los Angeles County cities like Huntington Park, which had the largest increase of registered voters per capita of any municipality in the state. You could trace the death of Anglo civic culture and the birth of its Latino replacement in Huntington Park in the statistics of the county Registrar of Voters. Back in 1964, when the city still had its white majority, 15,533 people were registered to vote in the election in which Lyndon Johnson defeated Barry Goldwater. By 1982, after a generation of white flight that left Huntington Park firmly established as an immigrant city, there were only 7,309 registered voters in its crowded three square miles of single-family homes and apartments. That paltry number remained more or less constant for the following decade. In 1994, for example, there were still only 7,861 voters. Then, within two years, the total increased to 10,118. In 2003, there were 12,658.

Just when the rush to registration was reaching its peak, I called up a political consultant and purchased a list of voters in the one Huntington Park neighborhood where more new voters had registered than any other. It was a few blocks west of Pacific Avenue, which functions as the Main Street of Mexican Southern California: when Mexico's national soccer team wins a big game in the World Cup, this is where people come to celebrate. Like a wanna-be councilman testing the waters, I walked door to door through a neighborhood of stucco homes, scattered apartments, and the occasional oversized, brand-new immigrant palace of faux Guadalajara arches and glass chandeliers. Even with all the new voters, on some blocks there were just a handful of names on my list. I met César Salas, a young man who worked as an usher at the local theater, where the patrons had recently risen up in revolt because *Titanic* had been screened without Spanish subtitles. "A lot of people can't vote. I think it's like a gift," he told me in English as we sat in the living room of his apartment. César was twenty-one, and according to my list he hadn't missed casting his ballot in any election since registering three years earlier, making him that rare breed consultants call a high-propensity voter. "They can take your vote away from you, the judge can if you do something bad. If you can vote, vote. While you can." A few blocks away, I met a sexagenarian couple, the Buenrostros, who had become citizens and registered to vote along with six other members of their family. "We've lived here for twenty-four years and it was time," Socorro Buenrostro told me in Spanish. "Even if the gringos don't want us, this is our *tierra*."

The rush to citizenship and voter registration was being accelerated by Proposition 187, the 1994 ballot initiative to prohibit public services to undocumented immigrants, which was what Socorro Buenrostro was referring to when she said, "Even if the gringos don't want us." For the better part of two years, the story of Proposition 187 dominated the Spanish-language media in California. The Mexican and Central American reporters of KMEX-TV's nightly news program issued breathless reports on the anticipated catastrophe in immigrant communities should the measure pass: mothers giving birth would be turned away from emergency rooms, kindergartens in barrio schools would be suddenly empty.

Governor Pete Wilson was running for reelection that same year, and his campaign ads featured images taken from security cameras at the Tijuana border, grainy black-and-white images of Latino men and women running into the United States past the guard shacks at the border and into the traffic on Interstate 5, the voiceover proclaiming with the ominous monotone of a horror flick, "They keep coming." It is difficult to describe—in controlled language—the visceral reaction that short piece of cinematic propaganda evoked among people of Latino descent in California. Roughly speaking, we had been equated with the rushing rodents of the movie *Willard*, a horde of small, voracious mammals whose sheer numbers make them an unstoppable force. Most Latino families have a crossing or a migration story in their past, be it over *el bordo* or up and down the farmworker valleys of the American West. Pete Wilson confronted us with the moment in our history at which we were small and meek. In response, almost 100,000 people marched against Proposition 187 some weeks before it eventually passed, easily the largest mass mobilization for a Latino cause in the history of the United States. It was one of those rare events in a community's history where the sense of threat becomes so overwhelming that the idea of protest is transformed from a cliquish conspiracy into a participatory festival. A civil rights movement was born. One afternoon, it reached Jefferson High School in central Los Angeles, brought by university activists who passed out flyers calling on the students to march to City Hall. At the announced hour, most of the student body headed for the exits, so many leaving at once they had trouble fitting through the open gates. One was then–sixteen-year-old Ana Soto, the daughter of a *mexicana* seamstress. She joined this crowd of rule-breakers as they marched north toward City Hall, an hour's walk away, a moment of communal power unlike anything she'd felt before, and that lingered with her long afterward, despite the disappointment that came when people started dropping out of the march to go home. "You feel pride, you're standing up for it," she told me when I talked to her two years later, after she became Jefferson High's student-body president. "You're doing something about it. You're not the person that's sitting there waiting for the decision to be made."

In the weeks, months, and years that followed, more Latinos decided they could no longer "wait for the decision to be made" without having their say; they signed up to be naturalized, hoping to escape the category "illegal aliens" or the less pejorative but still second-class "resident aliens," and become members of the fully protected category "citizens." In 1995 alone, some 250,000 California Latinos became citizens, a fivefold increase over the year before. The ceremonies were moved to the Los Angeles Convention Center to accommodate the crowds. I attended one about that time, the first naturalization ceremony I'd been to since my own mother and father were sworn in as Americans in the 1970s, when I was about seven years old, standing at the back of a downtown office building with a few dozen people. This time, three thousand people stood together in an arena-sized room, rising to their feet as one, and lifting their right arms to take the oath as they faced a man standing on a distant podium; if they had each raised their left arm too, the ceremony would have looked exactly like an evangelical revival. Outside, they walked up to rows of tables covered with voter-registration forms, and began chatting with volunteers for the Democrats, Republicans, Libertarians, and Greens. On the day they cast a ballot for the first time, they became citizens, too, people who had acquired a sense of themselves as Americans that will be forever colored by the time of conflict and uncertainty in which they received that ornately decorated piece of parchment from the U.S. government that is called a Certificate of Naturalization.

What it means to be an American citizen, and what makes you a citizen, has been a fluid concept throughout this country's history. In the early twenty-first century, San Francisco school officials contemplated a measure that would allow "resident aliens" the right to vote in school board elections; it was argued that the hundreds of thousands of tax-paying, immigrant parents deserved the right to have a say in the education of their children, that they should be citizens (in the broadest sense of the word) with respect to the school board. Throughout the seventeenth and eighteenth centuries, the time when most modern American political institutions were being founded, the dominant strain in political philosophy had it that only property owners were qualified to vote or hold office, because only they possessed, in the words of one historian, "reason and disinterested virtue." The propertyless "mob" was a slave to its passions and thus unfit to rule. Thomas Jefferson believed that wage laborers would always be servants to their masters and that the young American republic drew its strength from the yeoman farmer and independent property owner.

Probably Jefferson would have shaken his head knowingly if he had wandered into Bell Gardens and seen what was happening in that city of renters and working people. How could you expect people who worked sixty hours a week, people whose presence in the community is probably transitory, to dedicate the time and energy to build a government of "reason and disinterested virtue"? What was missing in the Bell Gardens I first visited was the citizen who dedicated himself to local rule in the way Tocqueville observed, a person who "acquires a taste for order, comprehends the balance of powers, and collects clear practical notions on the nature of his duties and the extent of his rights." Such people were in short supply throughout Spanish-speaking California. But here and there, it was possible to find a modern-day equivalent of Jefferson's yeoman farmer, people who were planting roots and giving themselves a political education.

A few miles up the 710 freeway from Bell Gardens is Maywood, a city shaped like a pistol on Southern California maps. On East Fifty-fifth Street, in a neighborhood of neat single-family homes and apartment duplexes, of ice-cream trucks whose speakers blare out "Guantanamera" and Ford pickups with gleaming stickers of the Virgin of Guadalupe on the back windows, is the property and home of Edauco Pulido, purchased for $225,000 about four years before he unexpectedly became one of the founders of the new Spanish-speaking township culture in Maywood. Behind the chain-link fence that marks the front boundary of Pulido's domain, he has planted succulents and cacti that grow from holes in the concrete, the kind of flora that many Mexican homeowners like Pulido find to be a cleaner, neater alternative to the crabgrass or fescues that were a status symbol for a previous generation of American homeowner. The plants appeal to his northern Mexican sensibility—the nopal cactus, after all, is on the coat of arms of Mexico's flag—and are also drought-resistant, which is important, because everyone knows that

Southern California is a desert and that everything green there grows with water borrowed from somewhere else.

Pulido's plants don't need much water, which was why he was surprised when he got his water bill one day and found it had nearly doubled. He was more surprised when he hunted around the outside of his house in search of his water meter, and found it covered with dust, suggesting that no one had read it for months. He talked to two other neighbors who had noticed the same high bills and unread meters. Together they took their water bills and walked four blocks to the headquarters of the Maywood Mutual Water District Number Two. The people in the front office made fun of their accents and pretended not to understand them. "What are you trying to say? What?" True, his English was not the best. But the way he was treated had nothing to do with language. Edauco Pulido was reminded of being in Mexico, and the disdainful, bored sneers of the lower-level bureaucrat behind his desk. In Mexico, the only way to deal with such people is to get in their face. So he and his friends pushed and argued their way into the office of the company president, Cleo Evans, a septuagenarian whose family had operated a trucking company in Maywood since 1931. Evans told Pulido and his friends to "first go learn English and then come back and talk with me."

"They treated us as if we weren't worth anything," Edauco Pulido told me in Spanish. They had been humiliated. "I don't like to stay quiet. I told them to be ready, because I was going to fill that place full of protesters." Mr. Pulido and his two neighbors went back home and came up with a plan. They pooled their money together to print some bilingual flyers. The English was a too-literal translation from Spanish, so that instead of saying "We invite you to the meeting," they said "We invite you to the reunion," because *reunión* means "meeting" in Spanish. Their translation of *"Juntos haremos la fuerza!!!!"* came out as "Together we will be the strength!!!!" Two hundred people joined Pulido and his friends when they returned to the water company office. "There were so many of us, the manager wouldn't let us in the door. He said we would have to move the meeting to City Hall." At City Hall, the company officials offered an explanation for the rising water bills: the state health department had ordered improvements in the system. This did not satisfy the Latino homeowners. Pulido took a look around at the people milling about City Hall after the meeting and told his friends, "I have a garage we can use to keep this going."

They named themselves El Grupo Pro Mejoras de Maywood, the Maywood Improvement Association. John Velásquez, a fifty-year-old grandfather, became its president. Gustavo Villa, a burly truck driver from Guadalajara with a bachelor's degree from the National Autonomous University of Mexico, became the group's strategist and thinker. He tracked down a copy of the water company bylaws and sat down to study it; he discovered that the company was publicly owned, with each Maywood property owner granted shares of stock. The stockholders voted to appoint board members, who in turn picked the president, who now happened to be that angry old gringo who had insulted them.

"The water company belongs to us," Villa told his neighbors in Spanish at the next meeting in Pulido's garage, as they munched on his wife María's *pan dulce*. Those of them who owned their home—and most of them did—could vote for the water company's board of directors, even if they weren't U.S. citizens. Being a property owner made Pulido a citizen with respect to the water company even though he was a "resident alien" as far as the U.S. government was concerned. Over the coming weeks, El Grupo Pro Mejoras gathered proxy votes from seven hundred Maywood households. With those votes, Gustavo Villa was elected the new president of the water company. "They want to get rid of me because I don't speak Spanish," Cleo Evans told me. "That I don't like, because this is America and you should speak English." He denied having made any disparaging remarks about Mr. Pulido's linguistic abilities. "They can speak English well enough, but they want everyone to speak Spanish. They operate a little differently because they're from a different culture."

With the revolution in the water company complete, El Grupo Pro Mejoras turned its attention to the city council. About twenty of them started going to the meetings; they would cluster together at the back of the chambers in the second floor of City Hall, in a long room with folding chairs that looked more appropriate for a lodge meeting. Afterward, they would go back to Edauco Pulido's garage to discuss what they had seen. They latched on to new issues, like the ballot initiative put forward by the council to raise money for street repairs. The members of El Grupo Pro Mejoras had been bitten by the local government bug; nothing else could explain their sudden obsession with the minutiae of bond measures and the public works budget. They put out new flyers, with markedly better English. "We all want a better Maywood," one read. "But the bond issue doesn't guarantee that your street will be fixed." They registered with the California secretary of state's office as a "general purpose committee" so they could raise campaign funds. El Grupo Pro Mejoras wanted to do things right, which meant following American law and also their Latin American traditions: they stamped most of their flyers with the "official" Grupo Pro Mejoras seal, a scale of justice superimposed on the letters GPM, because that's what civic groups do in Mexico. A generation had passed since Maywood had seen its residents trouble themselves with such an effort. Thanks to El Grupo, the city's bond initiative went down to defeat: needing a two-thirds majority to pass, Proposition 981 got barely a third of the votes, losing 671 to 1,291.

A fter wandering through New England in the 1830s and witnessing the town meetings of the early American republic, Tocqueville concluded that the ability to exercise local power was the cement that bonded Americans to their democracy and fed their incipient patriotism. "The New Englander is attached to his township not so much because he was born in it, but because it is a free and strong community, of which he is a member, and which deserves the care spent in managing it." In Maywood, in the first decade of the new Latin American democracy there, the citizen-activists of El Grupo Pro Mejoras de Maywood became mestizo equivalents of the nineteenth-century New Englander. They had come to see themselves as members of a free community and had come to believe they had a role in managing it, though how they saw their local government and their role in it was still colored by their Latin American experiences.

A week after their victory in the bond election, I stopped by Edauco Pulido's garage. As always, María Pulido passed out the *pan dulce*, the seashell-shaped *concha* rolls covered with pink sugar, and *cochinito* gingerbread. The twenty or so members of El Grupo wore name tags and sat in chairs arranged in a wide oval that started in the garage and opened into the driveway beyond. I sat just past the open garage door in the night air, looking up at the thin sliver of a crescent moon. The group had placed a file cabinet in one corner of the garage and the obligatory *mexicano* calendar of an Aztec prince carrying his princess past the Popocatepetl volcano. The prince shared the wall with a map of the Maywood Mutual Water District Number Two and a framed copy of Form 410 from the California secretary of state's office, El Grupo's official "statement of organization."

The big news that night was that several Grupo activists had been approached by one of the council members at the end of the last council meeting. Several members raised their eyebrows, others frowned skeptically. The city establishment, such as it was, had made a first move toward courting them.

"I don't trust any of those council members," one member said.

"The system is based on hypocrisy," another said. "I don't want to work with any of these people at all."

"They're like the presidents in Mexico. The money just disappears."

Velásquez suggested that since both Mayor Martin and his son were on the city council, the City of Maywood bore some resemblance to the dynasties that have ruled all or part of Mexico at one time or another. "They spend so much time in power, they forget about the community, another member said. "They start to think of themselves as kings." El Grupo would be better off keeping their distance from such people.

In late-eighteenth-century America, people believed that power, unchecked, could lead to a return of the kind of tyranny King George III had foisted upon them, a tyranny that could easily take new guises. The Maywood group saw the despotism with which they were most familiar lurking about everywhere: the one-party, political-boss system of "caudillos" and the all-powerful executive who picks his successor with the "pointing of a finger," a *dedazo*. It seemed entirely possible to them that any leader, American-born or Mexican immigrant, could take the guise of the *PRIistas* who had ruined Mexico, enriching themselves and their family at the public trough while *el pueblo*, the people, suffered in misery. The symbol of the PRI—the Revolutionary Institutional Party, which ruled Mexico for most of the twentieth century—was three letters inside a red-white-and-green circle; in the political campaigns of resurgent *mexicano* Los Angeles, it became a symbol of authoritarianism, appearing in mailers and posters in city council campaigns. In Pulido's view, the people of Maywood had already cast aside one such leader, Cleo Evans, leaving Villa in his place. Pulido seemed to feel that Evans should be taught a further lesson, that the group should move to reduce his pension or inflict some other punishment, seeking a pound of flesh for the abuses they had suffered.

"He never respected us," Pulido argued. "Why should we respect him?"

"Answering an iron hand with an iron hand doesn't work," Villa answered. His voice was trying to pull them in the direction of "reason and disinterested virtue," against impulses learned in the old country. Pulido looked back skeptically at Villa, at the opposite end of the garage. The tension between them at that moment would linger only briefly, dissolving in the optimism of the group's recent victories. But it was, in essence, symptomatic of the large conflict between the competing strains of thought and tradition that will define new chapters in American history in the century to come. Across the United States, in all the new places where Spanish-speaking immigrants are settling, in Dalton, Georgia, and Grand Island, Nebraska, the moment will come when simple demographics make Latino political power inevitable. Will the new pretenders to power in these towns surround their city halls with dial-a-crowds and hang the mayor in effigy? Or will they sit patiently in their garages studying bylaws and bond measures in a language they learned at night school? Will they embrace the iron hand (*la mano dura*), or will they take the Long March Through the Institutions of an Arturo Ybarra?

On the night I sat in Eduaco Pulido's garage, Villa successfully steered the discussion away from talk of vengeance and retribution. Instead, the group began to talk about breathing new life into the Chamber of Commerce and establishing an independent school district. "We're like people who've woken up from a long coma," Velásquez, who was sitting next to me, whispered in Spanish. "We want to do everything at once."

"Be careful, we're just a little *pueblito* now," Gustavo Villa would tell me later, using the Spanish word for "little village," because their movement was still small and isolated, like those places where they had been born, cities and towns and hamlets on the brittle plains of Jalisco and Michoacán. "But in ten, fifteen years, who knows? If this can happen in Maywood, it can happen in other places. This might be contagious."

There were many more scandals and upheavals in Southeast Los Angeles County in the years to come, but the steady rise in voter registration gave hope to a series of candidates who, having caught the civics bug I had seen in Maywood, successfully ran on anti-corruption slates. In Huntington Park, where I had walked the precincts to see why so many people were registering to vote, a mother of three from Mexico City was elected to two consecutive terms on the city council. Rosario Marín favored conservative wool dresses and wore glasses with thick frames, as if she had been cast to play the mother in a *mexicano* version of *Ozzie and Harriet*. In an overwhelmingly Democratic city, she was the only Republican official, and the party rewarded her loyalty by putting her on the lectern next to its presidential candidate at his "Hispanic" rallies. They also gave her a ticket to the Republican convention in Philadelphia. I got sent to the convention too, to do a story about black Republicans and other obscure topics. One afternoon, while squeezing through the throng on the convention floor in search of a black person to interview, I ran into Councilwoman Marín. "*¡Héctor! ¿Cómo estás? ¡Qué* *gusto verte!*" She gave me a hug and a friendly peck on the cheek, a warm Latino greeting that would have seemed incongruous, given the WASPy GOP setting, were it not for the Ricky Martin songs that played periodically on the loudspeakers and the group of black men and women in Stetsons standing over by the sign for the Texas delegation: that was the year the GOP embraced "multiculturalism." Later, the Mexican icon Vicente Fernández would belt out a tune on the convention's main stage, complete with his Mexican *charro* outfit. "*Adiós,* Rosario," I said. Pointing toward the Texans, I said, "I see the people I need to interview over there."

The election of George Bush as president of the United States turned out to be very a good thing for Rosario Marín. He appointed her treasurer of the United States: the barrios of Southeast Los Angeles County had produced their first national political figure. Millions of dollar bills, including the twenties sent down to Mexico by laborers in Alabama and the hundreds carried in the pockets of coyotes in Tijuana as they guide their charges past the Border Patrol, carry her signature, complete with the grammatically correct (in Spanish) ascending accent over the "í."

The threads linking American democracy to the prejudices and melodrama of little Latin American *pueblitos* like those that exist in the memory of Gustavo Villa are very much alive in the City Hall of the nearby town of South Gate. These connections are not immediately obvious when you approach South Gate City Hall from the parking lot and step in through the door. If you walk down the long corridor to the very end, you will find two long glass cases containing pictures of local men and women serving in the war in Iraq ("In Honor of Our Son and Daughter, Sgt. De la Cruz, Spec. De la Cruz"), and the snapshots of homes with elegantly trimmed hedges awarded "South Gate Beautification Awards." But if you turn to the right, you will find the office of the city clerk, Carmen Avalos, a woman with the oval face and cappuccino-colored complexion of central Mexico.

Step into Carmen's office and you come upon a collection of certificates and commendations (one with her name misspelled) that she has earned for an act of courage, performed in this office, that rescued the good name of South Gate city government. The story of Carmen Avalos's civic awakening begins, like that of Gloria Romero, with a humiliation, but it also has a prologue in a Mexican village, the site of an unbearable and thus long-secret family tragedy. Carmen begins to wipe tears from her eyes because she is seven months pregnant and the story of her election as city clerk and her battles with the "mafia" that until recently ruled South Gate has somehow led her back to the hamlet of San Joaquín, down the road from the town of Atotonilco, in the state of Jalisco, Mexico.

"When my father came to this country, he crossed over *el cerro*," up and over the mountain at the place where the Sonora Desert reaches the Pacific, she tells me in English and Spanish, which is the way she speaks for most of the two hours I spend in her office. Her father had the rest of the family brought over. When Carmen was old enough to go to kindergarten, they took her to English as a Second Language classes, and she has vivid memories of those first days at school, of the refurbished janitorial supply closet where the English instruction often consisted of watching Disney movies, and of the time she entered a room and the children erupted in laughter: to this day she does not know why, because much of what happened in the English-laden air around her was a mystery then. Maybe it was the braids her mother had worked into her hair. But she does remember vowing, in her five-year-old brain, "That's the last time anyone laughs at me because I don't know something."

Scroll quickly through the next dozen years of Carmen's California life, skipping past her moral triumph over a skeptical Honors English teacher in high school, and you arrive at the moment she receives the letters telling her she has been accepted to Stanford University and UCLA, and also at the moment some days later when she breaks down in tears because her parents have informed her they cannot possibly afford to send her to either place. Instead, teenage Carmen hops on the bus for the hour-long, daily ride to the decidedly less elite campus of East Los Angeles College. She is a teenager who feels she deserves better, and one especially frustrating day she decides at the bus stop to just give up, to return home and tell her mother she is going to drop out because "I don't belong at East L.A. College—I belong at Stanford." Her very traditional, very Mexican mother offers no words of sympathy. Instead, she says: "*Ay, mija* [my daughter]. Why study so much when your husband is going to tell you to stay home to cook and clean?" Those words stunned Carmen awake. "You know what?" she announced. "I just changed my mind."

Carmen got her degree at Cal State Dominguez Hills and became the biology teacher at her alma mater, South Gate High School, where she enjoyed the prestige Mexican families confer on *la maestra*, a symbol of culture, hope, and learning. Her life changed on the day a fellow teacher brought up the subject of city politics. A recall election was taking place that day, to remove the last Anglo from the city council, part of a blatant power grab by the strongman of South Gate, one Albert Robles, who would later be hauled into court for threatening to kill his opponents. Robles had moved to South Gate because of the opportunity represented by the new Latino majority there and the lack of people trained in American-style politics. "Nature abhors a vacuum," he told the *Times*. He was, in essence, a modern-day carpetbagger. One Robles foe had his home firebombed, another had been shot in the head, but Carmen confessed to her colleague to know nothing about any of this, to which he replied, "Carmen, you're one of the smartest people I know, and I can't believe they're trying to make a fool out of you too." This offhand remark upset Carmen so much that her students noticed when she went to her next class. "I'm nobody's fool," Carmen told them. The class discussion that followed ended with everyone present agreeing that she would run for office in the next election.

Her campaign was part democratic crusade, part situation comedy. Put succinctly: she had no idea what she was doing. Someone told her that the city clerk was responsible for the municipal elections, so she decided to run for that. When she showed up with her signed candidate petitions at City Hall, she very nearly walked out after discovering that the registration fee was $800, "more than half my mortgage." *Ni modo*, as they say in Mexico: What can you do? She plunked down the money. Her students walked door-to-door with her, dispensing handmade bilingual flyers. They were unaware they could obtain lists of registered voters from City Hall, so they knocked on everyone's door and quickly discovered that many people were ineligible to vote. Carmen spoke to one Mexican woman who listened to her campaign pitch with a look of guilt and embarrassment, an encounter that illustrates perfectly the reverse Latino political logic that would eventually help Carmen get elected. She relates this story in a mixture of English and Spanish: "This lady told me, '*Mija*, I wish I could help you, *pero no tengo papeles* [but I don't have any papers].' Then I thought to myself, how does our culture communicate? So I said, '*¿Sabe qué, señora?* Do you know someone who can vote?' '*Pues sí. Todos los hijos de mi comadre.* [Yes. All the children of my *comadre*, my child's godparent.]' So I told her, '*Entonces, ¿por qué me dice que no puede hacer nada? Tiene voz.* [Why do you tell me you can't help me? You have a voice.] Right?' She said, '*Sí.*' 'If you pick up the phone and talk to your *comadre*, that will help me tremendously.' And she said, '*Eso sí puedo hacer.* [That I can do.]' She got happy. She had power." Word of mouth, her position as *la maestra*, the friendship and family connections that came with having lived most of her life in South Gate—her mother's prayer group delivered an unexpected and multiplying sum of votes—added up to victory for Carmen Avalos.

A few days after the election, someone dumped a large teddy bear on her lawn, with its throat slit and limbs pulled apart. The city attorney, a Robles ally, refused to allow her to be sworn in—she showed up at her inauguration at the last minute, without a judge, because the city had kept her in the dark about when the ceremony would be. Once that had been settled, she found a newly built wall that cut her office in half. Most city employees wouldn't speak to her or look her in the eye. The Robles-dominated city council announced it would lower her salary from $72,000 to $7,200 but backed down when she threatened a lawsuit. One of her first responsibilities was to oversee another recall election—this one launched by community activists against Robles and his allies—but the city council voted to hire a private law firm to run the election instead. One of her assistants charged she was running the recall campaign out of her office— if true, a violation of the law—and the chief of police showed up to confiscate all her files. Finally, the Robles machine filed petitions to launch a recall against her too, which put her in the strange position of fighting to keep a job that had been stripped of its most meaningful responsibility.

At the moment when she was feeling most beaten down and isolated, when good sense should have dictated a retreat from City Hall, back to her life as a teacher and single mother, Carmen Avalos stood firm. She gathered all the evidence she still had in her possession of the political fraud and pillaging she was witnessing in South

Gate, and sat down to draft an impassioned letter to the state attorney general and the secretary of state. It was a manifesto and a plea written in that language she did not speak when her classmates broke into unexplained laughter all those years ago, a letter that began, "I was elected to bring fair elections to this city. . . ."

A few weeks later Carmen Avalos stood on the lawn before South Gate City Hall with Secretary of State Bill Jones for a press conference. Just as in a turbulent Latin American country, outside observers were brought in to ensure a fair and clean recall election. Albert Robles and his allies were run out of office, despite some desperate, last-minute efforts to sway the electorate in their favor, including the giveaway of a house in a raffle, in a carnival-like ceremony outside City Hall, a spectacle that invited widespread comparisons to the tactics of the PRI in Mexico.

Carmen Avalos kept her job as city clerk, was exonerated of the charges against her, and eventually regained her responsibility to run the city elections. Democracy was triumphant in South Gate, all thanks to her own stubbornness and that of a handful of leaders in the community. It was at this point in the telling of her story, for reasons I cannot explain, that our conversation drifted to the past, to her crossing at age two and those first days at State Street Elementary, to her father the truck driver and the lessons he passed on to her about dignity and tenacity. Her father taught her to say, *El hambre me tumba pero el orgullo me levanta*—Hunger knocks me down but pride picks me up. He was a man who grew up in a *rancho* and "wanted to be somebody in life" but who never got past the second grade, which is as far as the priest who came to his *rancho* could teach him. Leopoldo Avalos was one of twenty children, and he often told his daughter the story about how when his turn came to be the one to go to the big city and study third grade, as his older siblings had, it was decided that he could not go, because his family needed him to work, so he stayed there in the *rancho*, where the Avalos were pariahs because even by the standards of rural Mexico they had too many children, more than they could possibly feed.

When Carmen became an adult, she and her parents all traveled together to San Joaquín and to the *rancho*, where they walked along the desolate roads, past the old crumbling adobe buildings, her father suddenly distant, his mind elsewhere. He began to weep.

"Do you think it's fair," he blurted out, "for a seven-year-old boy to have to bury his one-year-old brother in a cookie box?"

In the next few minutes, the secret he had been holding for decades came flowing out as quickly as the tears pulsing down his sun-beaten cheeks. His baby brother had died of malnutrition, his mother was sick and delirious, and his father was elsewhere, so it fell to seven-year-old Leopoldo and his eight- and nine-year-old brothers to bury him. "Your uncles got scared," Leopoldo told his daughter, so he alone buried his baby brother, folding his little arms and legs because they wouldn't fit in the cookie box otherwise. Leopoldo had held on to that story and never told a soul until that moment, when Carmen suddenly understood what fed the font of his striving, the unflinching sense of personal honor that had rescued him from that place of horrors and brought him to the place of possibility and reinvention people call *el norte*. Somehow he passed on that strength of will to his children; it was the force behind Carmen's determination not to be belittled as a little girl, or humiliated as a woman and citizen. Determination was Leopoldo's legacy to his children; it was reborn in the younger daughter who went to USC and the son who went to Berkeley, and in the older daughter who could have gone to Stanford but didn't, and who instead won an election and became the city clerk of South Gate.

Part Four

E PLURIBUS UNUM

Chapter Ten

UNA NACIÓN UNIDA

Heroes of Another Fatherland

El Reno, Oklahoma · San Juan, Puerto Rico · New York, New York · Baghdad, Iraq

imothy McVeigh was in this prison. His stoic countenance, small eyes, and lanky, jumpsuited frame are with me as I approach the aggressive array of fences, and then walk underneath menacing whirlwinds of barbed wire and enter the first of several security passages. Just an hour away across the grainy red Oklahoma plains, the most famous inmate of the federal penitentiary at El Reno brought down a government building, leaving a monument of sorrow and a place of pilgrimage in its place. I have come to Oklahoma to see another convicted terrorist, a living relic from a bygone era that also produced the Weather Underground, the Symbionese Liberation Army, and all those other debating clubs of alienated young men and women who got it into their heads that they could transform places like Milwaukee and Berkeley into battlefields, in emulation of, and in tribute to, Che Guevara and his lonely band of revolutionary warriors. Timothy McVeigh had perhaps one other follower, maybe two if you counted his slacker roommate from Arizona who shared his antigovernment views but didn't want to blow up buildings. Elizam Escobar, on the other hand, was always part of a *movimiento*, one that has lived on for decades—sometimes vibrant, sometimes small and isolated, but never completely vanquished. In Puerto Rico, there are thousands of people who consider him a hero, as will become clear on the day he is set free and put on a plane to San Juan, to be received in the embrace of a tropical morning at Luis Muñoz Marín International Airport. But for the moment, he was alone in his Oklahoma cell, a former art teacher who had cast his lot with an isolated band of bomb throwers, the generically named Fuerzas Armadas de Liberación Nacional, the Armed Forces of National Liberation. They were said to be responsible for bombing the police headquarters in New York City, one of more than one hundred attacks that killed five people and injured dozens more. When the police finally cornered them, in Evanston, Illinois, Escobar and his comrades declared themselves "prisoners of war" and refused to participate in their trials. That had been a generation ago, when Elizam himself was a lean thirty-year-old with stringy black hair and a toddler son. I had in my possession a picture of him a few years after his arrest, his arms folded before him in a pose of proud defiance, the hair reaching to his collar, a man from the era of lava lamps whose cause, comrades, and victims had been forgotten to most Americans.

The Elizam Escobar I saw in the conference room was a much older version of that young man in the photograph. I was struck by his grayness, by the deep circles under his eyes. He exuded exhaustion, as if the prison jumpsuit he was wearing were a set of pajamas and I had roused him out of bed. In El Reno, he worked in the craft room on allegorical oil paintings with subtly political themes, or wrote in his cell, trying to tune out the noise of nearby cardplayers, wanting to build his own little universe of thought, art, and political struggle in the few square feet around him. He considers himself an intellectual, a man confined to a prison cell because he fought for the liberty of his country, which is about as powerful a self-image as you can have. Against this, there is the prison system itself, whose function is to shrink an inmate's self-image, to tame him of his bad behaviors. "I feel like a fish out of water here," he told me. The prison was an ecosystem of corruption, intimidation, and self-destruction, and he longed to rescue his artist's heart from the place before the flame inside it died forever. Prison, he said, is "a living death."

From the perspective of the prison conference room where we talked, there was something poignant about Elizam Escobar. He was a man who clung to the idea that he was a patriot even though the passage of time had reduced him to little more than a bureaucratic afterthought to the empire he fought, a human being filed away in a concrete container. The citizens of the empire he fought had long ago stopped fearing him—how many Americans know that in the last century Puerto Rican nationalists shot up Congress, and that they nearly assassinated President Truman? The idea that he and his small band of comrades ever constituted an "army" was a risible bit of hubris. As I sat there, just a few feet away, it was clear that the only trouble Elizam Escobar presented to the empire was the daily task of feeding him and paying the guards who reminded him to wash his paintbrushes.

It had all seemed bigger back in the 1970s, when Escobar and his comrades were detained after an armored car robbery and documents found in their possession suggested they were in town to kidnap a prominent industrialist. It was to be one more dangerous act at the service of an ideal, the liberty and dignity of the place where he was born, raised, and educated, Puerto Rico. We talked and Elizam began offering his explanations, the historical "roots of the struggle," and of course he could not do this without sounding like a man who had emerged from a time machine, from an era when the word "colonialism" was on the lips of people in East Harlem and East Hollywood. He invoked the 1898 Spanish-American War, Northern Ireland, Palestine, and the ongoing occupation of his own Caribbean island. "The only crime here is colonialism," he told me. "The treaty that handed over Puerto Rico to the United States is illegal. There is no lawful basis for the occupation of my country." Puerto Rico is a "commonwealth," a sort of in-between status, neither a colony nor the fifty-first state of the United States. Its residents are American citizens who cannot vote in presidential elections and have no representation in Congress, but who are free to travel back and forth to the United States. The question of Puerto Rican sovereignty repeatedly comes up at a United Nations committee on decolonization, alongside the question of the fates of Western Sahara and assorted Pacific islands. "How can I be accused of seditious conspiracy?" Escobar said of the main charge against him. "How can I be a traitor when I'm fighting for the freedom of my country?"

Truth be told, back in Puerto Rico, and in the Puerto Rican neighborhoods of New York City, these ideas were not quite the anachronisms they seemed to be from the perspective of that Oklahoma prison. Seventy-five thousand people had signed a petition to the White House demanding his release and that of the other FALN prisoners. Against this, there were the dead and the injured, including a New York police detective blinded by an FALN bomb who had stepped forward to say that President Clinton was "pandering" to the Puerto Rican vote by offering the prisoners an amnesty deal. In the name of the victims, congressmen and senators and police officials were pressuring the Clinton administration to withdraw the offer. They said the president was considering releasing the prisoners to further the ambitions of his wife, who was contemplating a run at the U.S. Senate in New York. The Puerto Rican vote was a key number in the equations of victory for a candidate in the Democratic primary.

Sitting in El Reno, glimpsing the news in between episodes of Jerry Springer and Oprah on the rec room television, Elizam Escobar had seen the debate about his crimes unfolding; perhaps he had winced at the sight of the blinded detective. "I lament, profoundly, every person who has been injured, regardless of their position," he said, sitting across from me with his palms on the surface of the table, looking at the back of his hands in contemplation. "We had a high respect for life and always took measures in that direction." Then he recovers himself, and the ideas at the center of his being here. "It's a cliché, but one person's terrorist is another person's freedom fighter. We are closer to the traditions of the American Revolution than any of these politicians. . . . All of a sudden we are very visible in prison, but we are being used by the politicians for their purposes."

To be set free, Elizam only had to place his signature on a piece of paper; then he could walk through all the maze of doors and bulletproof glass, out past the spools of razor wire and onto the Oklahoma plains. He could hope to see his son's imminent graduation from college. He would have accepted the offer but for the conditions attached, which he considered humiliating: he would not be allowed to engage in any political activity, or to meet with his former comrades-in-arms, or make any overtly political statements. "It's another test of fire. After twenty years, any offer of excarceration is a temptation," he told me in English, the use of the false cognate of the word *excarcelación* betraying his Spanish-speaking roots. "But we're here for the struggle of independence of Puerto Rico. That is our primary concern. . . . When I was arrested, I knew it was going to be for a long time. When you take a position of principle, you have to be willing to accept the consequences. I understood then that I might never get out of prison. And I still feel that way. I might have to wait until 2014, and I have no idea what the situation will be like then." He gave a quiet laugh at the absurdity of that number, 2014, by which time he would be a senior citizen, a rebel in retirement.

I left that meeting convinced Elizam Escobar would remain in prison for many years to come. It is impossible not to feel small, I thought, in the presence of someone who is willing to stay behind bars, to surrender sunlight and long walks across open vistas, to surrender the choice of what he will eat each day, all in the name of an ideal. His presence in that cell was a metaphor for Puerto Rican national identity and that to complain about his fate, or to accept a lesser freedom, would be a betrayal to anyone who believed in that identity.

But others in the group were tired of the long, lonely fight. A few days earlier, Escobar and the other eleven prisoners offered the amnesty had participated in a government-arranged conference call, the first time they had spoken as a group since their arrest two decades earlier. They had agreed to make "one, collective response" to the government's conditions. Escobar was a hard-liner, but a democratic one, and said he would respect the will of the majority.

In the end, the group decided to accept the government offer, and Elizam Escobar was set free.

I arrived in San Juan the morning of September 11, 1999, on a red-eye flight from Los Angeles via Miami, half-awake and startled by the sudden Caribbean heat and humidity. I was just an hour or so ahead of the emancipated prisoners, who were arriving at this same airport, so I ran quickly across the terminal to the spot where some two hundred people had gathered around a pair of glass doors, waiting for their heroes to step through. I could hear them clapping and chanting from a distance; as I got closer I could see they were being led by a smallish woman in blue jeans with a booming, raspy voice that sounded as if it were being transmitted over a loudspeaker.

"*¡Libertad, libertad!*"

"*¡Para los presos políticos ya!*"

The people in the crowd held old pictures of the prisoners, Puerto Rican flags, and hand-painted signs repeating the slogans in the chants. I talked to a seventy-eight-year-old teacher and *independentista* named Enrique Segarra who said, "It's a great triumph for the Puerto Rican people that we've been able to rescue eleven prisoners from the American dungeons." María del Pilar Cristián was not an *independentista*, but wanted to be there to honor the "freedom fighters"; she was there because it was a moment of island history, akin to seeing Nelson Mandela walk out of prison, even though she did not entirely believe in the cause of the emancipated prisoners. "I am a supporter of the commonwealth. But I understand that Puerto Rico should conserve its traditions, its culture, and its language." This seemingly contradictory way of thinking was, it seemed, how most Puerto Ricans felt that day. Even the pro-statehood daily *El Mundo* had written gushing stories about the return of prisoner Adolfo Matos the night before, the banner headline announcing, "He's home!" The mayor of the town of Lajas greeted Matos warmly, calling him "a hero who never killed anyone or stole anything. What he did was defend his country." The day the prisoners came home seemed to be one of universal celebration on the island. And yet in the last referendum on the issue, less than 3 percent of the electorate had voted for independence. Seeking to understand this paradox, I had spoken with Ronald Fernández, a sociologist and the author of

The Disenchanted Island. Puerto Ricans, he said, have a long tradition of embracing their most radical militants as symbols of national honor, even while rejecting the creation of a separate nationhood. "There's a tremendous groundswell for these people, because they're seen as defending the culture," he told me. "It's all about dignity and respect." Puerto Ricans think of their U.S. citizenship as a windfall that guarantees opportunity and success for their children, but retain the idea that they really are a separate, sovereign nation in hiding.

Throughout his life, my father has felt the same attraction and repulsion to Americanness. Like Puerto Rico, my father wanted to have it both ways: he wanted his son to go to college and ascend to the top of the American class, but he still wanted that free *centroamericano* republic to live on in his brain. He embraced his *latinidad* with more fervor even as his mestizo roots in Guatemala became more distant. Puerto Ricans, too, grew fonder of the *independentistas* as it became less likely the militants would achieve their stated goal. This was, of course, the same tension that informed the lives of the dozens of people I had met in my wanderings across North America. Gregorio, the onetime *mexicano* goatherd, embraced the American spirit and traveled from the Pacific Northwest to Alabama and the Carolinas in search of the money and adventure it could offer him, but he always found himself drifting back across the Rio Bravo del Norte to Mexico: probably he would spend the rest of his life that way, straddling a border that would become less meaningful each time he crossed over it. Cuban Miami had seemed to be ready to slip quietly into the American orbit, its old fighters fading into obscurity, until a little boy arrived across the water and pulled their spirits all back to the island. José García took the oath of American citizenship but kept his eye on the south, wondering if his brother might show up at the fence again, ready to jump over as so many others had. *Latinidad* was something inescapable: it was always there, just over the fence, just over the water, tattooed into your skin, in the blood of your defiant brother, in the ubiquitous portraits of El Che, and in the aging faces of men and women emerging from their prison cells.

Through the glass doors of the air terminal, I could see one of the freed Puerto Rican prisoners entering the baggage claim area, where she was greeted by a pair of young girls with flowers who reached up on their tiptoes to give her a kiss on the cheek. I sneaked past the distracted airport security guards, one of whom had a camera. A moment later this same guard was posing for a picture with Carmen Valentín, a convicted terrorist. Valentín then walked through the doors to a waiting bouquet of microphones arranged to capture her first public words as a free woman. She gave the impression of a person who did not know what to say, or who felt sadness at not being able to say the things that the airport crowd expected of her. She thanked the thousands of people who had helped win her release, and said she would spend time with her family, "to see all that we've missed these years being absent." She walked away, burying her face in her hands. The crowd began a new chant, assailing "the real terrorist": "¡El yanqui, imperialista, el verdadero terrorista!"

Elizam Escobar arrived later that afternoon. "I will do everything possible to behave in a way that is worthy of Puerto Rican history," he said in Spanish. "We will try to open new trenches in the struggle." It would be the most militant statement any of the former prisoners made that day.

I f Elizam Escobar had turned down the clemency offer from the Clinton administration, chances are he would have stayed in prison until the end of his term. Two years to the day after he was set free and arrived in Puerto Rico, a group of men crashed a pair of airplanes into the two tallest buildings in New York City. Like other such attacks over the past century of world history, including those of the FALN militants, it was an act intended to bring distant conflicts and grievances home to the comfort of an imperial capital. Unlike Elizam Escobar and his comrades, however, these men did not profess "a high respect for life." Such was the trauma inflicted upon the American psyche by the mass murder of that day that it is likely several decades will pass before an American president again performs an act of mercy on behalf of someone who has dared flirt with the label "terrorist."

Not even the most hardened FALN fighter could have imagined an act of such demented proportions. They would never have imagined that a small group of determined men could change how time was lived in New York City, that they could make its residents lower their gaze away from the proud and confident skyline, or cause the spiritual gloom of faraway and impoverished lands to fall like a cold rain over its modern avenues. When I arrived in New York on the night of September 13, it was to a strangely empty Midtown, a place that bore little resemblance to the vibrant place in my memory, where traffic moved to an Aaron Copeland score and the sidewalks were populated with young adults whose every footstep suggested purpose, impatience, and ambition.

Instead, I found sidewalk shrines by the Gap ads and the shop windows, little memorials of votive candles and flowers like those I had seen at the site of Los Angeles gang shootings, or Andean bus crashes. In Latino Los Angeles, as in the Andes and other Spanish-speaking places, the idea is to build the shrine at the spot where your beloved's soul ascended into heaven, but in New York that was not possible. Here the memorials rose from the bus stops where the dead once waited, and from the patches of street that greeted them when they walked out of their apartment buildings. Their faces, ren-

dered by ink jet, gazed back at you from lampposts, a moment of do-
mesticity or office camaraderie now captioned "MISSING." It was impossible to look at them without feeling your Americanness, a
quality that, in those days, seemed to attach itself even to people
who were not citizens. Ecuadorians, Colombians, Californians, and
Iowans: they had all chosen to place themselves in New York City,
the capital city of twentieth-century American reinvention, inside
or near its tallest monument to ambition and progress. It was for
that reason, and for that reason only, that they had been killed.

I ended up at Union Square, which was crowded with people
locked in prayer and debate, some kneeling before more shrines to
the missing and the dead. A hundred votive candles shimmered in
one spot, forming a glowing lake of wax and flame. Others gathered
around people holding a stick that functioned as a symbolic bull-
horn, listening to the speeches with the kind of innocent earnestness you never associated with New Yorkers. "If we go to war, we
have to be ready, we have to be prepared to make sacrifices," one
speaker said as he gripped the stick. I listened for a while, until one
of the photographers who had traveled to New York with me pulled
me away, a look of urgency on his face.

"We need to get to Ground Zero," he said.

"Isn't it closed off?"

"Put this on," he said, pulling a thin yellow raincoat out of his
camera bag that matched the one he was wearing. "They'll think
we're rescue workers."

We walked around the first barricades just past Union Square,
down the trafficless streets around NYU, toward a bank of floodlights in the distance. With each block we walked, the grayish powder on the ground became thicker, until rain began to fall and the
dust evolved into a mud the texture of wet cement. A thunderstorm

was passing through, and with each flash of lightning a white cloud appeared over our heads, then disappeared into blackness. We approached a barricade on a pitch-dark street where a single female soldier in a green poncho stood, assaulted by sheets of rain. "Look down, don't make any eye contact. Just pretend you belong," the photographer said. He was a wiry man with bad teeth, and a famous *L.A. Times* newsroom eccentric, and I listened to him because "shooters" always do this kind of thing. The soldier, a National Guardswoman, had slunk down inside her poncho, and a few steps later the photographer and I had passed her.

We entered a realm that was not of our own time, but rather from some future epoch of scrap steel and fossilized concrete. Here, a blue mailbox whose paint had been blasted away on one side to reveal naked metal; there, a building whose steel skin had been ripped to shreds so that each gust from the storm caused it to crinkle like a wind chime. The wind kissed another building, and the building gave a deep sigh, sending a few lethal shards of glass crashing to the pavement. In a peopleless plaza that had the eerie stillness of an archaeological site, we came upon a United Nations flag flapping in the breeze. We found a graffito finger-traced into the dust covering the windows of a Brooks Brothers store: AN EYE FOR AN EYE. Firemen ascended a small hill of rubble in a line, as if they were Alpinists attempting to summit a peak of concrete and rebar. I stood there for the rest of the night and into the very early hours of the morning, hiding the photographer's extra lenses, shivering against the unexpected cold and the rain, telling myself I would be in an excellent position to tell the story should the rescuers in front of me pull out a survivor, though they never did.

No one had been found alive after the second day, a full twenty-four hours before I arrived at the scene. Later that week, I was on the phone talking to families of the disappeared, trying to dance around this heavy, inescapable fact. The daughter of Norberto Hernández, a pastry chef at the Windows of the World restaurant at the top of World Trade Center One, had refused to give up hope. She had tried to sneak through the police barricades at Ground Zero to search for her father but had been turned away. Norberto was a native of Puerto Rico who had come to New York decades earlier, as young men from Latin America do, with little capital but big hopes. When he disappeared, thirty-three years later, he had three U.S.-born daughters and three grandchildren, a home in Queens, and a job with a veneer of prestige to it, working atop the tallest building in the city, a man with a craft, a pastry chef who some days made his desserts above the clouds.

His daughter Jacqueline was twenty-five years old and she sounded angry, confused, and determined all at once. "They say there's people stuck underneath," she told me. My mind turned back to the site, to the rubble, to the impossibility that anything as fragile as a human body might have survived the physics of so much falling mass. "I don't know. I'm not going to give up without a fight. I'll do whatever I can to see my father." The family had put up a thousand flyers with his face across the city. "Together forever" was Norberto Hernández's motto. His cousins and many brothers and sisters were holding a vigil by the phone, waiting to see if someone would call. Family filled his home in Queens, and by now Jacqueline's young children were growing suspicious at all the weary and stunned adults around them. They kept asking her "Where's Coco?"—it was the nickname they knew their grandfather by.

"He's in Puerto Rico," Jacqueline would tell them. "He's in Puerto Rico, baking cakes."

In the minds of his grandchildren, Norberto Hernández lived those September days back on the island that was the family homeland. He had left Puerto Rico in 1968, and come to New York City to work as a dishwasher at about the same time my father was parking cars in Beverly Hills and I was carrying the flag at my school parade in kindergarten. He was one of dozens of Latin American men and women to go missing on September 11, most of them in service jobs like his, helping to keep the Trade Center's moneymaking engine running, cleaning windows, delivering packages, keeping the water in the bathrooms flowing. The Mexican immigrant organization Asociación Tepeyac assembled a list of them: Fabian Soto, a janitor from Ecuador who played soccer on the weekends in Newark; Sonia Ortiz, a former seamstress from Colombia, who ran one of the building's freight elevators . . . Their biographies fell into a familiar pattern: The World Trade Center was the locus of their striving, the good-paying job that was the destination on their résumés, a place where you could work and make enough money to leave something to your family. Their stories had now been united into a larger narrative, what the network television anchors were calling the bloodiest day on American soil since Pearl Harbor, while others reached farther back in history to the fallen at the Civil War battles of Gettysburg and Antietam. The immigrant dead had become the modern equivalent of the bodies on the battlefields in Matthew Brady's famous photographs, martyrs of the ATTACK ON AMERICA, as CBS called it on the caption that ran on the screen during their round-the-clock coverage, fallen civilians to be avenged in AMERICA'S NEW WAR on CNN. The caption on Univision, the national Spanish-language television network based in Miami, was made up of three words filled with contradiction and possibility: UNA NACIÓN UNIDA.

Which united nation is this? If a resident of Iowa or Idaho who has never spoken a word of Spanish in his life is told he is a member of *una nación unida*, will he comprehend this fact and accept the idea of a union with Univision's viewers?

Can he ever be truly *unido* with the truck driver Gustavo Villa in Maywood, the newspaperman Humberto Luna in Georgia, and several million other people who live, work, and even govern themselves in this country without surrendering their native tongue? I wondered about this a week later when I saw a Mexican street vendor selling American flags at an intersection in the Latinified Los Angeles suburb of Pico Rivera: She sold me my flag in a very businesslike way. She did not stop to comment on the tragedy in New York, or how we all had to stand against the terrorists; she just gave me change for a twenty and said, *"Sale,"* which means "done," and let me go on my way. I would also wonder what *una nación unida* could mean the Saturday afternoon I spent in Jersey City, watching the FBI raid a brownstone apartment building filled with Middle Eastern immigrants.

I happened to witness this raid by accident. The FBI did not then and does not now advertise its raids beforehand. I was climbing the front steps of a Muslim community leader's home when something down the street caught my eye, a crowd of people standing by a barrier two blocks away. FBI agents in blue shirts and blue windbreakers were filing in and out of the brownstone, bringing out boxes of evidence. From a second-story window, a pair of Arab women watched the agents on the street, one holding a baby and weeping profusely, looking down at a gathering crowd clamoring for vengeance. Later I would walk inside this building, knock on its doors, and find it a crowded immigrant tenement, thick with almond-eyed children. A man was led out of the house in handcuffs, another with his head covered with a blanket, prompting a loud cheer from the crowd.

"Get 'em!" someone shouted. "Get 'em all!"

"Woo!"

"Burn in hell! You're going to burn in hell!"

On that day, less than a week after the attacks, you could stand at the Jersey City shore and still see the cloud rising above the tip of Manhattan, as if the towers were still falling, filling some bottomless chasm with a cascade of concrete dust, burying and reburying the thousands beneath. You could say that many Americans felt betrayed, even Americans who were not technically Americans, because a group of invited guests—men from the Middle East here on student and tourist visas—had murdered their hosts. "Unfortunately, Jersey City is full of that kind of person," a man from Colombia told me in Spanish. He was referring to the Arabs, people with black hair, women who covered their heads with scarves but who might have been mistaken for Latin if they decided to take a walk through Spanish Harlem or East Los Angeles. That neighborhood on Tonnele Avenue was one of the most diverse in New Jersey, a tossed salad of people with Italian surnames, South American citizenship, and Middle Eastern origin. The outrage over the attacks on September 11 called into question the wisdom of the open-mindedness and relatively relaxed policies that had brought this diversity into being. In the days and months that followed, the efforts of the Mexican government and immigrant activists to win some kind of amnesty for the several million *mexicanos* living illegally in this country would come to a halt.

In the years before the towers fell and afterward, Mexican janitors and cooks and housekeepers, and working men and women from other Latin American countries, staged an elaborate piece of street theater at the tip of lower Manhattan, on behalf of the notion that they deserved at least a sliver of citizenship. They begin on Good Friday with an immigrant Jesus carrying a cross toward Bowling Green, persecuted by mock Border Patrol guards in the place of Romans. At Federal Plaza, Jesus is condemned to death by Pontius Pilate, he is nailed to the cross at Museum Green and Broadway, and in between the faithful in the procession stop to give true-life testimonies. They speak, for example, of a fourteen-year-old from Oaxaca who was killed by gang members in East Harlem and of a fifteen-year-old from the Bronx who works around the clock to support his nine brothers and sisters in Mexico. The actors in the troop yell at Jesus— "Illegal, we're going to deport you!"—and he falls under the weight of his cross on Wall Street, and is lashed while the patrons of a Starbucks look through the front window. "We too are crucified and humiliated," the immigrants following the procession call out. The crucified immigrant Jesus later ascends into heaven at the Statue of Liberty, underneath her huge bronze toes and the words of Emma Lazarus.

The march of the penitent Mexicans was part of a long and largely forgotten history of radical street theater staged at the lower tip of Manhattan. In 1766, approximately eight hundred yards from the future site of the World Trade Center, a group of patriots raised a liberty pole in defiance of colonial authorities. Some years later, when the ambassador of the new French republic visited newly independent New York, he was feted and carried through the streets; red liberty caps became all the rage, and enthusiastic republicans (in the eighteenth-century sense of the word) erected a model of the guillotine the Jacobins were using to execute the enemies of the Revolution. Here, too, New York's workingmen burned effigies and gathered in taverns to argue the case for universal male suffrage in the early nineteenth century, and Irish working men and women formed the Convention of Irish Societies, transforming the St. Patrick's Day parade into a celebration of Irish identity and militancy. In 1853, the Irish marched to Greenwich Village holding aloft a banner showing George Washington shaking hands with Daniel O'Connell, "The Liberator." Each one of those acts, like that of the cross-carrying *mexicano* Jesus, was an attempt to give the common man more "citizenship," and to expand the Rights of Man to an ever larger universe of people.

The creative force behind the Via Crucis del Inmigrante, the Stations of the Cross of the Immigrant, was Joel Magallan, a brother of the Jesuit order. I met him at the association's office on West Fourteenth Street, in an office with the group's logo on one wall, a stylized Virgin of Guadalupe looming over the New York skyline. Magallan had been summoned to New York when the Irish priests ministering in the Bronx noticed larger numbers of *mexicanos* in their parishes, a sprinkling of Olmec faces amid the Dominican and Puerto Rican families. After a reconnaissance mission to the Indian villages in Puebla and Oaxaca where a majority of Mexican New Yorkers had their roots, Magallan helped create the Asociación Tepeyac, named for the hill outside Mexico City where the Virgin of Guadalupe appeared to the Indian Juan Diego—the moment when Mexican Catholicism was born. "Tepeyac is the place where the Virgin of Guadalupe comes to announce that *indígenas* are to be accepted with dignity. She speaks to the *indígena* Juan Diego, and he passes on her message to the bishop. She says, 'The Church that I want is one that provides compassion, help, and defense of the oppressed.' She says that the Church has to allow the people to have their traditional celebrations, to speak their language, to keep their culture."

Magallan gave the Virgin of Guadalupe a Liberation Theology coloring, and the Asociación Tepeyac recruited thousands of families to demonstrate for amnesty. It also raised money so that children would not go hungry when a father was injured on the job, or to send a son or daughter back to Mexico to be buried there. Here, too, *mexicanos* were keeping alive a long New York tradition; you don't have to scroll that far back in the city's history to find similar work being done by German bunds and the Sons of Italy, by Irish leagues and Jewish *Landsmanschaften*. For all those other groups, New York City was a starting point, a place where traditions and organizations were born that would spread across the United States. *Mexicanos* approached New York from the west, reaching the city as part of a great eastward and northward advance across the continent.

The creation of the Asociación Tepeyac marked the arrival on the East Coast of the tide of Mexican-dominated immigrant activism I had first seen in California. Over the course of a decade or so, farm laborers, university students, priests, construction workers, and others had taken Mexican ideas and institutions and spread them across a wide swath of the United States, from the Brown Belt of the old Southwest into the Heartland states of Kansas, Nebraska, and Iowa, then into the states of the Confederacy, finally reaching the cities of the Northeast. In imitation of this eastward advance, the members of the Asociación Tepeyac each year carry a torch from Mexico City to New York, hundreds of runners following a route overland from the shrine of the Virgin of Guadalupe in what is the northern reaches of Mexico City's sprawl, to the border at Brownsville, and up through Louisiana, Alabama, Georgia, and other states to New York City, where thousands of Mexicans await its arrival at a mass at St. Patrick's Cathedral.

In the new Gotham, *lo mexicano* ("that which is Mexican") meets *lo dominicano, lo colombiano,* and *lo puertorriqueño,* adding more Latinness to the city's ethnic mix. The various Latino threads meld together in communities like Spanish Harlem, still the heart of Puerto Rican New York. In Spanish Harlem, I watched one of those blacktop basketball games for which New York is famous, only with two teams made up entirely of squat *mexicanos* in knockoff Knicks and

Tar Heel uniforms. I passed young men in replica jerseys of the Mexican soccer league, the Red Devils of Toluca, and my old team from my Mexico City days, the Pumas of the Universidad Nacional Autónoma de México. I saw mestiza women pushing baby strollers south along Second Avenue, toward the distant Midtown vanishing point on the horizon, rolling past grocery stores that sold tamales and chocolate for making *mole*.

I headed for a restaurant called La Fonda Boricua, a gathering place for East Harlem's Puerto Rican art and politics crowd, to meet Pedro Pedraza, a longtime Puerto Rican activist and researcher at Hunter College, and his partner, Enercida Guerrero. "The governor of Puerto Rico came here to eat," Pedro told me as I admired the abstract paintings on the walls. "And Marc Anthony did a *Good Morning America* show here." "El Barrio" is the epicenter of Puerto Rican New York, and its streets have names of *boricua* heroes like Tito Puente, but it is no longer exclusively Puerto Rican, thanks to an influx of poor Mexicans ("they pack eight people into one apartment and split the rent," Pedro says). At the same time, El Barrio is being gentrified, making Spanish Harlem another world from the community Pedro and Enercida remember from their youth. Both lived in El Barrio and in the Bronx in the 1970s, in neighborhoods with Italians, blacks, Irish, Jews, and Puerto Ricans. Those New York neighborhoods defined a twentieth-century notion of American identity; they were a landscape painting whose central elements and basic composition would be copied and reinterpreted in cities across the continent. Today, New York City has a new pan-Latino feel. At Hunter College, Pedro's students are Puerto Ricans, Hondurans, Ecuadorians, and Colombians, and Enercida says, "All of my daughter's friends are Mexican."

After dinner, we walked around Spanish Harlem, early on a Wednesday summer evening, an hour when families and young people spill out onto the streets under purple skies and the horizon lights up with rectangles of light. Pedro took note of the *mexicano* basketball players I had seen earlier. "They still can't beat the Puerto Ricans and the blacks, because they're too short," Pedraza observed. "But maybe one day . . ." I remembered how, when I was a boy, my father told me that the United States would make me taller, and my children taller than me, and I wondered if this generation of height-challenged basketball players would pass on to their children the same article of faith. *Eat this American food and eat well, and you will grow and achieve "air." You will fly over the blacktop like I never could.* We turned north on Lexington Avenue and headed toward Pedro and Enercida's apartment. A sandwich board on the sidewalk caught our eye. It advertised a series of poetry readings and other events inside a café called Carlito's Gallery. "This is a new place. I haven't seen it before," Pedro said. Carlito's Gallery was planning to host a "Viva Ecuador" reading and a concert of "Afro-Peruvian music," offered regular Spanish classes, and had just finished screening a movie, *Los Últimos Zapatistas: Héroes Olvidados,* The Last Zapatistas: Forgotten Heroes. Through the window I could see a group of people, Latinos of various adult ages, locked in a quiet and intense discussion about the film, which recounts the story of the Zapatista rebels of old, whose leader was a dark-skinned farmer with a drooping mustache, and the Zapatistas of today, whose leader is a college professor with a pipe spouting from a hole in his ski mask. They sat on couches and lounge chairs, their posture and expressions suggesting the great themes of justice and revolution that were being discussed there. It was a scene like countless others in the history of a city whose citizens have debated the ideas of Robespierre and Danton, held aloft the portraits of O'Connell and Michael Collins, and mourned the deaths of Rosa Luxemburg and the Spanish Republic. Today, the latest Jacobins celebrated in New York are men and women from Mexico, and the symbols of liberty and resistance are not red caps but rather the woolen hoods with which guerrilla fighters cover their faces in a distant, dreamy tropical place called Chiapas.

I n the barrios of East Harlem, Brooklyn, the Bronx, and Queens, in the spring and summer of 2002, parents worried as their sons and daughters marched off to war. One of the Latino soldiers of New York was Marcos Arvelo, a native of Brooklyn and the son of Puerto Rican and Dominican parents, who had joined the army because his father suggested he do so. Braulio Arvelo was retired from the NYPD and encouraged his son to follow him in his career. Go to John Jay College, his father told him. So young Marcos went there. Maybe you should join the Army, become an MP, it will look good on your résumé, his father said, you will learn discipline and what the Americanos call teamwork. So Marcos had signed up, while he was still engaged. "All of a sudden he comes out with this, that he's going to sign up with the army," his fiancée Cynthia would tell me much later. They got married anyway and went to the Dominican Republic on their honeymoon, and then he got shipped out to Europe. Marcos Arvelo was on a training mission somewhere in a German forest when the news came of September 11. The destruction of the World Trade Center set in motion a chain of events that ended two years later with Specialist Arvelo on a plane to the Middle East. Thousands of Latino soldiers set off for the Persian Gulf, leaving from most of the places I had visited during my travels across the new Latin American republic of the United States.

One Saturday morning, a few days after the first U.S. and British ground troops had crossed from Kuwait into Iraq, the phone rang with a call from my father. "I need to tell you a story," he said. My father and I still almost always talk in Spanish, even though his English is excellent. *"No me lo va a creer,"* he told me. You're not going to believe it. His story was about a longtime friend, a coworker during his many years in the hotel business, a woman from Ecuador called Nora. She had taken in a foster child a few years back, an orphan from Guatemala who had crossed overland from Central America to California, where he had ended up in the custody of various institutions and temporary guardians and eventually in Nora's home. This young man liked to write poetry. My father and Nora were then in the process of starting a business together, and each time they met, the subject of José came up. Of all the children who had passed through Nora's home, José had left the strongest impression. He was very bright and told horrific stories about his journey, at the age of sixteen, from Guatemala to Los Angeles, riding on top of trains across Mexico. My father had told Nora that José and I should meet one day; there aren't too many published Guatemalan novelists in Los Angeles, or many Guatemalan-American journalists, and in my father's mind I am a *guatemalteco* celebrity. If you meet my father and talk to him for ten minutes, chances are he will tell you about his son the writer. My father told Nora that I was out of town, but that he would try to persuade me to pay José a visit the next time I was around. Soon afterward, Nora reported that José's mood had turned sullen. He moved out of her house. A few weeks later, he signed up with the Marines.

"Oh, no," I said, in English, because it had suddenly become crystal clear where this story was going.

On the same day that the first combat deaths were being announced on the television, my father continued, he had another meeting with Nora. She was worried because news had come of two Marines killed in a town called Umm al Qasr. My father told her not to worry: there were thousands of Marines in Iraq, after all. What were the odds that it would be José? Later that evening, just before midnight, Nora called my father at home. Three military officers had just come to her door: representatives of the Marines and the Navy, she said. José Antonio Gutiérrez was dead, killed in combat at Umm al Qasr, Iraq.

Within a matter of days the picture of José's squat Guatemalan face tucked underneath his white Marine dress cap would be circulating throughout the U.S. media, and then in Latin America and the rest of the world. A week after my father's phone call, I picked up a newspaper in Buenos Aires with José's picture on the cover. Back in California, five of my colleagues at the *Los Angeles Times* went to work at recreating the epic tragedy of José Gutiérrez's life, from the deaths of his mother and father to poverty and alcoholism in the slums of Guatemala City, to his stints in Guatemalan orphanages and jails. "I come from a place where the angels reside in misery," he wrote in a letter my colleagues found and published. "They are clothed in filth and they devour dreams." José Antonio Gutiérrez survived with a combination of wiles and striving; stealing food when he was a street urchin, lying when he had to, and applying himself to his studies when the opportunity of an American education presented itself. He graduated from a Southern California high school and conquered the mental and physical rigors of the Marine Corps. He was the "brother alien" and the "brother citizen" wrapped into one, though he actually received his naturalization papers only in death. One of many U.S. "resident alien" Marines posthumously granted citizenship by an act of Congress, he was buried in Guatemala City with a Marine honor guard and an American flag on his coffin. "We need to be prepared to make sacrifices," I had heard someone say in Union Square in New York City, when the World Trade Center was still smoldering. Here was one sacrifice, made by a young man who had crossed into the United States by defying the barriers of steel and electronics meant to keep him out.

In the weeks that followed, more immigrant Marines died in combat, their stories forming an irony-tinged narrative of cultural conflict and ambiguity that unfolded, one chapter at a time, in my hometown newspaper. There was Lance Corporal Jesús González, who had been raised, as I was, by radical parents who took him to farmworker rallies when he was a boy. His story, like those of the other "green card Marines," as they came to be known, suggested that he joined the military because it offered a shortcut to the kind of traditional American success and citizenship José García achieved. Like José, Jesús was ambivalent about this thing the *americanos* called patriotism. In Indio, a city in the same desert where Gloria Romero had learned about community and injustice a generation earlier, Jesús had walked about his high school wearing a beret and telling people he considered Che Guevara to be his role model. He helped lead a march on Indio City Hall against Proposition 187, went to college, but dropped out. For reasons that were not entirely clear to his family and friends, he ended up in the Marines; mourners carried United Farm Workers flags at his funeral, with the same black eagle that symbolizes Chicano militancy and that rises at the César Chávez Monument in San Fernando. In Escondido, not far from the Tijuana neighborhoods where he had been born and raised, another Lance Corporal named Jesús was buried with a Mexican flag draped over his coffin. Jesús Suárez del Solar had been a fan of Los Tigres del Norte and Eminem; his father proclaimed him "our Aztec warrior" (*nuestro guerrero azteca*) in a letter to the Spanish-language media, saying his sacrifice had united "thousands of hispanos" across the United States. He led the mourners at his son's funeral in a tearful rendition of the Mexican national anthem—"*¡Mexicanos al grito de guerra!*"—while a Marine honor guard stood at attention with the Stars and Stripes.

Even a decade earlier it would have been inconceivable that

funeral services for American soldiers killed in combat would be transformed into expressions of *mexicano* patriotism and Chicano militancy. This was a new United States, where people of Latin American heritage felt more confident every day with the notion of their binational identity. *Latinidad* could assert itself in the most unlikely settings, with the Marine color guard and a seven-gun salute of American rifles at the ready, with a young man inside a coffin wearing an American military uniform. To live in the United States and be Latino is to have an understanding of your national and cultural identity that is colored by the idea of resistance. You could feel this even when your family had made the ultimate patriotic sacrifice to the United States of America. There is no single word that describes this way of feeling about yourself and your family, so people used dozens of synonyms: Latino, *hispano,* Chicano, *dominicano, mexicano,* or "Hispanic" if you live in New Mexico. When people use these words it is a shorthand way of saying they have preserved and nurtured a sense of who they are and how their life stories fit inside a larger narrative of colony and empire, of exodus and displacement. That self-definition was what drove Gloria Romero to the State Senate, it was the rallying cry around which María Chacón united her troops and built an incipient machine in Bell Gardens, it was behind the sense of pride that enabled even pro-statehood Puerto Ricans to celebrate the liberation of Elizam Escobar, the *independentista.*

Eventually, I wound up in Iraq myself. I'm an addict for chaos, for the spinning whirlpools of crime and conflict, and the human debris that circles in its vortex, and for rifles and pistols and tear-gas canisters. I arrived at the Al Hamra Hotel in Baghdad, a capital city that was at once liberated and occupied, a place of violent paradoxes. "You must be an Arab," people told me in English, or in Arabic through my interpreter, Samir. I heard this everywhere I went in Iraq—it was my mustache and my goatee, the coloring of my skin, Samir told me. "If you do not open your mouth, you are an Iraqi."

"Probably you have an illegal father who is an Arab," a Bedouin man told me near the Syrian border, as we took a break from the subject that had brought me to his home in the moonscape of Iraq's Western Desert—the presence of an American tank battalion on the next ridge, occupying half of his village, days after another American unit had bombed it. "Perhaps," I said. "My great-grandfathers were from Spain, and that country, as you know, was once controlled by Arabs." If you could have taken off the helmets, the kevlar, and the camouflage from all those Mexican-Americans, Mexicans, Puerto Ricans, Cubans, Guatemalans, Peruvians, and assorted other Latinos in Uncle Sam's army, they probably would have had similar conversations. Unfortunately, those soldiers could not experience Iraq as I did, free of any uniform or rank, without any other responsibility than to be a storyteller. They could not know that underneath the deep hostility toward the American occupation, there were people who could greet you with the sincerity, the hospitality, and the lack of pretense that are considered good manners not only in Qaim, Iraq, but also in places like Ponce, Puerto Rico, and Liberal, Kansas.

"You are an American too, but you are different," an imam in Baghdad told me, after describing an encounter with American soldiers in the same mosque we were now sitting in, shoeless, our legs folded on the carpet. "You have come here as a guest."

At that moment, I was suddenly overcome by a sense of sadness and futility around me. A few minutes earlier, the imam's aide had wept while recounting the story of the mosque's invasion, a deep and embittering humiliation. The American soldiers tramped in with their boots on—they did not take off their shoes at the entrance as I had. I was tired, exhausted from the heat and the unrelenting fear, and couldn't help but weep too. We both felt helpless, the imam's assistant and I, before the violence unfolding before our eyes, a tragedy that threw together earnest and frightened young men and women from my country with the humiliated and frightened people of his. Like the American soldiers, I was deaf and dumb here; I looked out at the landscape of men in dishdash robes and veiled women and wondered who might be friend or foe. When I wandered the streets with my Iraqi translator and driver, inside the skin my illegal Arab grandfather had bequeathed me, I saw a city ruled by tanks and men in khaki space suits with automatic weapons who told us, with curt hand gestures, to stop our car and step out and barked obscenities at us until I opened my mouth and started talking to them about California and baseball and everything was cool. This is what imperial wars feel like, I told myself—this is what they have always felt like. To be an American in Baghdad those days was to feel you were a character in a Graham Greene novel, walking about a landscape of shrapnel-pitted office buildings and fading luxury hotels with foreign correspondents drinking bad wine, and covert agents and shadowy rebels who disappeared into the sunflower fields and the reeds by the edge of the Tigris River. It was a situation analogous, I thought, to all those invasions and wars by proxy that had characterized United States history, from the occupation of Mexico City in 1847 to the intervention in the Dominican Republic in 1965, all of which had helped provoke the migrations and displacements that would help fill large chunks of the United States with brown-skinned peoples.

I remember standing inside a base on the outskirts of Baghdad, talking to a National Guardsman from suburban California. "You know, you're the first real human being I've talked to in three months," he told me. A little while later it sank in that this observation described not only the way he felt toward the Iraqi civilian population but also how he felt about his fellow troops: what he meant to say, I think, was that the *situation* was inhuman, that being a solider in this place so far from home, a warrior thrust among hostile natives, negated his humanity. This was the situation, roughly, in which I found Specialist Marcos Arvelo, at an Iraqi police station in the Al Bayaa neighborhood of Baghdad.

Specialist Arvelo was a tall, thin man with overheated reddish-brown skin, standing behind a wall of sandbags with a machine gun on top facing the street. I walked up to his post the way I walked up to every other American base in Iraq: very slowly, speaking very loud and very colloquial English. "How's it goin'? I'm a reporter. An American." My interpreter and I had come to check out a story that an American solider had been killed in Al Bayaa, but neither Arvelo nor anyone else at the police station—a cube of crumbling, damp concrete that resembled a set from the movie *Midnight Express*— knew anything else about it. Probably there had been no such attack. So I walked back toward the entrance and fell into a relaxed, shoot-the-breeze, how's-Baghdad-treating-you conversation with Arvelo and his buddies in the Military Police unit.

"You think we're going to be able to get jobs when we get back home?" a solider from Texas asked me. "We hear there's this recession going on."

"Are you kidding? If anyone will be able to get jobs, it'll be you guys," I said. "You can say you were MPs in Baghdad. What police department wouldn't hire you? People will be in awe of you when you get home."

Specialist Arvelo said things in Baghdad weren't so bad. He'd learned to communicate a bit with the Iraqis. He'd discovered that the Iraqi gesture in which you bring out your two index fingers and rub them together means "friend." "At first, I thought they were saying I was gay. I'd say, 'No, look,' and I'd show them pictures of my wife and daughter." His wife Cynthia is from South America, he told me. Of himself, he added, "I'm Puerto Rican–Dominican."

I told him I was writing a book about how Latinos were changing the United States.

"Hey, I did a paper about that at John Jay College!"

"That phone you got in your pocket work here?" The Texan interrupted. "And can you call the States with that?" During those early days in Iraq, calling home was a rare privilege. You could go weeks or months without getting your hands on one of the phones set up in the bases. My satellite phone was called a Thuraya, which means "star" in Arabic, and it did indeed reach across the planet to Texas and other places. I lent it to the Texan. "Man, you made my day," he shouted after he'd finished. "You made my month! I talked to my mom today!" Arvelo said there was a Mexican guy who would want to use it too: *"¡Díaz! ¡Ven acá!"* he shouted, Come here! Arvelo went to his tank to look for his wife's new phone number: she had moved back to New York to live with her parents while he was away and he didn't have the number. He returned from the tank a few minutes later looking stricken: he'd left the number at the base.

"Just use it to call anyone," I said.

He called his home in Brooklyn. It was about four A.M. in New York, but no family of an American solider minded getting a call from a son or daughter in Iraq, no matter what the hour. A moment later Arvelo was speaking with his father in a mixture of English and Caribbean Spanish.

"¡Mira qué suerte que están ahí!" he shouted happily into the phone. Cynthia had spent the night at her in-laws' house; she was

there, in Brooklyn, with Marcos's parents. So was their baby daughter. Now Marcos changed into the voice of "Papi" to talk to the daughter who was still in diapers, getting a chance to be a father for a minute or so as he stood in front of an Iraqi police station, a few feet from his unattended machine gun. When he got off the phone, he beamed with a wide smile and a Gomer Pyle overbite.

"She was there, with my parents," he said, still in a happy trance.

I told him I was going through New York on my way home and could stop by and visit his relatives.

"Arvelo!" a soldier shouted from the police station doorway. "The captain says, 'The post! The gun!' And put your helmet on too!"

Specialist Arvelo twisted his face into a New York scowl. "I know! I was doin' sumthin' here!"

I didn't get a chance to ask Specialist Arvelo any of the deeper questions I might have posed to him. I didn't get a chance to ask him what he had written in that paper at John Jay College. He was on duty and he needed to get back to his post and his gun.

W hen I got to New York I telephoned the Arvelo household in Brooklyn and talked to his mother, Isabel Frías. She was grateful for the few minutes she had had with her son over the phone in Iraq. *"Muchísimas gracias,"* she said. But she didn't want to talk to any writers: she was worried that if her son's picture or name was in any newspaper, it might invite a terrorist attack of some sort against him. In New York, in those days, people worried about those kinds of things.

"I understand," I said. "Could I talk to your husband, briefly, just to say hello?"

Braulio Arvelo said he would be happy to talk to me. "Come on over."

I took the subway from my Manhattan hotel to Brooklyn and got off at the Crescent Street station, and walked down a block of narrow houses, and gardens just big enough for a pair of lawn chairs, to the Arvelo family home.

I was greeted by Braulio and his son, two daughters, and daughter-in-law. (Isabel had left for a few hours, too nervous and worried to talk to me.) I told them the story of my encounter with Marcos, how he looked, and the general situation in Baghdad, putting the most optimistic spin on things I could without lying. Braulio Arvelo said he spent long hours watching the news in Spanish and was an emotional wreck: every day there was news of another American soldier killed in Iraq, another bit of information to broil into an incipient ulcer of worries in his stomach. Before I'd let Marcos use my phone that afternoon in Baghdad, the last time Braulio had spoken with his son was when he was in Kuwait and "about to cross the line" into Iraq.

"Ever since I have been asking myself what I would do if the military officers come to my door. What would I do when they came up those steps?" he told me in Spanish. "Would I start yelling at them to leave? Would I tell them, 'Get out of here, I don't want to hear it, I don't want to know.' Or would I run up and embrace them and begin to weep?" He told me this with tears welling in his eyes and then dripping down the salt and pepper stubble of his cheeks.

I listened and nodded and wondered what I should say next, looking around at the room we were sitting in; it was the bedroom of another of Braulio's sons, Marcos's younger brother, who had put up Puerto Rican and Dominican flags on the walls. Finally, I said to Braulio in Spanish, "Well, God is great. [*Dios es grande.*] He did send a stranger to come knocking at your door. But it wasn't a military officer. It's me, a civilian. And I've come with the news that your son is safe and that no harm has come to him."

Braulio gave the faintest of smiles. We switched topics, to the one subject no Latino I've interviewed ever tires of talking about: the family history. Braulio had arrived in New York in 1959, and in those early days the most difficult thing was not the small rooms he lived in, or adjusting to the cold winters, but the unending sense of loneliness. He traveled around the United States following a variety of jobs, then circled back to New York to work as a subway conductor. He met the tall, beautiful young Dominican woman whose picture I had seen in the hallway coming in and married her. He joined the NYPD "to keep on making progress" and served there twenty-five years. His dream had always been to return to Puerto Rico, and he even bought a piece of property near his hometown.

"I would have liked for Puerto Rico to be an independent country. But now, with the passing of the years, I know it probably could not survive. It's just a small island." Like so many other people I'd met on my travels across the Spanish-speaking United States, Braulio Arvelo, a retired cop, was of two minds. Having grown up on an island occupied by a foreign power gave him a special insight into what his son was going through in Iraq, he said. "There's a lot of people who don't want him there. That's the way it is in my country. They say, 'Gringo, go home.' The gringos are the bad guys." For decades Puerto Ricans on the island, in New York, and elsewhere united to protest the U.S. Navy's use of a corner of their country as a bombing range. Braulio saw the parallels; he understood the Iraqi anger. "I don't blame them for that," he said. "If it were me, I'd be fighting too. When I was growing up, I had a strong national pride [*orgullo nacional*]. But the rest of my family were supporters of Luis Múñoz Marín and I could not go against them." Múñoz Marín was the architect of Puerto Rico's in-between "associated free state" status, whereby it remained a part of the United States with a semblance of its own separate national identity. "I am a patriot of the two countries," he told me in Spanish, "of the one over there and the one here." He'd heard on the Spanish-language media a report on the immigrant soldiers that used a phrase he liked that described his son's mission in Iraq—*héroes de otra patria,* heroes of another fatherland.

I thanked Braulio for his time and said good-bye to the rest of the family, to Marcos's brother and sisters and his wife, Cynthia, and his daughter, Illyana, who was still in diapers. "Marcos named her," Cynthia said, "from a character in the X-Men comic books." Cynthia was Peruvian-Ecuadorian; she'd been born in South America and had migrated to New York as a child. That made Illyana Arvelo, the daughter of Cynthia Arvelo and Specialist Marcos Arvelo, a Puerto Rican-Dominican-Ecuadorian-Peruvian-American, and also a New Yorker. She was a citizen of the Americas whose *papi* was off in a distant land, armed to defend the Stars and Stripes. He was most recently a voice she had heard on my satellite phone, bouncing off the stars.

CHE AND THE THREE MONKEYS
Che y los tres monos

**La Higuera, Bolivia · Buenos Aires, Argentina
Los Angeles, California · Ashland, Alabama**

1. THE VILLAGE

On the day I enter La Higuera, Bolivia, the air is flavored with ash from fires burning fifty miles away and the peasants tell me it has not rained in a year. The cattle are turning rib-cage skinny and the fields are littered with the brittle yellow stubs of cornstalks hacked, harvested, and left to bake in the sun. People lean from their doorways and gaze out at the dirt road that runs through their village, where chickens peck aimlessly and where a famous man once limped past, a bearded and bedraggled Argentine in floppy sandals whose battle fatigues were dissolving into rags. Today the people say, without a trace of self-consciousness, that they pray to this man. They light candles to him, place flowers at the shrine built to him in the village square, they murmur his name to the rainless sky. "If you really believe in him, if you have full faith, your prayers to him will never fail you," a *campesino* named Juan Pablo Escobar tells me. The bedraggled man ascended to heaven in this very place, on the dirt floor of the schoolhouse where the children took lessons from a teacher who was a bad speller. Handfuls of pilgrims come from the great unknown world beyond this village to touch the spot where the man died, and to scratch messages on the wall and the door outside. POR ESTA PUERTA SALIÓ UN HOMBRE A LA ETERNIDAD. Through this door, a man walked out into eternity.

La Higuera is the portal through which Che Guevara passed from human being to myth, where the complications and contradictions of his thirty-nine-year life dissolved into the haze of legend. I've come to the scene of his last battle and his execution, hoping to gain some insight into the real human being whose life story is a pillar of *americanismo,* that construction of stories, ideas, and hopes in which the Spanish-speaking Americas are one, from Tierra del Fuego to the farms and forests of Maine. Standing before the denuded, drought-stricken mountains that form the sides of a bowl rising around La Higuera, I grasp for the first time the scale and absurdity of Che's ambition: he believed that two dozen men walking through these sparsely populated canyons would somehow ignite a revolution that would spread across the hemisphere. Che had come to liberate the peasants, to join their forgotten village to a more just world, but when he was alive they feared him, they believed he and his band of bearded warriors to be wizards and enchanters.

Three decades onward, the peasants are still as poor as when Che passed through. Outsiders have built a museum in the old schoolhouse to help bring some cash to the village, but little La Higuera (population 150) is too far away, too isolated, the roads too precarious to ever bring more than a trickle of tourists. People are leaving the village, just as they leave thousands of other villages across the length and breadth of the Americas. The *campesinos* of La

Higuera migrate in search of work to the cobblestone and dirt streets of Vallegrande, population 15,000. In Vallegrande, I touch the concrete laundry basin where Che's body was put on display behind the town hospital, and later sit in an Internet kiosk next to two young women *chateando* online with their boyfriends who have gone to work in the city of Santa Cruz, the business capital of Bolivia, a five-hour drive away on cattle-clogged roads. In Santa Cruz itself, the sun is a tangerine disk shimmering through the smoky haze created by peasants who have set hundreds of fires on the edge of the city; they believe the ashes of the old crop will make the land fertile for the new one. In Santa Cruz those lucky enough to sort out a U.S. visa quickly buy tickets on Lloyd Aereo Boliviano Flight 900, non-stop to Miami, and then travel onward to the Bolivian enclave in Washington, D.C., the largest in North America. When they arrive, the expatriate Bolivians will search for the Internet cafés, the public libraries, to *chatear* with the people back home, because these days there's hardly a town in Bolivia, or Latin America, that isn't connected.

Bolivia's fate is linked more than ever to the United States. Not a few people believe the American embassy is really running their country. Bolivia's most recently elected president now lives in Miami, having been chased out of office by an Indian-led insurrection I witnessed after entering the besieged capital city of La Paz on the back of a bicycle, which was the only way to get around the cobblestone barricades. From Miami, the disgraced former president Gonzalo ("Goni") Sánchez de Lozada speaks to the Bolivian media in English-accented Spanish that Bolivians find alternately endearing or annoying. Goni was born in Bolivia but raised in the United States and graduated from college there, then returned to Bolivia to make a fortune and become president: like my own Spanish, Goni's was a tongue he reacquired later in life.

In all honesty, my own Spanish is actually better than that of the exiled president of Bolivia. When I go to Bolivia and talk to people in Spanish (mine is now a mixture of Mexican, Guatemalan, and Argentine inflections and idioms), no one can quite place where I am from. "*¿De dónde es usted?*" they ask.

"Guess," I say.

"Colombia?" is the most common answer. And sometimes "*¿Centroamérica?*" No one guesses "*Estados Unidos.*" When I was in La Paz, watching Goni's police try to force the Indians out of the city, and the wind shifted and tear gas filled my eyes, causing me to double over in panic and pain, a man came to my aid, placing a vinegar-soaked rag over my eyes, speaking instructions in Aymara. He looked into my Los Angeles face and saw something Indian. For the same reason, the woman at the anthropological museum in Vallegrande refuses to believe me when I tell her in Spanish, responding to her query, that I am "*americano, un yanqui.*" "You don't look like an American," she answers in Spanish.

"What does an American look like?" I shoot back in Spanish.

"Not like you," she says.

America is a different country now, I explain, a lot of Americans look like me. There are parts of the United States filled with people who look like me. I pull out my passport, its cover faded after so many travels, and open it up to the page with my picture and the martial eagle of the Great Seal of the United States. I start chattering away in English. She finally believes.

"Ah, *señor*, I wish I could speak English like that," she says in Spanish with a bright smile. "Such perfect pronunciation! That's what I'm missing."

2. THE GREAT METROPOLISES

These days my life is a series of up-and-down trips across the Americas, from South America to North America and back again, over the Amazon and across the Caribbean, the names of jungle outposts and mountain ranges passing on the small video displays attached to the seat backs of jumbo jets. I live in Buenos Aires, the southernmost major metropolis of the Western Hemisphere. My wife and I moved down here, in part, so that our sons would be certain to learn Spanish, and now, when my boys kick the ball around our backyard, they mimic the calls of Argentine television announcers, shouting out *caño!* (literally, "pipe," which is what South Americans say when a player dribbles the ball through an opponent's legs) and *golazo!*—the celebratory chant of the goal scorer. Sometimes I can hear a slight *porteño* accent in our boys' speech, and I wince, because in Mexico and California that accent is associated with pretentiousness, though here it is the speech of all classes, rich and poor.

My life now has a permanent link to South America. Our daughter was born on a full-moon night in Buenos Aires. She is a binational citizen and the obligatory holder of U.S. and Argentine passports: when she travels from Buenos Aires to Los Angeles, she'll need both. Days after she was born, I sat in the offices of the National Registry of Persons, watching a series of Argentine officials, all women, copying my daughter's vital statistics and name by hand from one ancient ledger book to the next—*Luna Tobar, Luna Tobar*—because the National Registry of Persons doesn't have computers and may never get them. After a week, I returned to the office and was handed an official copy of our daughter's birth certificate, the name and every other detail written out by hand. I called my wife from the office to tell her. "It looks like the temporary driver's license

I got in L.A. when I was fifteen, but they say it's official." Someday soon we will take her to see her grandparents and aunts and uncles in California.

We will visit Los Angeles at least once a year, because as I have told you before, that city is my *tierra*, my homeland, the place to which I will always return. We go home to big enchilada meals, to backyard swimming pools and barbecues with propane gas attachments, and hamburgers sizzling on the grills, and twilight baseball games at Dodger Stadium, where the home runs never reach the palm trees rising beyond the bullpens, and where I once collected an autograph from the Hall of Fame pitcher Don Sutton. When I return to Los Angeles, I find a place immediately recognizable, and always disconcertingly different; it's never quite shaken its addiction to newness and to change. The newest stadium in town is a soccer stadium, which in the coming season will be shared by two teams of Major League Soccer: the Los Angeles Galaxy, whose star player is a Guatemalan named Carlos Ruiz, and a new outfit called Club Deportivo Chivas USA, an American clone of the most beloved club team in Mexico, the Chivas [young goats] of Guadalajara. Chivas USA is promising to field the first all-Mexican and Mexican-American team in the history of U.S. professional sports. The arrival of Chivas USA is a matter of great excitement to my brother-in-law Paul Garnica, who never really has been much of a soccer fan (he asked me to explain some of the rules to him), but whose professional life happens to be linked to the sport. Paul runs the concessions at a handful of Southern California arenas, including the new soccer stadium, the Home Depot Center. He is excited about the prospect of a stadium full of Spanish-speaking Chivas fans because his years in the food-concession business have taught him an important axiom: Mexican families spend double or triple on food and drinks at the ballpark what non-Mexicans spend. "An American family will pack their own sandwiches and bring their own bottled water so they can save. But for a Mexican family, a night at the soccer game is a big deal, it's the big family outing. So they go all-out. They spend big-time."

Paul is a guy from East L.A., a second-generation Mexican-American, who worked his way up from bar bouncer to corporate management. We talk in his company BMW, and I listen to him place a cell phone call to one of his cooks in halting Spanish that is not nearly as good as that of the exiled president of Bolivia. His parents didn't talk much Spanish to him when he was a kid: they wanted to be sure he learned English, because that's how you got ahead back then if you lived in the barrio. He's learned that in the new Los Angeles, achievement can take you deeper into a Spanish-speaking world. He's on the board of several charitable organizations and also a member of the Latin Business Association. "There's all these executives and people from companies like Univision, and even though they can all speak English, when we meet, everyone starts blabbing away in Spanish. It's a kind of a status thing. Sometimes it's hard to keep up, but you gotta do what you gotta do."

Paul is very busy, so he doesn't make it to my reading a few days later at a San Fernando Valley bookstore, Tía Chucha's, *tía* meaning "aunt" and "Chucha" being the diminutive for the name "Jesusa." Nearly everyone in the audience is a friend or family member, including my cousin the undocumented immigrant, whom I haven't seen in eleven years, since the day my wife and I got married in Guatemala. My friend Michele, having heard about the book I'm writing, hands me a flyer she's found near the Tía Chucha's bulletin board. "Girl Scouts of the San Fernando Valley Presents—A Taste of Salsa. Featuring salsa making, tasting, and dancing." Can a Girl Scout earn a Salsa pin now, I wonder, to place on her uniform alongside her Cookie Sale Activity pin?

After the reading, my sons pester me to buy some exotic objects they've discovered in one corner of the bookstore: for example, stick-on tattoos of low riders, broken hearts, and crucifixes; and inch-tall plastic figures called Homies, which pay tribute to various barrio stereotypes. They are cartoonish mini-dolls dressed in classic *cholo* clothing with names like "Cruzer," "Sir Grumpy," and "Sad Girl." I tell my sons I will buy them these things. A young Chicana woman rings up my purchase and I notice there is a small wooden pendant dangling from her necklace. From a distance it looks like a religious medallion. I gaze closer. Is it the Virgin of Guadalupe? Jesus? No. It is Che Guevara.

3. ANYTOWN, U.S.A.

On my most recent visit to the United States I stop by Ashland, Alabama, the town where I once worked in a chicken plant and where I learned how the truly devout take Holy Communion. On a pleasant summer Sunday at St. Mark's church, I meet a Puerto Rican couple (they have driven from Birmingham for the day to help out with the church prayer group), a Panamanian (he came from Miami to work in the chicken plant), some resettled Californians (the family of Socorro Ibarra), and Roxana Ramírez, who came to Alabama from Oaxaca, Mexico, after a brief stint in the tomato fields of Immokalee, Florida. Roxana owns a small grocery store in Ashland called Monte Alban, after the ancient ruins of the Zapotec culture. A Guatemalan family has arrived in town recently, too, I am told. The church priest, who is from Colombia, says the rolling hills and green farms around town remind him of his country.

Ashland, Alabama, has become a crossroads of Latin America. The routes into the interior of the North American continent that begin in Los Angeles, Mexico, Miami, South America, the Caribbean, and other Spanish-speaking places meet here just as they do in other American towns with water towers and Baptist churches and volunteer fire departments like this one. I watch the Ibarra children kick a soccer ball around the back of Saint Mark's; they tell me they are all fans of the Chivas of Guadalajara, but the biggest of the boys plays center on the Clay County High football team and dreams of wearing the uniform of the Alabama Crimson Tide. It is a time of great change and new happenings in Ashland, population 1,965. What will Ashland look like in a generation? How will this time be remembered? Will the stories of hardship and perseverance of the chicken workers be taught in the American history lessons at Clay County High someday deep in the twenty-first century? What language or languages will they be written in? I know this for certain: the movement of peoples is a quintessentially American story, repeated again and again, from the Pilgrims to the Gold Rush to the Dust Bowl. Leaving St. Mark's, driving through the center of Ashland and then accidentally out of town, I come across a historical marker on the side of the road. HERE LIES A BABY GIRL WHO DIED WHILE HER FAMILY WAS TRAVELING WEST, CA. 1860. I remember Carmen Avalos and her father Leopoldo, and the baby boy buried in a cookie box in Mexico, and the family's journey northward across the border, a tale that is hidden within the very recent history of the California city of South Gate, though only a few people who live there know it.

I circle back to Ashland, looking for a phone to call home to Buenos Aires, to let my family know I have finished here and am on the way home. In the very center of town, across from the courthouse, I see a storefront with a collection of signs in Spanish, including an advertisement for international calling cards. MI CUATE GEORGIA is the brand of one of the cards: "My Georgia Buddy." I step inside to find a man with a shaved head behind the counter. It is

Juan Valdez, the former *balsero* from Cuba. He has moved out of the chicken factory and bought his own store; it is not the first catering to the Latinos who live here, but it is the newest one, the shelves only half-covered with cans of mango juice and black beans and bags of tortillas. Juan is happy to be an entrepreneur. He tells me that when he went to register his business at the state tax office, they asked, "What are you going to call this store of yours?" He wrote down "Los Tres Monos" because he had three monkey statues he wanted to decorate the store with. The official behind the counter frowned and asked, "What does that mean?" wondering if maybe they were Spanish swearwords; Juan explained with an innocent, disarming smile that belies his shaved head and the barbed-wire tattoo on his biceps. Now the tiny monkeys are sitting in the store window, neither speaking, nor hearing, nor seeing any evil.

Juan is all alone behind the counter in Los Tres Monos until his old friend and fellow *balsero* Gerardo Mir walks in, not to buy anything but just to talk and pass the time. Mir is dressed up for the part of Southern sidekick, wearing a floppy fisherman's hat and a pair of suspenders, and at Juan's prodding he tells his stories of Guantánamo, of the failed crossing of the Strait of Florida, of the riots at the refugee camp. Juan announces that he doesn't think everything about the Communist regime was bad. "They fed me, they educated me," he says in Spanish. Gerardo seems very upset that his *compatriota* is speaking this sacrilege to a writer, to a man scribbling down notes. "There is no freedom under Fidel. None!"

I am in a two-stoplight town in the Alabama hill country, in the heart of the Bible Belt and Crimson Tide football mania, listening to an old-fashioned, heated argument between Cubans like the ones I've heard in Little Havana in Miami, but the moment very quickly loses its sense of strangeness and cultural dissonance. This is what America is like now—North America, I mean, the United States. The craziness of *cubanos* and *mexicanos* and *guatemaltecos* can find you just about anywhere. Juan's smile turns a little mischievous as he reaches into his pocket and pulls out his wallet, searching for something stuck between his driver's license and his Alabama gun license. It is a picture slightly larger than a postage stamp of a line of marching rebels on horseback, the portrait of Che Guevara looming behind them. "He was brave, he had his ideals," Juan explains, gripping his crotch to say this is what Che had—*cojones*. He never backed down from a fight. This is really a bit much, I think: Che and his saintly gaze are following me everywhere. I am about to tell Juan, "You're a Cuban exile—you're supposed to hate this guy," but Gerardo jumps in first.

"Guevara was a cosmopolitan adventurer," he says with a look of weary disgust, *un aventurero cosmopolita*.

Juan shrugs his shoulders, unbothered and happy to have made his point, and puts Che safely back in his wallet. He is thirty-four years old and carries Che with him wherever he goes. In Communist Cuba, Che is the saint in the schoolhouse, children are taught to emulate his hard work and sacrifice, and Juan Valdez is not willing to surrender that part of his himself, not yet, if ever. Yes, it took him three tries to escape Cuba and seek a better life, but that doesn't mean he has to let go of his nostalgia for the bright sunshine of his childhood schoolyards, for the voices of his teachers passing on lessons about the man who died in Bolivia alongside other men with nicknames like Chino and Pacho, a story that becomes more of a fable each time it's told, like the stories of George Washington chopping down the cherry tree. That's what freedom is to Juan Valdez: the right to worship heroes other people despise, and to believe he can be the same person in the Alabama hill country as he is in the Cuban city where he was born and raised.

I bid the two arguing Cubans good-bye and head out the doorway into Ashland's Courthouse Square, which is empty of cars and pedestrians. I cross the street and look up at the gray dome of Clay County Courthouse. The National Register of Historic Places says it was built in 1900, at the dawn of a century that began with bricklayers and masons crafting the steps of this civic edifice in the center of their town. That same century ended with Spanish-speaking chicken workers and furniture makers building the Catholic Church that rises on the edge of town, on a hill overlooking the forests where, in still other centuries, men with bayoneted rifles marched into battle, and Creek Indian women washed clothes in the rivers.

ACKNOWLEDGMENTS

The essayist and comedienne Sandra Tsing Loh tells the only joke I've ever heard about Guatemalans in Los Angeles. "Hillary Clinton said it takes a village to raise a child. But in the case of Los Angeles, it's a Guatemalan village." That joke was a kind of acknowledgment: these women from a faraway place are the designated caregivers in the better-off half of our city, it said. Let's give them their due. In a similar vein, the author would like to say that it's taken a village—made up almost entirely of non-Guatemalans—to keep him writing long enough to finish this work. I wouldn't be writing books at all if it weren't for Jay Mandel and Virginia Barber, my longtime and unfailingly optimistic literary agents. And almost every day I write, I hear the voice of Joy Johannessen, who years ago bought my first novel for a small literary house and whose wise and uninhibited use of a red pen taught me how books are put together. Thomas Keneally and Judith Grossman first guided me away from the safe world of daily journalism with the two-year prize of an MFA in creative writing at UC Irvine. Stuart Dybek and John Calvin Batchelor, two itinerant professors at that institution, were early and enthusiastic supporters of my work, and I remain indebted to them.

At the *Los Angeles Times*, I owe thanks and *abrazos* to too many editors and colleagues to be able to mention them all. Scott Kraft first signed me on to the National Desk and never ordered me back home, even as my wanderings took me to such increasingly exotic destinations as Saginaw, Michigan. Thanks too to National Desk editors Tom Furlong and Bret Israel. My first city editor, Peter H. King, believed that my tales about immigrants belonged on the newspaper's front page, and Bob Baker edited the stories in my "American Democracy in Latino L.A." project. Simon Li signed me up for the Foreign Desk and thus gave me the opportunity to wander into dozens more Latin American villages and cities than those I already knew. Marjorie Miller and Mary Braswell sent me to Baghdad and made sure that I made it back alive—and almost as important, they granted me the time and freedom to finish this manuscript. Thanks to onetime Metro colleagues Stephen Braun and Judy Pasternak, for their support when I was a rookie reporter with an uncertain future. And all of us Latino writers at the *Times* owe much to the late Frank del Olmo, who, during his sadly truncated life in the newspaper business, never stopped advocating on our behalf.

A certain very small group of editors and writers played roles in the somewhat unlikely series of recent events from which this book was born, although I am sure none of them know they did so: Sue Horton, my boss at *LA Weekly*, who introduced me to the world of literary journalism; Dorothy Wickenden at *The New Yorker*, who solicited the essay that helped me find this book's central voice; Steve Wasserman, at the *L.A. Times Book Review*, and Tom Hayden, whose advocacy on behalf of my first book helped ensure I would write a second; and Adrienne Miller, who set off my undercover foray into Texas and Alabama.

In Buenos Aires, thanks to Jessica Boianover and Andrés D'Alessandro for their daily collaboration and companionship in our South American news bureau. Thanks too to Paula Burns in Dallas for transcription and to Annie Nisbet for legal research into the shenanigans in Bell Gardens, and to Robert J. Lopez at the *Times* for access to his files on the case of the "green-card Marine," José Gutiérrez. Thanks as well to Jesse Katz and my *compadre* Roberto Lovato, for the gift of friendship and insight.

I owe a big and very long *abrazo* to Sean McDonald, who saw in the germ of my not especially well-articulated book proposal what an entire book might look like. Sean is the midwife of the village that raised this book, and for his calm and intelligent presence during its delivery I am eternally in debt.

Finally, completing this book would have been a very hollow accomplishment indeed but for my wife, Virginia Espino, who held our family together during my repeated absences, and during the countless hours I spent in the trance of my computer screen. This writer finds his talents inadequate before the depth and persistence of her commitment to the values of truth, home, and justice. She means more to me than I can ever put into words.

NOTES

Chapter One

I was able to fill in the details of Ernesto "Che" Guevara's life thanks to Jon Lee Anderson's seminal biography, *Che Guevara: A Revolutionary Life*.

The passages from *The Labyrinth of Solitude* by Octavio Paz are from the 1985 Grove Press edition (Lysander Kemp, Yara Milos, and Rachel Phillips, translators).

The newspaper stories and column quoted in this chapter include: "Kentucky Ties Help Mexican Town," from the series "Una Vida Nueva—A New Life," Lexington, Kentucky, *Courier-Journal*, March 30, 2003; George Rede, "A World Away," Portland *Oregonian*, February 13, 1994; Josie Huang, "Pain and Desperation," Portland, Maine, *Press-Herald*, December 8, 2002; and Steve Lopez, "Finding L.A. Roots in the Dust of Mexico," *Los Angeles Times*, June 16, 2004.

On José Antonio Gutiérrez, see Mark Arax, Rich Connell, Daniel Hernandez, Robert J. Lopez, and Patrick McDonnell, "Death of a Dream," *Los Angeles Times*, May 25, 2003.

The citations from Alexis de Tocqueville's *Democracy in America* are from the two-volume Vintage edition of 1990.

Chapter Two

Some of the details on the suffering of the border crossers in the desert and the detritus they leave behind come from Susan Ferriss, "Mexican Migrants Dream, Die," *Austin American-Statesman*, August 12, 2001.

Chapter Three

On Los Tigres del Norte and the rise of the *narcocorrido*, I consulted Elijah Wald's *Narcocorrido* and Sam Quiñones, "The Tigers' Tale," *Los Angeles Times Magazine*, December 16, 2001.

Translations of the Tigres' song lyrics are mine.

Chapter Four

On the indictments in the chicken-worker case, see "Six Tyson Officials Accused of Smuggling Illegal Workers from Mexico," Memphis *Commercial Appeal*, December 20, 2001; and Jeffrey Gettleman, "Town Not Surprised by Tyson Charges," *Los Angeles Times*, December 21, 2001.

The translations from Juan Rulfo's *El Llano en Llamas* in this and other chapters are mine.

Chapter Five

On the Klan in Siler City, North Carolina, see Barry Yeoman, "Hispanic Diaspora," *Mother Jones*, July/August 2000.

The academic paper, "Mexican Immigrant Communities in the South and Social Capital: The Case of Dalton, Georgia," was published as "Working Paper No. 64" by the Center for Comparative Immigration Studies at the University of California, San Diego.

Homero Luna has since sold *El Tiempo*. At last report, he was working in the beauty salon business.

Chapter Six

David Bacon's "Kill Floor Rebellion" appeared in the July 1, 2002, issue of *The American Prospect*.

Chapter Seven

On Cindy Montañez's first campaign for council, I consulted Marc B. Haefele's "City Limits" column from the January 15–21, 1999, *LA Weekly*.

On San Antonio's "War of the Purple House," see Jesse Katz, "Purple Passions Swirl About Texas Adobe Home," *Los Angeles Times*, August 11, 1997.

The "overboard" quotation about the new public library is from former San Antonio city councilwoman Helen Dutmar, as reported in *The New York Times*, November 29, 1995.

Chapter Eight

On the electoral fraud in Miami, I consulted and cited the Pulitzer Prize–winning story "Dubious Tactics Tilted Mayoral Votes," published February 8, 1998, in the *Miami Herald*.

Chapter Nine

On the shenanigans in Southeast Los Angeles County, I consulted Sam Quiñones, "The Savage Politics of South Gate," *Los Angeles Times Magazine*, July 8, 2001; Richard Marosi, "City Hall Plays Santa," *Los Angeles Times*, December 16, 2001; and Megan Garvey and Richard Marosi, "Southeast L.A. County Gets a Civics Lesson," *Los Angeles Times*, March 11, 2003.

Chapter Ten

On the history of New York City, I relied on Edwin G. Burrows and Mike Wallace, *Gotham: A History of New York City to 1898*.

Some details on the life of Norberto Hernández come from an article by Peter Cheney in the September 22, 2001, Toronto *Globe and Mail*.

Articles on the "green-card Marines" appeared in the *Los Angeles Times*, May 25–28, 2003.

About the Author

The son of Guatemalan immigrants, Héctor Tobar is a Los Angeles–born novelist and journalist. He has served as a national and foreign correspondent for the *Los Angeles Times* and was part of the writing team that won a Pulitzer Prize for the coverage of the 1992 L.A. riots. He has also written for *The New Yorker* and *LA Weekly*, and is the author of a novel, *The Tattooed Soldier*, that was a finalist for a 1999 PEN Center USA West award.